RUGBYNOMICS

Using Data to Tackle Rugby's Biggest Myths and Misconceptions

Chris Carter

© Chris Carter 2024

The moral rights of the author have been asserted. All rights reserved. No part of this publication may be reproduced, stored in or introduced into a retrieval system or transmitted in any form or by any means (electronic, mechanical, photocopying, recording or otherwise) without the prior written permission of the copyright owner of this book.

Rugbynomics

For my little champions, Lucas and Ella—may you always play, question and dream boldly.

'It's only when you risk failure that you discover things.'

—Lupita Nyong'o

Contents

Kick-off 7

1. Were You Born to Play Rugby? 12
2. Living for the Game: Rugby as the Elixir of Life? 37
3. Tackling Titans: The Rise of Rugby's Heavyweights and Their Sporting Rivals 53
4. Try and Triumph: The Constantly Shifting Strategies of Rugby 89
5. Winning Time: Where Matches are Won or Lost 129
6. Underdogs Unleashed: A Comparative Look into Upsets 158
7. No Roar, Same Score? Rugby's Home Advantage During the Pandemic 180
8. Navigating the Knockout Gauntlet: The Importance of the Rugby World Cup Draw 191
9. Rugby's Global Stretch: Should the World Cup Have 24 Teams? . 212
10. Regressing to the Mean—Of Rugby Players and Fighter Pilots .. 222
11. Black Tide Rising: Flipping the Script in the All Blacks vs Springboks Saga 233
12. Cap-italising on Position: Which Rugby Positions (and Locations) Offer the Best Path to International Fame? 255

Fulltime 265

References 267

Acknowledgements 269

Kick-off

I absolutely love sport.

Why? I'm hopelessly addicted to the uncertainty of it. The fact that you never really know what's going to happen next—if the hero or the villain will prevail in the end. After all, matches are not scripted in Hollywood. They play out on fields, pitches, tracks and courts where absolutely anything can happen.

I also like the fact that sport is drenched in data. That's what informs us how players and teams are performing. And, on the down low, I quite like data too. After all, it's been my profession for well over 20 years (and counting).

So when sport and data combine, I'm like a pig in the proverbial. My first inkling that they could come together in a lasting union was watching cricket in the 1980s. Players were measured in averages, strike rates and economy rates. There were graphs of 'Manhattan skylines' (showing the runs scored per over) and worms (charting the teams' score progression) wriggling their way to the top-right corner of the screen. It was marvellous stuff for a data-minded kid.

Of course, growing up in New Zealand in the 1980s, my number one sport was preordained to be rugby. It had to be; there wasn't really another option. Boys who didn't want to play rugby at my primary school were told to play netball with the girls. It was a Catholic school, and 'soccer' was considered one of the most sacrilegious words of all back then. It was a different era. An unfortunate lack of size, skill, speed and talent precluded me from playing the game to any high level. But like most New Zealanders, I grew to adore watching the sport.

However, what *really* turbo-charged my relationship with sport and numbers was my move to the United States in 2009. This was the heyday of the *Moneyball* era, and I found a merging of data and sport taken to a whole new level. Anything and everything that could be measured was communicated to the audience, who themselves had become increasingly data obsessed. Stats were a key part of the television broadcast armoury. From yards after contact to earned run average on a Wednesday night after three days of rest, U.S. broadcasters refused to withhold any bit of data they thought audiences would appreciate. The seemingly more obscure, the better.

The American sports fans loved it. Because guess what? From my experience, as much as people deride metrics, numbers and figures, deep down most people actually quite like data. Many just don't know it yet. People love a good graph that easily explains to them which thing is performing better than that other thing. They love a metric that illustrates what is happening. We are a curious species and we love knowing. And data is the fuel for this fire.

No doubt part of American sports fans' fascination with data is thanks to fantasy sports. What's fantasy sports, you might ask? (No, it has nothing to do with the Lingerie Bowl. Settle down.) It's a competition where normal people (like us) manage a hypothetical sports team made up of real players in a specific league. Success as a fantasy team 'manager' is based on the actual measured performance of your teams' players on the real sports field.

Fantasy sports is now a multibillion-dollar industry, spawning dedicated primetime TV shows and radio stations promising to tell you—and millions of other listeners—who to draft, who to start and who to bench. And Americans play fantasy sports for practically everything; there's even fantasy NASCAR stock-car racing. But the undisputed king of fantasy sports is National Football League (NFL) football.

NFL football (aka American football) is similar in many ways to rugby. In fact, it originated from rugby (along with soccer). However, the measurements and data recorded during NFL games is in a different league. Every yard gained is measured, analysed and communicated to the audience. Fans eat it up. After all, this data powers their fantasy teams.

Rugby is ever so slowly heading in this data-driven direction, albeit kicking and screaming. Now that the game is professional at the highest levels, teams have certainly embraced the sports data revolution and have screeds of internal data at their disposal. A lot of it is real-time player data garnered from GPS units in each player's jersey.

But access to rugby stats and analytics, while increasingly available to the general public in recent years, still lags well behind rugby's professional sport peers. A web search for 'rugby analytics' books quickly ends in coaching and rules' titles. The same search for sports like baseball, basketball, American football, cricket and football (soccer) offers more book results than ChatGPT could digest in, well, seconds probably. But it's still a lot.

Rugbynomics is my attempt to introduce the rugby fan to the sports analytics' revolution. My aim is to make illuminating and often fascinating statistics as easy to read and accessible as possible, even to the data-phobic among you.

There are graphs, tables and metrics in here. But I try to explain them as simply as possible. They are there just to communicate trends and results, not to overwhelm you with the methods of statistical analysis that produced their findings. So rest assured: you'll only find *p-values* mentioned sparingly. But for the fellow propeller-heads among you, there should still be plenty here to sink your teeth into.

It's important to point out that this book focuses on the men's game only. As I mention later in the book, much of the growth in the game is coming from the women's side, which is tremendous to see. Crowd attendance records are being regularly broken, with almost 60,000 watching England secure a Six Nations Grand Slam against France in 2023. However, historical data on the women's game is just not available right now, at least not enough to perform the level of in-depth analyses I provide on the men's side. Hopefully that will come in a future edition of the book!

With that caveat out of the way, let's dive into the data to answer those burning rugby questions that, I'm sure, have been keeping you up at night, such as:

- Does it matter when you're born?
- How big do I need to be to play international rugby?
- How much has the game actually changed in recent years?
- Is home advantage real? And if so, what causes it?
- Should I take the penalty kick or go for the try?
- Are upsets more or less likely in rugby than other sports?
- Does the World Cup draw matter?

Ready? It's time to set the first data scrum.

1. Were You Born to Play Rugby?

There are many factors that go into being a great or even good rugby player. Size, speed, strength, skill, bravery and dedication are some of the most obvious ones.

But there are also some subtle markers that go beyond these core ingredients. They give ever-so-slight advantages that can help determine if we were born to play top-level rugby in the first place. In this chapter, we'll focus on these not-so-little extras.

Happy birthday?

The significance of relative age effect (RAE) has been well documented across numerous sports. Being born in the months immediately after a selection cutoff period gives a player a relative advantage over their peers who are born shortly before that cutoff period. This effect is most pronounced at younger ages. For example, if September 1 is the cutoff date for a child to be selected in an age-group team, a ten-year-old born on September 1 will be practically a whole year older than a child born on August 31 the following year. Both children qualify for the same team, but the child born on September 1 is ten percent older than the child born on August 31, and on average five percent older than all other children eligible to play on the team.

1. Were You Born to Play Rugby?

The theory is that this age-effect bias is carried through the years, as children born in those first months are selected for the best age-based teams and get access to the best resources and coaching. A paper by Barnsley et al. in 1985 famously quantified this effect among age-grade ice hockey players in Canada. Since then, there have been numerous studies on how the effect has played out in sports leagues around the world, including on the All Blacks in a paper by Simons and Adams (2017). One finding was that the larger the pool of players, and the more competition there is for finite resources, the larger the impact of RAE (Grondin et al., 1984).

We know that the effect matters, but I wanted to dive a bit deeper into where and when it's most prevalent. As part of my research, I examined the birthdates of every All Black[1] and member of the England rugby team.[2] I chose these teams because they have large player bases and are from opposite hemispheres—and, crucially, they also have different selection cutoff dates.

New Zealand All Blacks

The selection cutoff date in New Zealand is January 1, and indeed there is a significant relative age bias when looking at the birthdates of all 1,200[3] players who have been part of the All Blacks between 1884 and the end of 2023 (Figure 1.1). You can clearly see there is a substantial bias towards being born in the first four months of the year. 37 percent of All Blacks were born during this

---

[1] From the www.allblacks.com website.
[2] From Wikipedia—restricted to all England players with a Wikipedia page.
[3] 11 records were removed as no reliable birthdate could be found.

time period, whereas for the population as a whole the figure is 32.5 percent.

There's also an interesting pattern around June and July. Only 7.3 percent of All Blacks were born in June, compared to the general population's 8.0 percent, while in July the All Blacks' births slightly exceed the population as a whole. July 1 is the school year cutoff date in New Zealand, and children are allocated into school years based on whether their birthday is before or after that date. Therefore, children born in July would be in the same school class as children born almost a year later in June. As school is where a lot of sporting development and identification occurs, the July spike could indicate a mini-RAE around the school year cutoff as well.

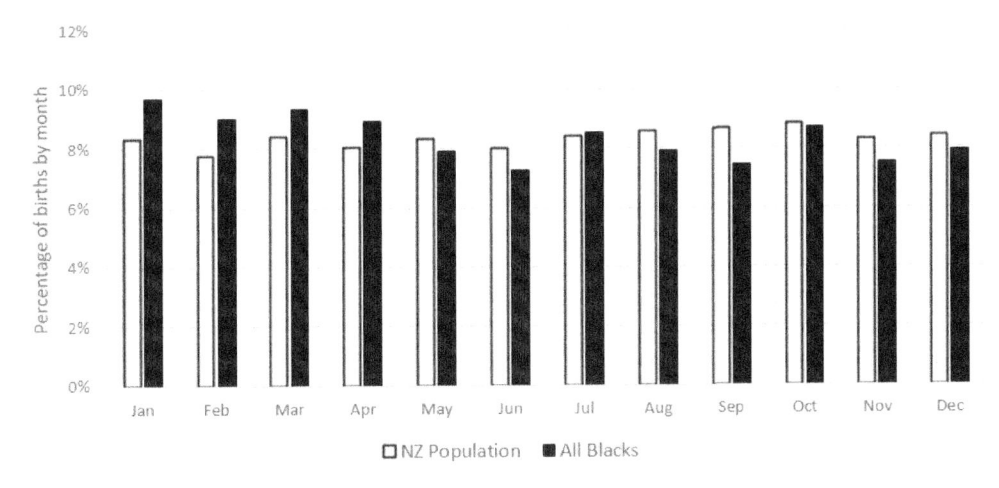

Figure 1.1. Actual birth month of All Blacks vs. the birth month of the general New Zealand population (from stats.govt.nz).

1. Were You Born to Play Rugby?

Of course, not every member of the All Blacks was born and grew up in New Zealand. This is particularly the case in the team's early days when many were immigrants from the U.K. and may have grown up in a different RAE environment. More recently, an increasing number of members have been born in the Pacific Islands. To that end, Figure 1.2 only includes the 1,100 All Blacks born in New Zealand. While the trend is the same as it is among the complete All Blacks roster, the RAE effect is more pronounced when restricted to New Zealand-born All Blacks only. You can see this in Table 1.1, which indicates that 37.5 percent of NZ-born All Blacks were born by April, five percent more than would be expected if no RAE was at play.

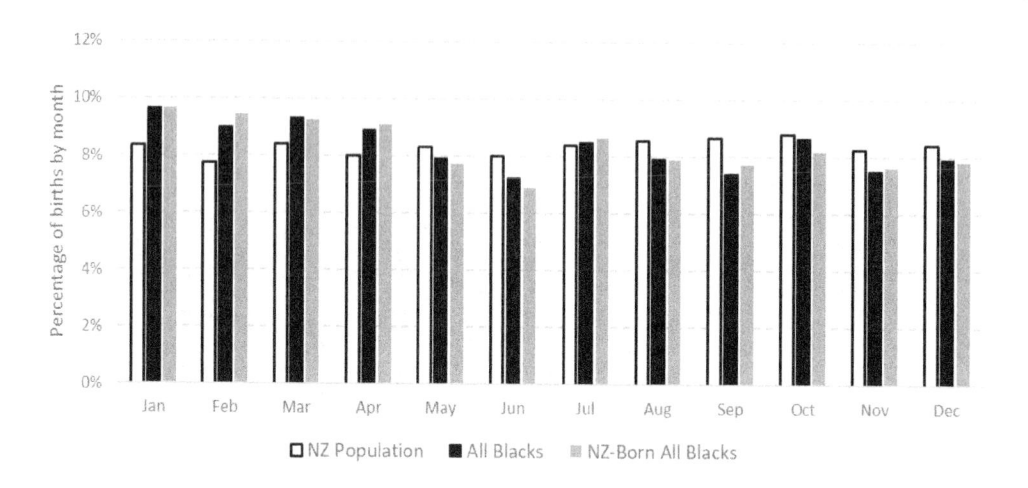

Figure 1.2. Actual birth month of All Blacks (all and NZ-born only) vs. the birth month of the New Zealand population (from stats.govt.nz).

Table 1.1. Cumulative percentage of players born up until the end of each month of the year compared to the broader NZ population (from stats.govt.nz).

Month	NZ Population	All Blacks	NZ-born All Blacks
Jan	8.3%	9.7%	9.6%
Feb	16.1%	18.7%	19.1%
Mar	24.5%	28.0%	28.4%
Apr	32.5%	36.9%	37.5%
May	40.9%	44.8%	45.2%
Jun	48.9%	52.1%	52.1%
Jul	57.3%	60.6%	60.7%
Aug	65.8%	68.5%	68.6%
Sep	74.5%	75.9%	76.4%
Oct	83.3%	84.6%	84.5%
Nov	91.6%	92.1%	92.2%
Dec	100.0%	100.0%	100.0%

I was also interested in exploring whether RAE has persisted over the last 150 years, or if it's a more recent phenomenon. Has the advent of the Professional era and the increased focus on talent identification that followed exacerbated RAE in New Zealand? To help figure this out, I divided player data into three broad but very distinct periods in international rugby:

- **Pre-War**—players born before 1930, likely to have debuted before World War II.
- **Amateur**—players born between 1930 and 1980, likely to have developed in the age-group system prior to the game turning professional in 1996.
- **Professional**—Players born after 1980, who would have developed in the age-group system during the Professional era.

For simplicity and clarity, I've restricted Figure 1.3 to the 'RAE period' of January–April where its impact is most apparent, since the charts begin to get more complicated with multiple bars. Figure 1.3 shows that while there is a mild RAE in both the Pre-War and Amateur eras, RAE really became significant in the Professional era. Indeed, *47 percent* of All Blacks in the Professional era were born in the first four months of the year, compared to 32.5 percent of the overall population. This is in line with the findings of Simons and Adams (2017), who also found a marked increase in RAE during the Professional era.

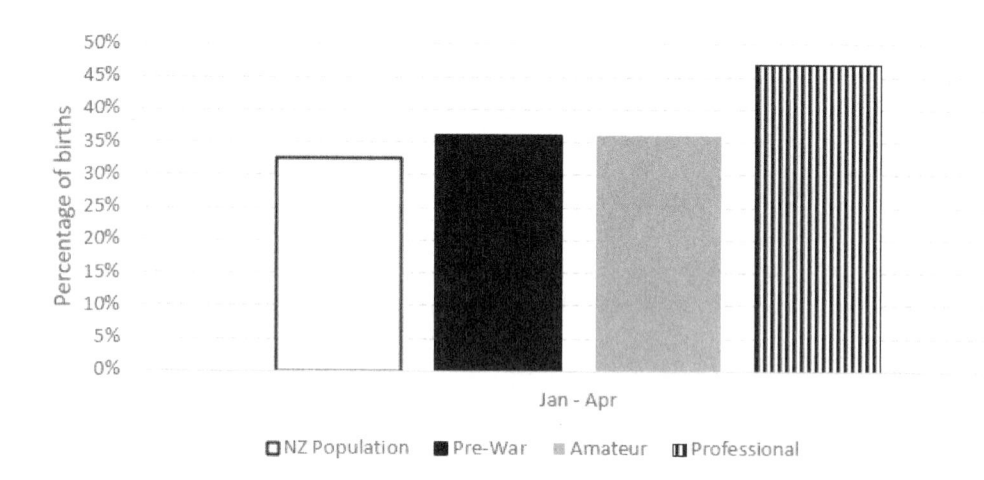

Figure 1.3. Comparison of New Zealand-born All Blacks who were born between January and April across the three different time periods (Pre-War, Amateur and Professional).

I had assumed that forwards would be the big beneficiaries of RAE, given the big size advantage that RAE should give older children as they develop. But it's actually the backs who have shown a more pronounced RAE over the years in All Blacks rugby (Figure 1.4). Speed and skill are also elements that develop with age, which may explain the more pronounced RAE among backs.

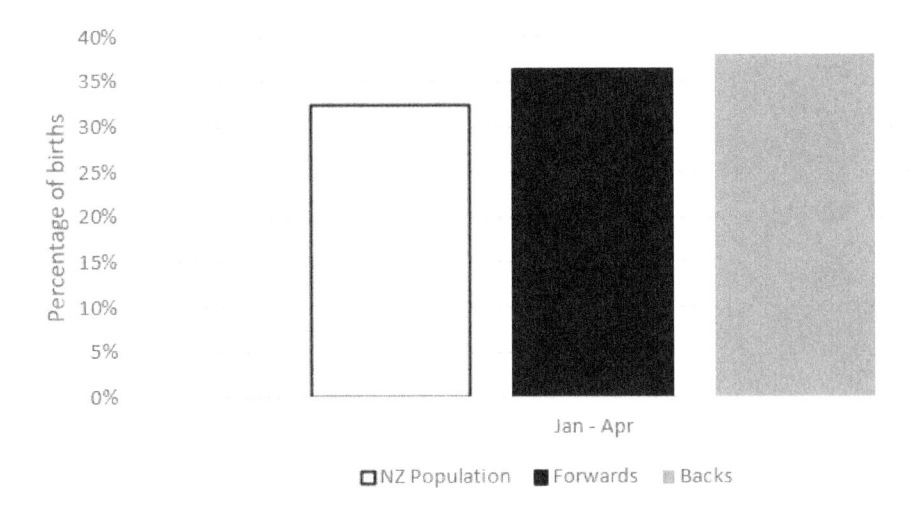

Figure 1.4. Comparison of New Zealand-born All Blacks who were born between January and April by forwards versus backs.

However, if we isolate this analysis to the Professional era only, a completely different picture forms: the RAE is much larger in forwards (Figure 1.5). A whopping 51 percent of Professional-era All Blacks forwards were born between January and April, a finding that may not be surprising given how much stock began to be placed on size at the dawn of the era. It is worth noting, however, that only 145 NZ-born players in total have taken the field in the Professional era, so the data starts to slice quite thinly when we divide things further into forwards and backs.

1. Were You Born to Play Rugby?

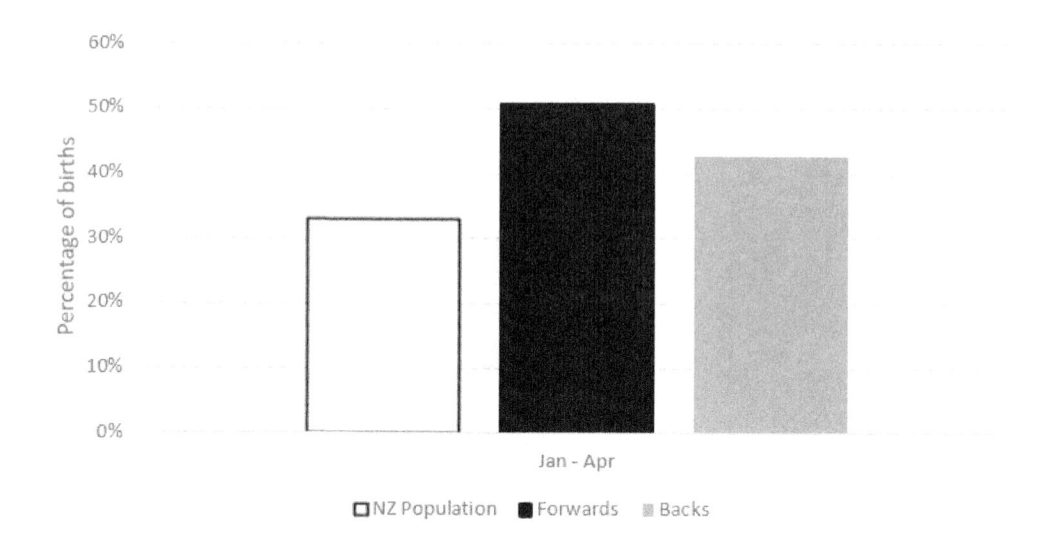

Figure 1.5. Comparison of birth months of Professional-era, New Zealand-born All Blacks who were born between January and April by forwards versus backs.

England

So how does this compare to the other side of the globe? In England, the school year is the exact opposite of New Zealand. More importantly, the traditional cutoff for age-grade rugby teams in England has been September 1. Accordingly, as we can see in Figure 1.6, there is a huge spike in English international rugby players born in September and, to a lesser extent, October.

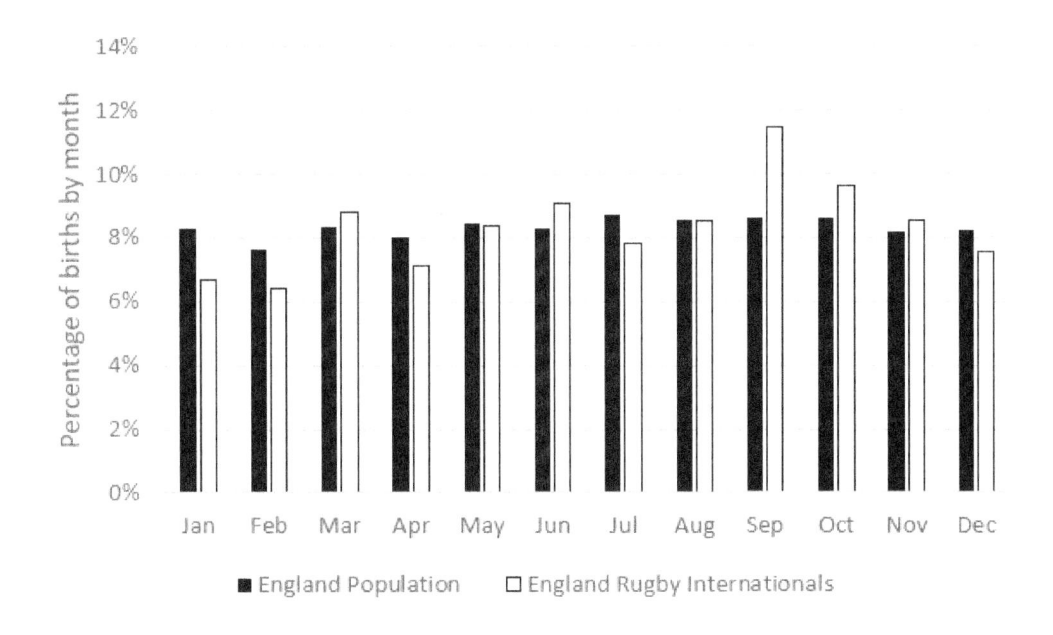

Figure 1.6. Actual birth month of England Rugby Internationals vs. birth month of general population in England (from ons.gov.uk).

Almost 30 percent of English players were born in the three months after the cutoff period (September–November), whereas the statistical expectation is that it would be 25 percent. This gap is slightly more pronounced than it is with the All Blacks, although the pattern of both nations is very similar (Table 1.2).

1. Were You Born to Play Rugby?

Table 1.2. Cumulative percentage of players born each month after the age-group cutoff in New Zealand versus England.

Month after Cutoff	All Blacks	England Internationals
1	10%	11%
2	19%	21%
3	28%	30%
4	37%	37%
5	45%	44%
6	52%	50%
7	61%	59%
8	69%	66%
9	76%	75%
10	85%	84%
11	92%	91%
12	100%	100%

In England, the relative age effect is well and truly driven by the forwards (Figure 1.7). Again, for simplicity and clarity, this and subsequent charts are restricted to the first four months of the English 'RAE period' of September–December. The effect on forwards is highly statistically significant, whereas for backs it is non-existent. This differs from New Zealand, where we still saw a relative age effect for backs, even in the Professional era. (The cheeky New Zealander may opine that perhaps it doesn't require a relatively older child to stand outside the fly-half in an English backline and never see the ball during the game. I'll try to stay above that kind of discussion here though!)

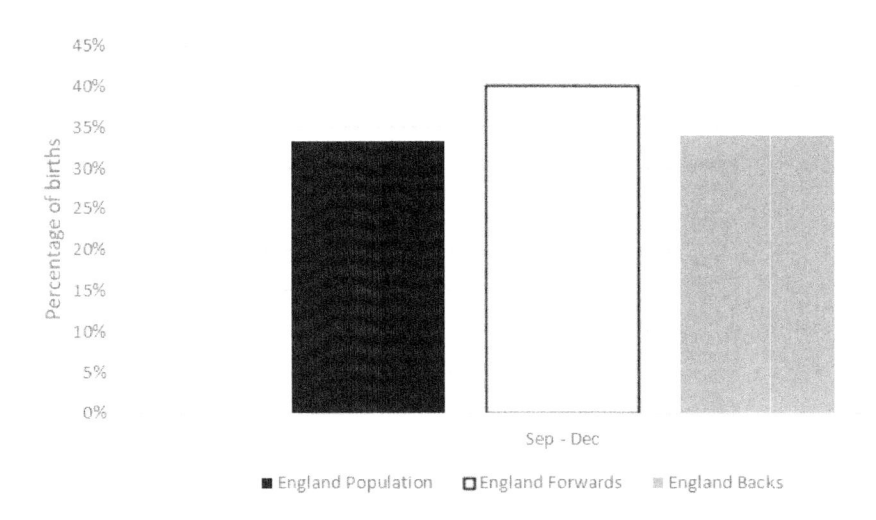

Figure 1.7. Comparison of England rugby internationals who were born between September and December by forwards versus backs.

When comparing the various periods (Pre-War, Amateur and Professional), a completely different picture emerges with English players (Figure 1.8). The RAE from September to December was most pronounced (and statistically significant) during the Amateur era and has completely disappeared in the Professional era.

1. Were You Born to Play Rugby?

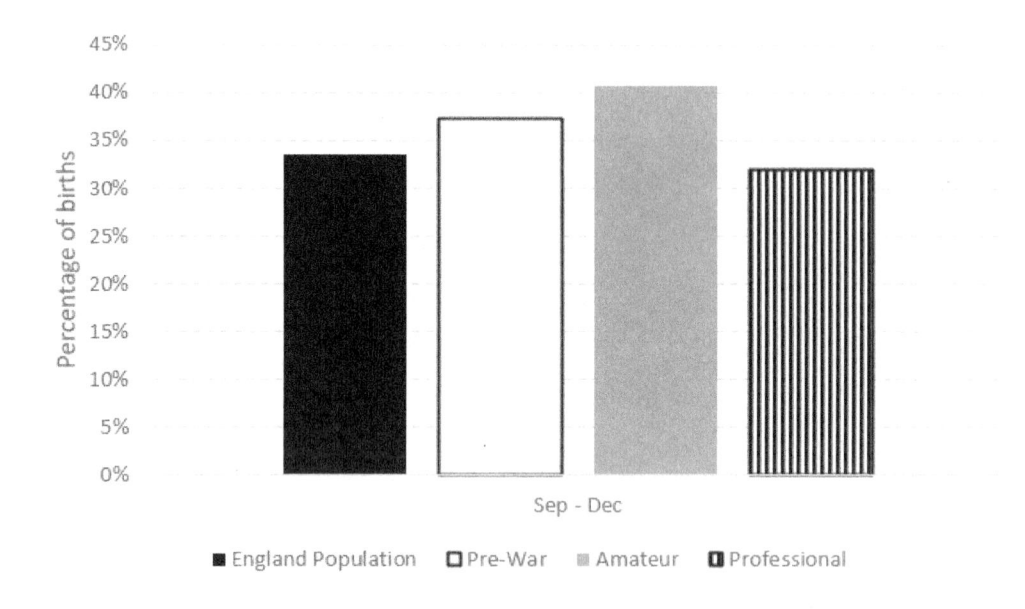

[Bar chart showing Percentage of births (0%–45%) for Sep–Dec period across four categories: England Population (~33%), Pre-War (~37%), Amateur (~40%), Professional (~32%).]

Figure 1.8. Comparison of England rugby internationals who were born between September and December across the three different rugby time periods (Pre-War, Amateur and Professional).

This is in line with the findings of Kelly et al. (2021), who examined the impact of RAEs on current England players from age-group play to professional play. They found that while there was a pronounced RAE at the age-group level, it had disappeared by the time players reached the international level in England.

Interestingly, this suggests that English rugby has adopted successful strategies to mitigate the impact of RAE in their player development pathways. Conversely, in New Zealand RAE has been exacerbated in the Professional era. 'This tells us there may well be promising players born at the 'wrong time' who are slipping through the New Zealand development system.

It's worth mentioning here that the relative age effect is ultimately mild—and not insurmountable. It conveys an ever-so-slight advantage of a few percentage points to people born at a stage when they are relatively older than their peers growing up. Most talented players will overcome this handicap, and there are still a decent number of players born in the months immediately before the cutoff. Richie McCaw, arguably the All Blacks' greatest player ever, was born on December 31—statistically speaking, the worst day for a rugby player to be born in New Zealand!

A family affair

One of my favourite pieces of rugby commentary was during an All Blacks vs Canada pool game in the 2019 Rugby World Cup. The three Barrett brothers were on the field for New Zealand, and there was a lengthy passing interplay exclusively between the trio of brothers before the ball unfortunately went to ground. 'Ohhhh, he's run out of Barretts!' was how commentator Scotty Stevenson described Scott Barrett's inability to find a fellow All Black teammate.

In retrospect, it's incredible to think that a single family could provide not two but *three* players, or 20 percent of the starting lineup, for the most fabled international rugby team in the world. And the Barrett brothers are not alone in making membership in the All Blacks a family affair. The Ioane brothers, Reiko and Akira, have been part of the same 2020s All Blacks teams, alongside the

1. Were You Born to Play Rugby?

Saveas (Ardie and Julian). Three Whitelock brothers played test rugby for the All Blacks in the 2000s, including the most capped All Black of all time, Sam. Prop Nepo Laulala's brother Casey played two tests at centre in the early 2000s. Add to this cohort Caleb Clarke and Ethan Blackadder, both of whom had fathers who played for the hallowed black jersey. The father of prop Tyrel Lomax represented New Zealand in rugby league, and Hoskins Sotutu's father played rugby for the New Zealand XV (as well as Fiji).

In fact, the All Blacks starting 15 to face Ireland in the third test in Wellington in 2022 included seven players whose siblings had also represented New Zealand: Nepo Laulala, Sam Whitelock, Akira Ioane, Ardie Savea, Beauden Barrett, Reiko Ioane and Jordie Barrett. Of the 124 All Blacks' debutants since 2009, 14 are immediate family members (brothers or sons) of fellow All Blacks.

And New Zealand is not alone in having strong family ties among the national team (Table 1.3). In the same time period (2009–2023), England selected 12 players with immediate family ties, Australia seven, France six and South Africa five. There have even been multiple sets of brother trios playing international rugby for Tier-1 countries, with the Fainga'a brothers of Australia and the du Preez brothers of South Africa joining the Barrett brothers of New Zealand.

Table 1.3. Prevalence of immediate family members in national team selections.

Country	Eligible Players	New caps between 2009 and 2023	Players with immediate family members also in team	Percentage of new caps with immediate family members	Approximate likelihood of selecting so many family members[4]
New Zealand	33,500	124	14	11.3%	1 in 1,000
England	131,399	141	12	8.5%	1 in 650
Australia	39,380	136	7	5.1%	1 in 500
France	124,079	146	6	4.1%	1 in 400
South Africa	113,174	131	5	3.8%	1 in 150

As can be seen in Table 1.3, there's a very small likelihood that so many family members would be selected to play international rugby purely by random chance. There's something bigger at play here. The phenomenon of disproportionate family connections has been well documented in many other sports and, with the Table 1.3 data, we can add rugby to the list. Whether it's nature or nurture, genes or backyard competition (it's probably a combination of all of these), having a relative who is also a rugby international greatly increases your chances of becoming one.

Naming rights

Believe it or not, there is widely documented evidence that the first letter of your surname is linked to your academic success. The effect is called 'alphabetism'. (We'll return to rugby in a moment, I promise!) In a 2018 study, researchers Zax and Cauley examined a group of people who had identical attributes such as IQ and academic performance. After crunching the data, they found that subjects with surnames later in the alphabet had more negative academic and life outcomes until they reached their 30s. The probability of

---

[4] Approximated based on estimated number of rugby-playing family members.

being designated an outstanding student by high school teachers dropped by ten percent for every ten surname letters. People with 'early' surnames were always at the front of the list and, presumably, top of mind. (Importantly for this book and its analysis, the study was also conducted purely on men.)

This got me thinking: could there be a similar alphabetism at play in rugby? Could players with early surnames benefit from some sort of priority bias? It's hard to think that this might be the case, but let's see what the data says!

(First, the caveats: accurate population-scale surname information is difficult to obtain. And surname distributions will also change ever so slightly over time. I have detailed where I obtained the surname letter data in each figure caption.)

Fascinatingly, for England rugby internationals we get a clear reverse-alphabetism trend. In other words, England rugby internationals *under*-index relative to the broader population when it comes to early surname letters (Figure 1.9).

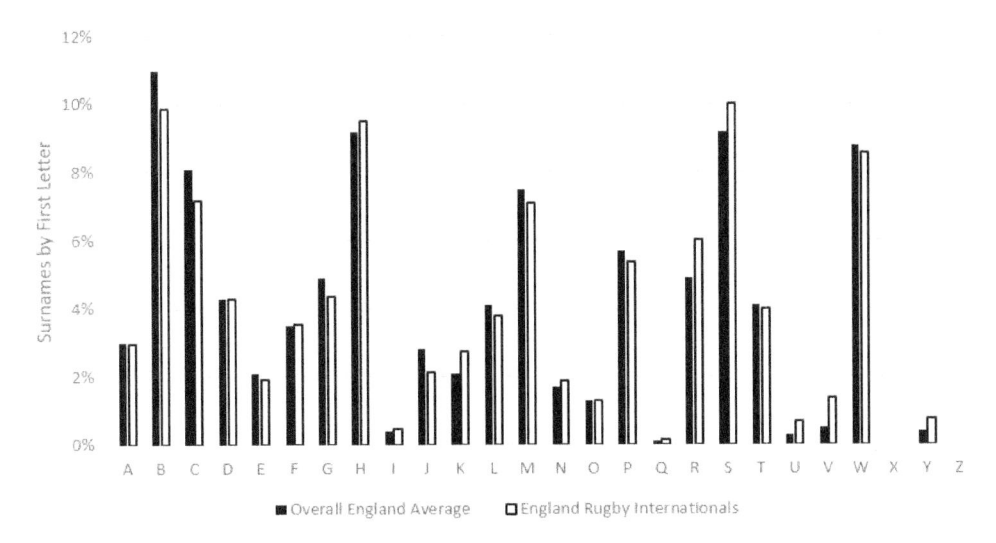

Figure 1.9. Distribution of the first surname letter of England rugby internationals compared to the overall England population average. Population average derived from Electoral Register of 1957/8, courtesy of one-name.org.

Looking at the cumulative chart as we progress through the alphabet (Figure 1.10), you can see that until reaching surnames beginning with V, England players are less represented than would be expected. 3.2 percent fewer England rugby players have surnames beginning with the letters A to P than would be expected, equating to 47 missing players out of a total of 1,449.

1. Were You Born to Play Rugby?

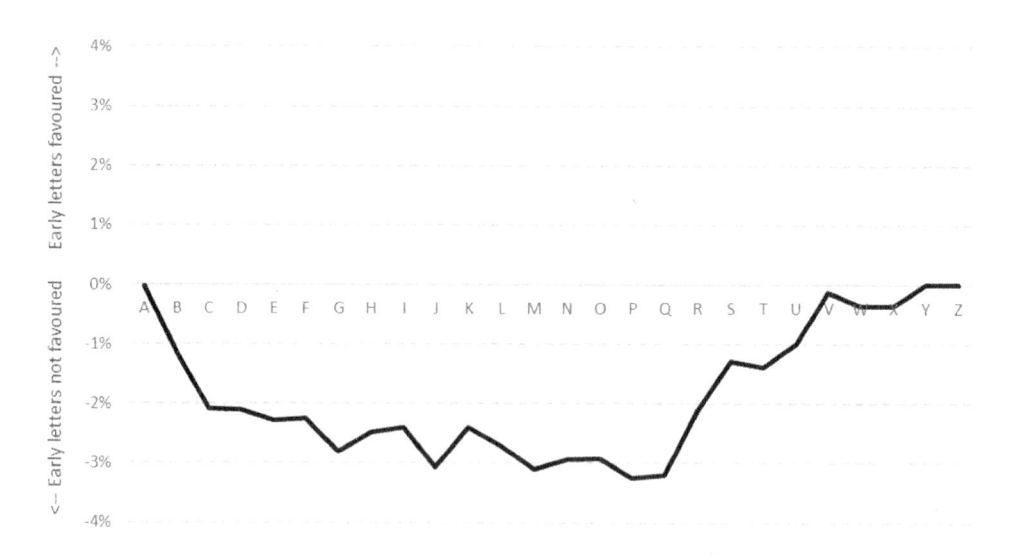

Figure 1.10. Cumulative comparison, moving sequentially through the alphabet, of the distribution of the first surname letter of England rugby internationals compared to the general England population average. Population average derived from Electoral Register of 1957/8, courtesy of one-name.org.

However, despite this 3.2 percent deficit in England player surnames from A to P, England rugby internationals still quite closely reflect the letter-by-letter peaks and troughs of the overall population (Figure 1.9). This means the discrepancy isn't considered statistically significant. But it's certainly interesting and worth exploring elsewhere.

If we move on to New Zealand, we again see a disadvantage in early-letter surnames (Figure 1.11).

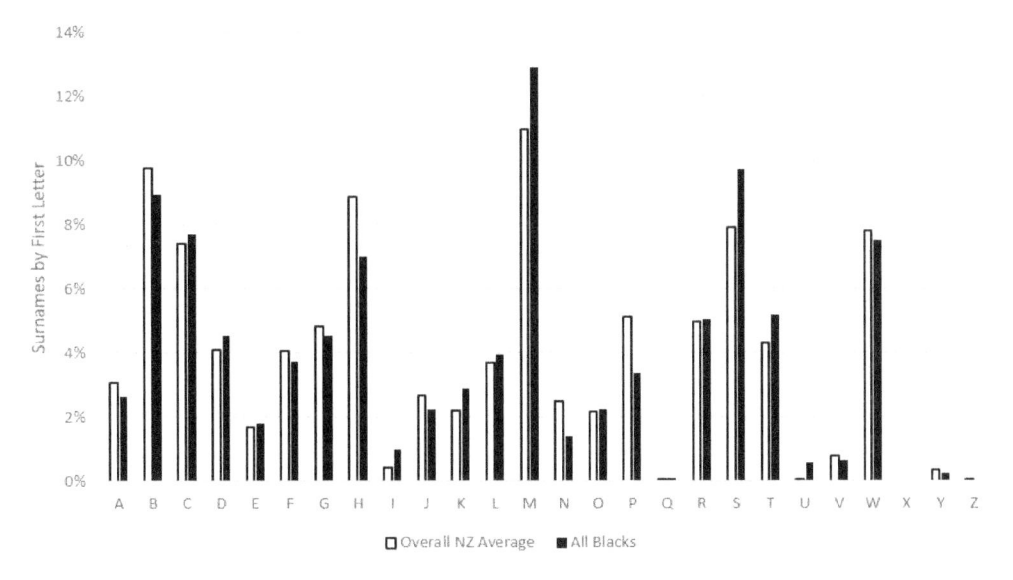

Figure 1.11. Distribution of the first surname letter of All Blacks compared to the overall New Zealand population average. Population average derived from cemetery plot data on data.govt.nz.

This early-letter disadvantage briefly crosses the horizontal axis at M (Figure 1.12), before finally breaking through for good at T. The cumulative discrepancy is 2.9 percent by the time we reach letter H, and 2.8 percent at letter P. Incidentally, the peak you can see at letter M is exclusively due to the vast number of 'McAllBlacks'. In a testament to New Zealand's Scottish heritage, 5.2 percent of All Blacks to date have had surnames beginning with 'Mc' or 'Mac', versus the population average of only 4.1 percent.

1. Were You Born to Play Rugby?

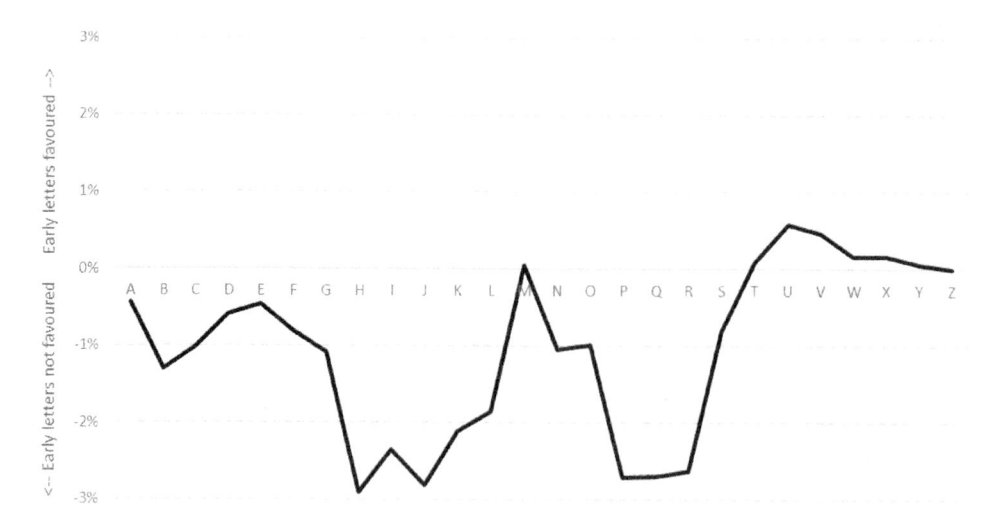

Figure 1.12. Cumulative comparison, moving sequentially through the alphabet, of the distribution of the first surname letter of All Blacks compared to the general New Zealand population average. Population average derived from cemetery plot data on data.govt.nz.

In Australia, the late-letter preference is even more pronounced (Figure 1.13). Australians with surnames beginning with the first four letters of the alphabet are 5.3 percent less likely than expected to make the Wallabies.

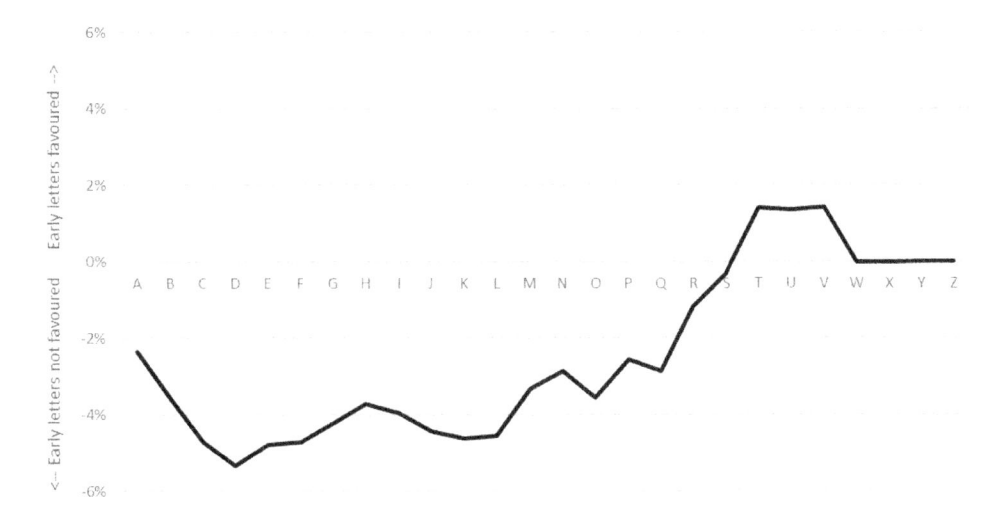

Figure 1.13. Cumulative comparison, moving sequentially through the alphabet, of the distribution of the first surname letter of Wallabies compared to the general Australia population average. Population average derived from Hughes, Colin. Alphabetic Advantage in the House of Representatives. The Australian Quarterly. Vol 42, No. 3, (Sep., 1970): 24-29.

We can even find the same effect with the U.S. Eagles, the United States' national rugby team (Figure 1.14). They are not exactly a global superpower of the game (yet), but a nation chosen for this analysis due to its availability of surname data!

1. Were You Born to Play Rugby?

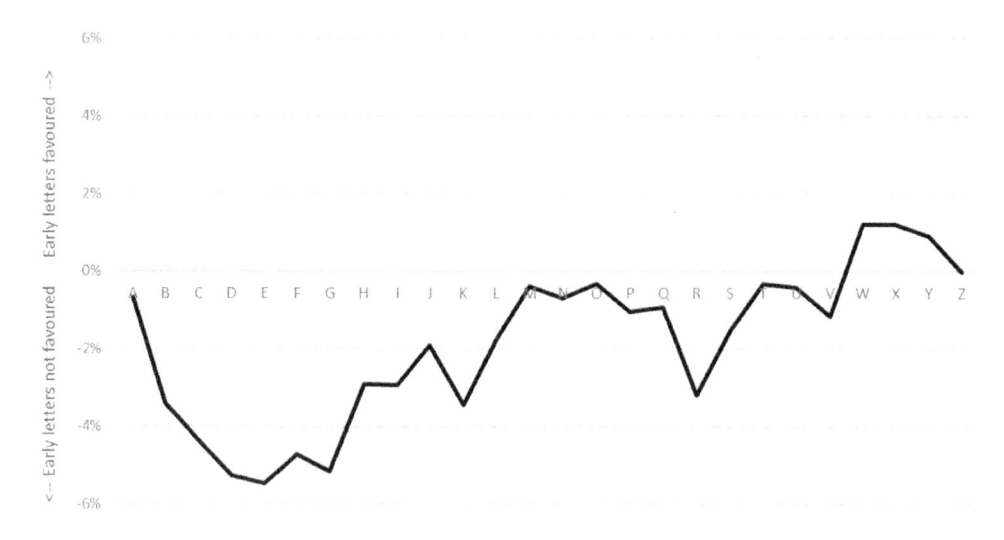

Figure 1.14. Cumulative comparison, moving sequentially through the alphabet, of the distribution of the first surname letter of U.S. Eagle rugby players compared to the general U.S. population average. Population average derived from the U.S. 2000 census table of all valid surnames appearing at least 100 times (covering 90 percent of total responses).

However, this reverse-alphabetism doesn't hold in all countries examined. Early surname letters are actually favoured in Wales (Figure 1.15) and Scotland (Figure 1.16).

Rugbynomics

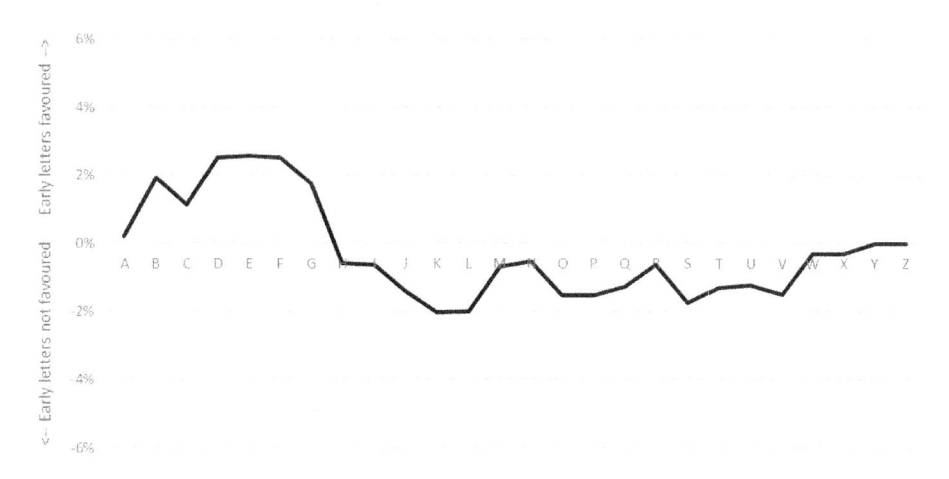

Figure 1.15. Distribution of the first surname letter of Wales rugby internationals compared to the general Wales population average. Population average derived from Electoral Register of 1957/8, courtesy of one-name.org.

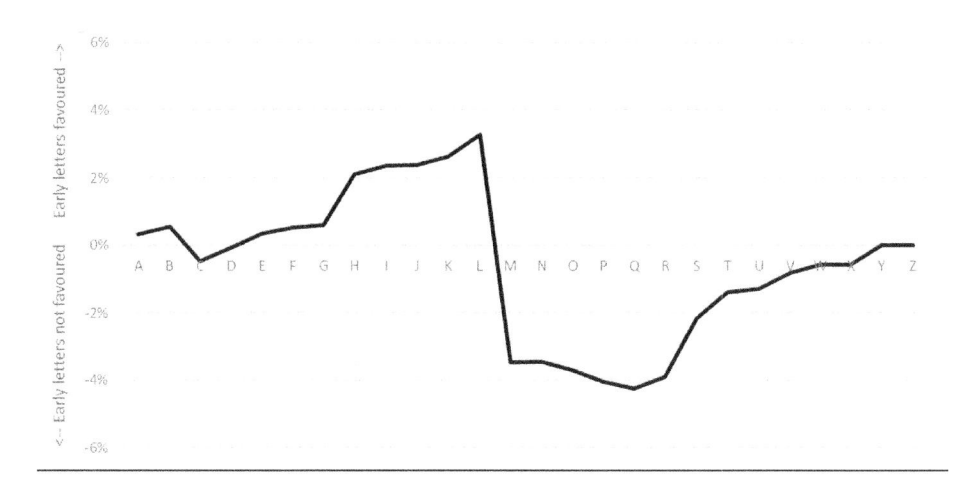

Figure 1.16. Distribution of the first surname letter of Scotland rugby internationals compared to the general Scotland population average. Population average derived from Electoral Register of 1957/8, courtesy of one-name.org.

1. Were You Born to Play Rugby?

For Scotland, there is a big drop at the letter M, where Scottish rugby players dramatically under-index. The proportion of overall Scottish surnames starting with M is 21 percent, making it easily the most popular letter for Scotland; in certain rural counties, namely the Highlands and the Islands, this proportion is closer to 40 percent. The fact that Scottish international rugby players tend to come from the cities likely explains why they are so underrepresented when it comes to patronymic surnames (Mc and Mac).

The breakdown

The jury is still out on whether there is an alphabetism (or reverse-alphabetism) effect in rugby. While there is evidence of the latter in most of the countries I examined, it's not universal to all countries and isn't considered statistically significant.

Supposing a reverse-alphabetism effect definitively did exist though, what could be the driving mechanism behind it? The clue might lay in Zax and Cauley's (2018) study on academic alphabetism, which found that people with later surnames had decreased academic attainment and satisfaction in high school. Could it be that the ever-so-slight academic penalty from having a later surname pushes those kids to focus more on their sport instead? Time will tell, but I for one think it's an intriguing proposition.

Even more intriguingly, if we take both reverse-alphabetism *and* birthdate into account, the effect on international rugby players increases enough to become statistically significant. The following matrices (Figure 1.17) show the percentage differences of international players versus what would be expected based on population averages. As you can see, All Blacks players who have a late surname and were born between January and April beat the population average by a whopping 19 percent, while England's rugby internationals who have a late surname and were born between September and December beat it by 14 percent.

All Blacks

Surname

Birthday	A - L	M - Z
Jan - Apr	7%	21%
May - Aug	-9%	-1%
Sep - Dec	-6%	-9%

England Internationals

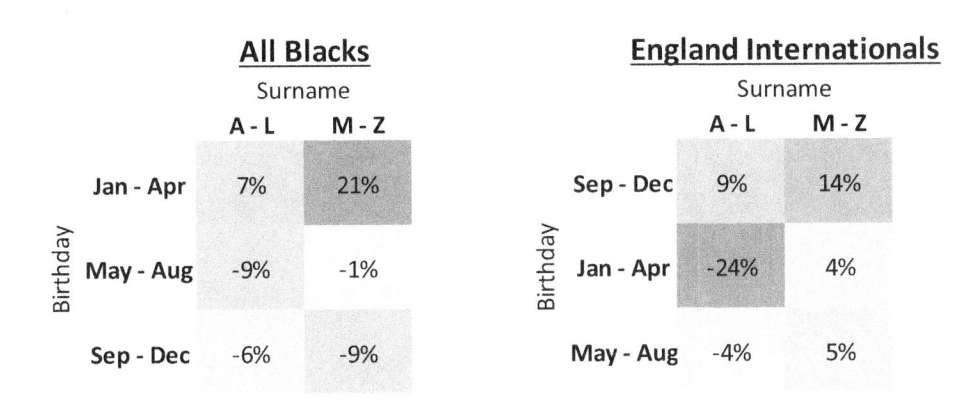

Surname

Birthday	A - L	M - Z
Sep - Dec	9%	14%
Jan - Apr	-24%	4%
May - Aug	-4%	5%

Figure 1.17. Comparison of the distribution of surname and birth month of All Blacks and England rugby internationals versus their respective country's population averages.

So while my birthday in early January puts me in prime All Blacks territory, perhaps my surname balanced things out and led me down the academic path instead. That's what I'll console myself with anyway!

2. Living for the Game: Rugby as the Elixir of Life?

As the saying goes, to the victor go the spoils. But could part of those spoils be sweet life itself? In a fascinating 2001 study, researchers Redelmeier and Singh found that Oscar winners have outlived nominees who didn't win by more than three years! This was true even when factors like age, gender, wealth and country of birth were factored in. What's more, the more Oscars someone wins, the longer they tend to live. A study by Rablen and Oswald (2008) found a similar longevity effect in Nobel Prize winners for science, who outlived nominees by an average of two years.

The exact cause of this longevity effect for prize winners is not completely known. Some have attributed it to the impact that 'winner' status confers. Others speculate that psychological satisfaction of the winners makes them more resilient to all types of stress as they age.

The obvious question for me, of course, is whether there is a similar effect for rugby players. To investigate this we have to go back a long way, to the first half of the 1900s, as most of those players born after the 1950s are (thankfully) still with us today.

New Zealand

As always, before we can make an analysis, we must define our metrics. What would the rugby equivalents of Oscar winners and runners-up look like? In my mind, the most relevant comparison is between New Zealand's international test players and players who reached first-class level but were never selected for the New Zealand national team. These two groups should be virtually identical in age and health metrics.

Getting accurate data on first-class rugby players who didn't represent New Zealand from the early 1900s is difficult. Back in those days, top-tier rugby players obviously didn't document their every move (and occasional body part) on social media and the internet. A website called rugbydatabase.co.nz, which does a great job of documenting known first-class and international players from the New Zealand scene, was my primary data source. However, it doesn't provide a comprehensive list of all the first-class players of yesteryear. So we must take a leap of faith that it offers a representative sample. On the other hand, data on every international All Blacks player in history is readily available on the official All Blacks website.

The data I used is restricted to players born between 1940 (the earliest first-class players we have data about) and 1960. I also removed first-class players who tragically died prior to turning 40, as I didn't want to bias the fact that they may have been on track to be selected for the All Blacks. This left a fairly small data sample of only 26 first-class players compared to 58 All Blacks. Be that as

2. Living for the Game: Rugby as the Elixir of Life?

it may, the results are quite incredible, with a ten-year average lifespan difference between the two groups. The average lifespan of All Blacks players in that time was 63 years, compared to 53 years for the first-class players (Figure 2.1). Given how different the lifespan distributions are (Figure 2.2), this is highly statistically significant.

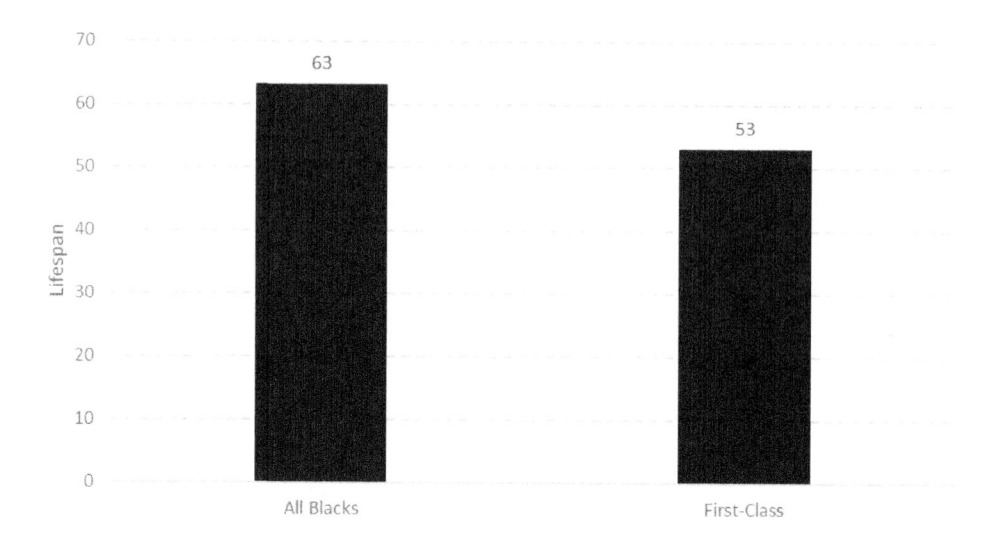

Figure 2.1. Average lifespan of New Zealand international rugby players (All Blacks) and first-class players from New Zealand who didn't attain international status, born between 1940 and 1960.

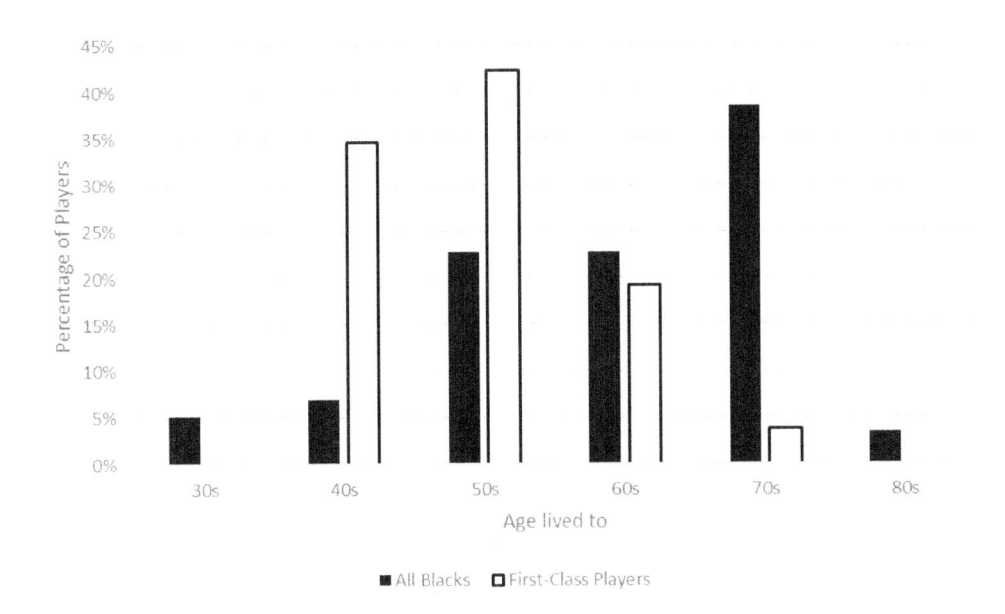

Figure 2.2. Lifespan distribution of New Zealand international rugby players (All Blacks) and first-class players from New Zealand who didn't attain international status.

This discrepancy seems far too vast to be true, so I have to concede that the first-class sample may be either too small or not representative enough. We may be better off taking a slightly different tack and using international caps as a metric instead.

While international tours are not as prevalent today, in the Amateur era extended tours were the backbone of bilateral series. Some players were selected to go on tour with the national team, but only played the midweek matches against local club sides. These players, affectionately known as 'dirt-trackers', did not earn an official 'test cap' for the midweek fixtures. Test appearances are

2. Living for the Game: Rugby as the Elixir of Life?

the pinnacle and thus reserved only for full-fledged internationals drawn from the best players from each country.

For purposes of this analysis, I considered dirt-trackers 'nominees' and test players 'Oscar winners'. Just like with the Oscars, could there be a longevity difference between those who achieved test status and the dirt-trackers?

In fact, there is—and it's remarkably similar to the gaps between Oscar winners and their nominees and Nobel Prize winners and their nominees. Capped All Black players born between 1900 and 1950 lived on average three years longer than uncapped players born during the same time period (Figure 2.3). This longevity difference is statistically significant.

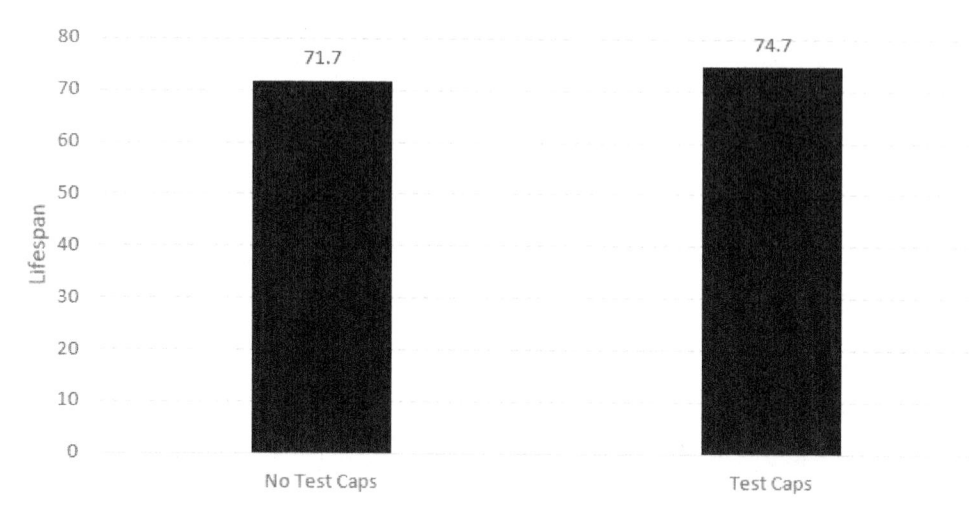

Figure 2.3. Average lifespan of All Blacks rugby players, born between 1900 and 1950, who received international test caps versus those who did not.

Even when the data is stratified by decade of birth (to account for the fact that more uncapped players were born earlier in the 20th century when life expectancy was lower), the effect is 1.9 years in longevity difference (Figure 2.4). However, this result is not statistically significant due to the paucity of data per decade.

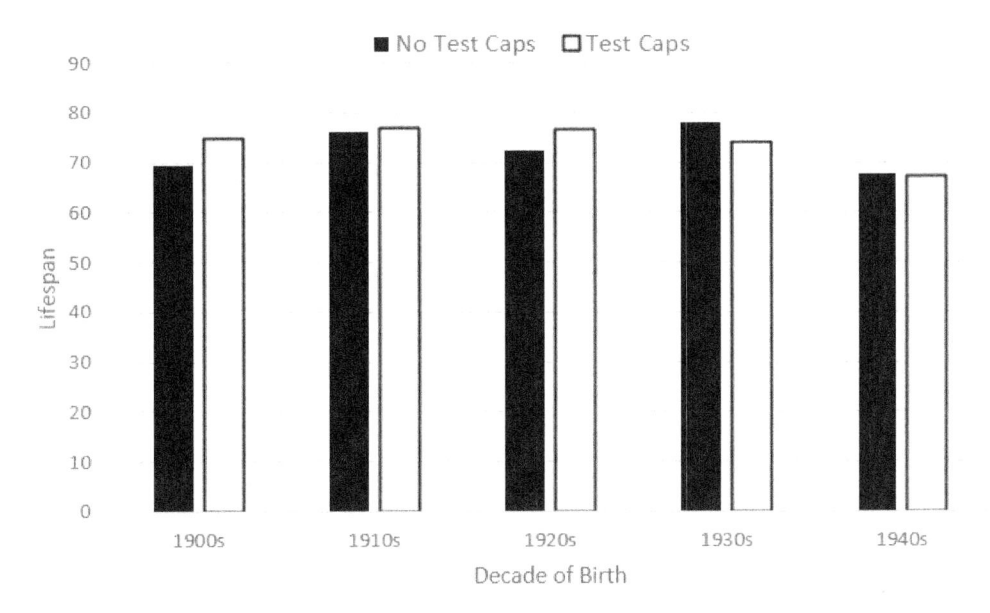

Figure 2.4. Average lifespan of All Blacks rugby players who received international test caps versus those who did not, by decade of birth.

What about the relationship between the number of test caps and longevity? To answer this, I built a statistical model which factored in decade of birth and number of test caps. The results were that each additional test cap equated to an average of 0.12 extra years of life. However, it should be noted that due to the wide variability in player lifespans (and the factors that determine them), neither decade of birth nor test caps were considered statistically significant determinants of longevity in the model. Still, the results of the model suggest that, all things being equal, every eight additional test caps equate to an extra year of life. They weren't kidding when they called Sam Whitelock a rugby immortal!

So there's evidence of a longevity effect when it comes to New Zealand rugby players. But does this effect apply elsewhere in the rugby world?

Historical data is not as easily available for players of other nations, but Wikipedia is a decent source (with the caveat that only around two-thirds of international rugby players born between 1900 and 1950 have their own Wikipedia page).

England

We'll begin, again, with a few notes about my criteria. For this analysis, I once again excluded players who passed away prior to turning 40, as well as the numerous players who switched allegiance to play the rival rugby league code during their playing careers, rendering them ineligible for further test rugby selection. For readers who aren't familiar with the sport's history, rugby league is a separate sport to rugby (also known as rugby union). Rugby league branched off in the 1890s to become a completely different professional code as opposed to rugby union (the sport we're interested in here), which remained amateur for another 100 years. While players switch back and forth between the two sports nowadays, back in the amateur days of rugby (union), it was not considered acceptable for a player to cross the divide to play professional rugby league.

Interestingly, I found no clear relationship between the number of test caps earned and longevity for England players. You can see from Figure 2.5 that the longevity trendline actually slopes ever so slightly downwards (though not significantly so) with additional test caps. Thumbing through the various Wikipedia pages of the players, you soon get a sense why. For players born in the first half of the 1900s, representing England in rugby was more like a gentleman's pastime than a life-defining pinnacle. This explains why there were so many lords, barons, marquises, ministers, major generals, Olympic medallists and a plethora of first-class cricketers among the ranks.

This cohort could of course be self-selecting, in that the players who were successful outside of rugby back then are the only ones who have Wikipedia pages. But it also fits in with rugby's status in English society at the time, which was vastly different than it was in New Zealand. Rugby was traditionally an elitist sport in England, played primarily by upper-class public-school pupils (English private schools) —an amateur pursuit played for the honour of the game, not for athletic distinction like it was in New Zealand.

2. Living for the Game: Rugby as the Elixir of Life?

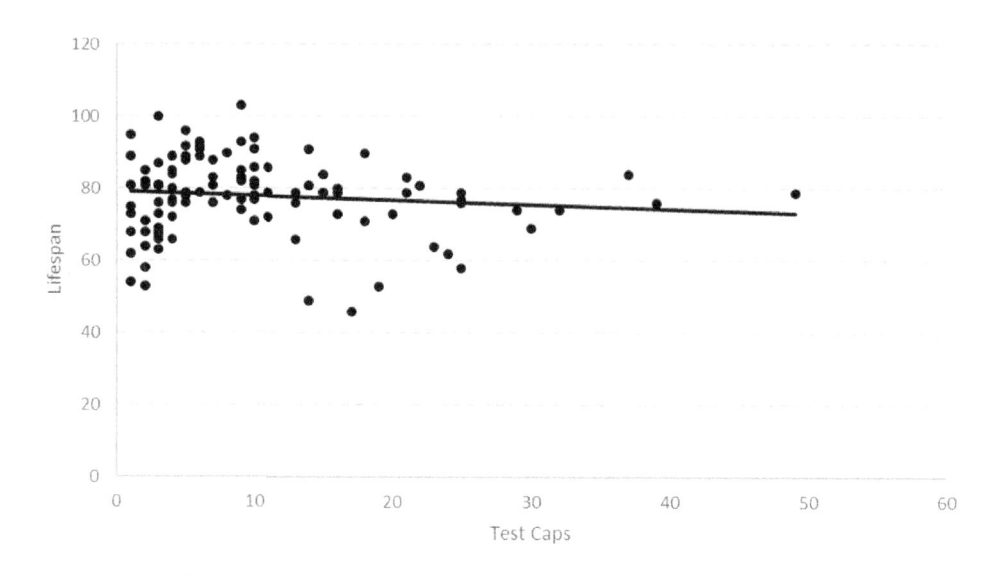

Figure 2.5. Lifespan of England international rugby players born between 1900 and 1950, by test caps.

We can't find a longevity effect in England. But perhaps things were different in countries more like New Zealand, where playing rugby bestowed an elevated status (and not vice-versa)?

Wales and South Africa

Wales and South Africa are the two other major test-playing nations where rugby could be considered the national sport (albeit for the white population only in South Africa, historically speaking). Looking at these countries individually, we can see a positive relationship between longevity and test caps by decade of birth. However, this effect is not statistically significant.

Combining the three similar rugby-mad countries together (New Zealand, Wales and South Africa) increases the statistical power, and we do find a subtle but significant overall impact of test caps on longevity in a statistical model incorporating all three nations. Figure 2.6 offers a good way to visualise this. Each dot represents a player, and you can see that, predictably, there is great variability in their lifespan and test caps; there are players who lived long lives with a small number of test caps, and players who lived short lives and had many test caps. Test caps are not the *biggest* predictor of lifespan, and we would never expect it to be. In fact, the model of test caps and birth decade only explains 6.7 percent of the overall variation in lifespan. Nevertheless, test caps are a statistically significant predictor of lifespan in this model. More test caps equate to greater longevity on average (as shown by the trendline in Figure 2.6 sloping upwards).

2. Living for the Game: Rugby as the Elixir of Life?

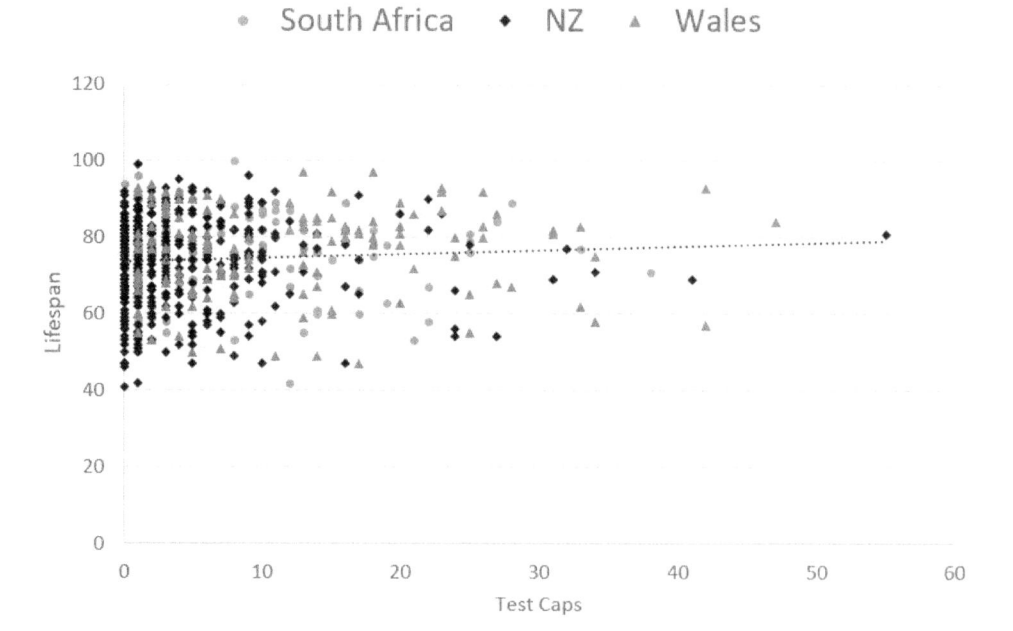

Figure 2.6. Average lifespan of South African, New Zealand and Welsh international rugby players born between 1900 and 1950, by test caps.

The roar of the Lions

There is another level of rugby achievement that is available to Welsh players but not to New Zealanders or South Africans. Selection for the British & Irish Lions, composed of the very best players from all the home nations of the British Isles (England, Wales, Scotland and Ireland), is a step up from national team selection. These tours are quadrennial nowadays but were more sporadic in the early 20th century. The data shows that selection for the Lions was associated with an increased lifespan for Welsh players of 2.7 years on average

(Figure 2.7). Statistically speaking, there is a 90 percent chance that this effect is real and not caused by chance.

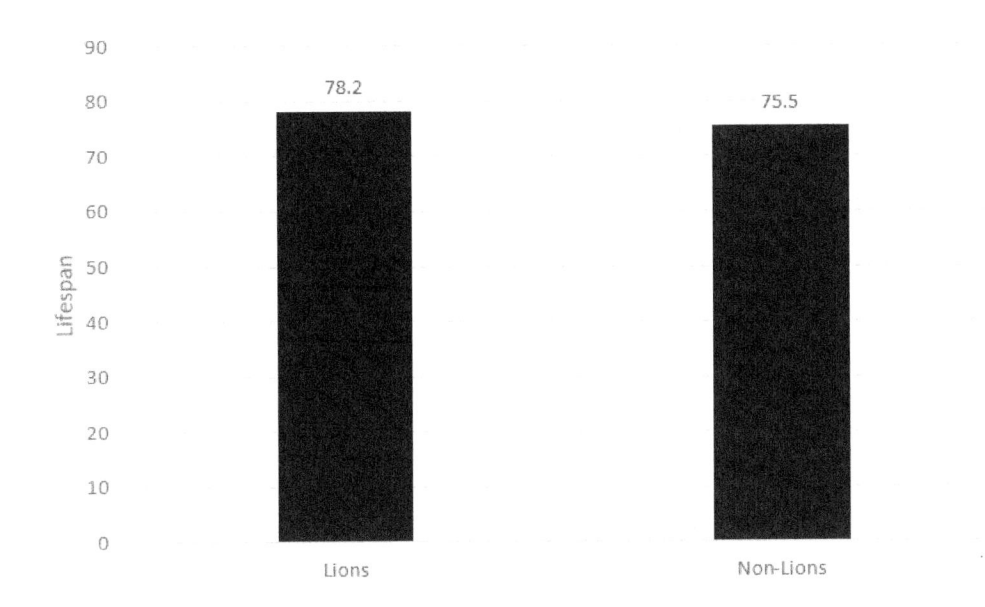

Figure 2.7. Average lifespan of Welsh international rugby players born between 1900 and 1950, by Lions test status.

Overall longevity

One thing that struck me while compiling this data was the longevity of these international rugby players of yesteryear. The majority of players born in the early to mid-1900s lived well into their 70s, 80s and even 90s—a rare achievement for people born in those times. Even if we include any players who died prior to turning 40, the average lifespan of rugby players from New Zealand, England and Wales far exceeds the life expectancy for males in those

2. Living for the Game: Rugby as the Elixir of Life?

countries at the time (Figure 2.8).

However, this is not a strictly apples-to-apples comparison. It's both staggering and heartbreaking to think that in the U.K. in 1900, the child mortality rate (under five years of age) was 23 percent; today that number has mercifully dropped to 0.4 percent. So when comparing the pure lifespans of international rugby players to the broader population, we are selecting men who had already passed that considerable hurdle of reaching adulthood in the early years of the 20th century.

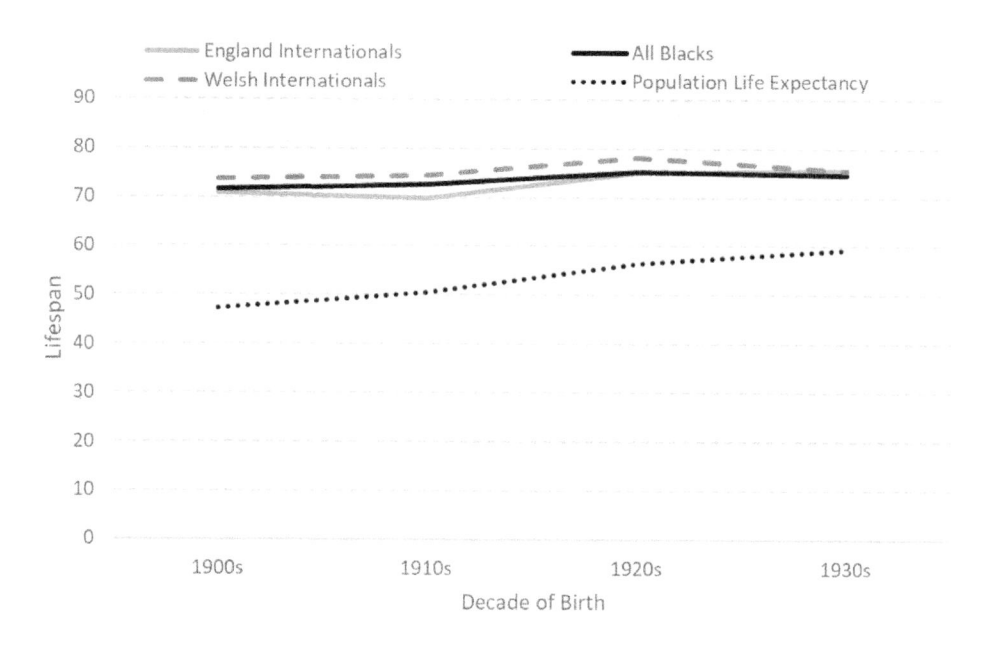

Figure 2.8. Average lifespan of international rugby players born between 1900 and 1940, versus the combined average male life expectancy of these countries from that era.

Accordingly, someone might reasonably object that these statistics are a bit skewed since no one who dies before age five can be counted as an international rugby player! That's where modal mortality, which relies on the mode rather than the average, comes in. Lifespan mode means the most common age at which people die. Since this number only includes people who have made it to adulthood, we can use it to make a more relevant comparison between international rugby players and the broader populations' modal lifespan. Grouping the three countries together ensures that the mode is not an outlier and is more robust.

The results show that even when we rely on mode rather than average, top rugby players considerably outlived the broader population (Figure 2.9). Their difference in lifespan is seven years on average during this period. This is in line with the numerous studies that have shown a longevity advantage for elite athletes over the broader population, with the levels varying by sport. Probably unsurprisingly, this advantage has been attributed to the athletes' high level of fitness and the lowered risks of cardiovascular disease and cancer that it brings.

2. Living for the Game: Rugby as the Elixir of Life?

Figure 2.9. Average modal lifespan of international rugby players (from New Zealand, England and Wales) versus the broader male U.K. population. Only the U.K. population's lifespan is plotted because it was nearly identical to New Zealand's over the same range.

The breakdown

There's always uncertainty in data, and the statistics presented in this chapter are no exception. Primarily this is because we're dealing with a cohort of players from a long time ago, about whom information is incomplete. It's certainly not ironclad that success on the rugby field leads to greater life longevity, as has been found in other fields. But the results suggest that it *may*, which is fascinating and tantalising to think about.

By necessity, this analysis had to be restricted to players from the Amateur era. But the game has changed dramatically since then (indeed, the focus of the next chapter is on how much bigger the modern international rugby player has become). Will the longevity effect still apply to the players of today? The force of the collisions is much bigger nowadays, although the sports science used to get players primed to compete and heal from injuries has also greatly advanced. Whether any effect will continue for players of the Professional era remains to be seen.

3. Tackling Titans: The Rise of Rugby's Heavyweights and Their Sporting Rivals

Go to any rugby pub around the world and it's amusing to look at the old team photos from yesteryear framed on the wall. The poses are the same as they are today—staunch players with arms folded and not a hint of a smile. But that's where the similarities between then and now tend to end. Because when you look at the old-time players, they look surprisingly... *normal*, at least from a size perspective. They're not at all like the behemoths that grace the pitches today.

It's tempting to date the turning point to 1996 when the game 'officially' went professional, meaning that players no longer needed to toil away at 40-hour-a-week jobs on top of training and playing. They could focus full-time on rugby, harnessing modern sporting science and professional expectations to boot. Accordingly, I thought it would be fascinating to examine what effects professionalisation has had on the physiques of today's players, which is why it's the focus of this chapter.

Player Weight

The most surprising thing I discovered when looking at the data is that by and large, rugby players have tracked the general population's weight increase over the last 100 years (Figures 3.1a and 3.1b). Rugby players have always been larger than the average man, even back in the 1930s, but their increase in size over time has been roughly proportional to that of the wider population.

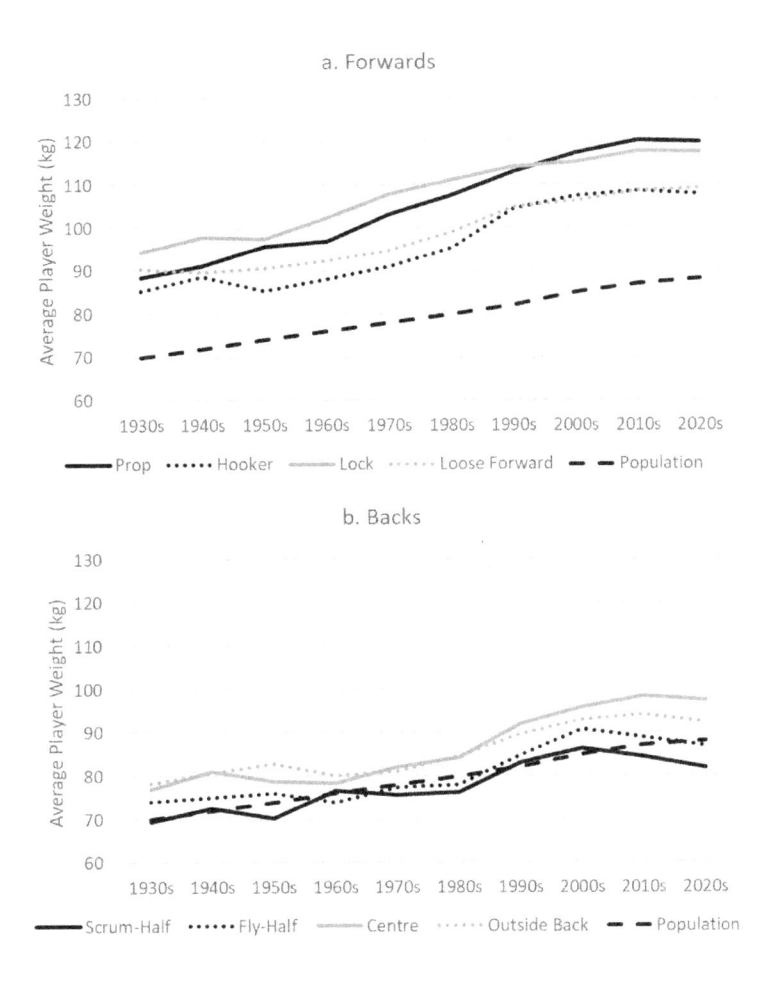

Figure 3.1. Average weight of Tier-1 international players by position; 'population' represents the average male adult in OECD countries. Figure 3.1a shows the forwards by position, and Figure 3.1b shows the backs.

3. Tackling Titans: The Rise of Rugby's Heavyweights and Their Sporting Rivals

By far, the largest growth in size over time has been among the props, whose weight increased 34 percent by the 2010s–20s compared with the 1930s–40s (Figure 3.2). The rest of the positions are either in line with broader male population growth or even substantially below it, as is the case with the 'skilled positions' of fly-half, outside backs and scrum-half.[5]

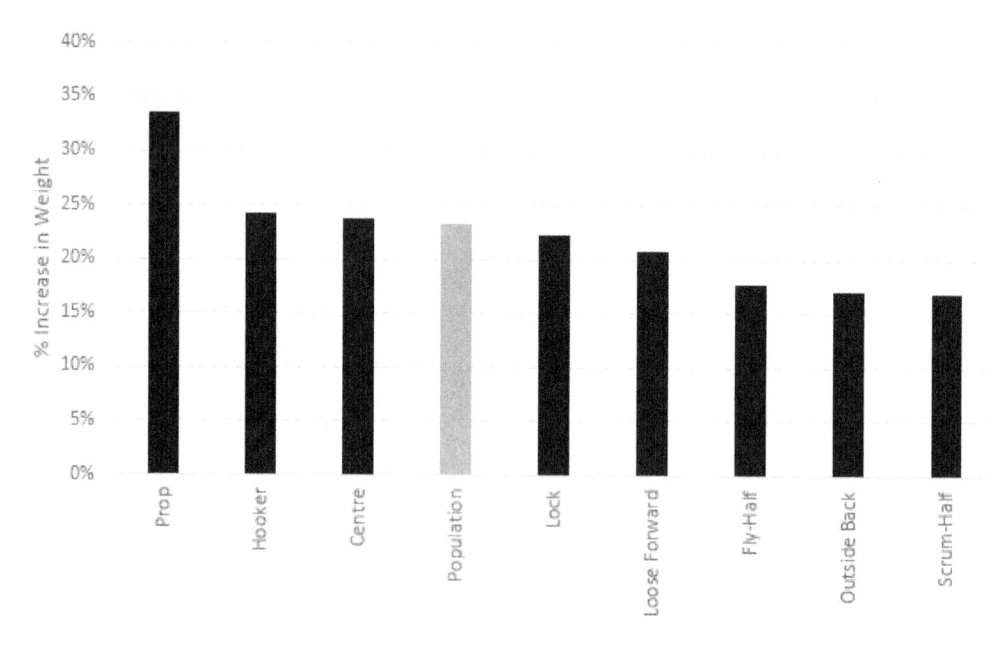

Figure 3.2. Average increase in weight by Tier-1 rugby internationals from the 1930s–40s versus the 2010s–20s. 'Population' represents the average male adult in OECD countries.

---

[5] I'm using the World Rugby convention for position names in this chapter. Common variations for fly-half are first five-eighth or out half, and the scrum-half is also called the halfback.

Now, as the average couch potato will attest, there are different types of weight increase. Nobody is concluding that the weight gain experienced by the broader population in OECD countries over the last 100 years has generally been a healthy increase in muscle mass! However, since the Professional era, rugby players have been piling on the pounds in the places that are most beneficial to their performance on the field. You just need to compare a modern-day prop to their forefathers of yesteryear to see how much their physiques have changed.

With rugby known as 'the sport for all body types', prop was traditionally the position occupied by the rather rotund players. (While they showed plenty of courage and guts in getting stuck into the very 'dark arts' of front-row play in the Amateur era, it has to be said that most of those guts were hanging out the front of their ill-fitting cotton rugby jerseys.) The average prop has gone from weighing 89kg in the 1930s to 120kg today. But even this huge gap in average weight hides some pretty stunning comparisons. Take for example Cyril Pepper, who debuted at prop for the All Blacks in 1935, weighing just 80kg. 80 years later, Uini Antonio was selected to start at prop for France, tipping the scales at a mammoth 149kg. That's nearly two Cyril Peppers! Here's how ChatGPT thinks a hypothetical meeting between the two would look:

3. Tackling Titans: The Rise of Rugby's Heavyweights and Their Sporting Rivals

Sometimes the change in body shape can happen rapidly, spurred on by the success of specific players. Terry Wright and Jonah Lomu were All Blacks wingers in adjacent eras. Wright's last test for the All Blacks was in 1992, whereas Lomu debuted in 1994. Wright was nicknamed the 'Cheetah', and he needed to be bloody quick to escape any trouble, since he tipped the scales at 75kg when dripping wet. Lomu, on the other hand, who rapidly became a global phenomenon and is still perhaps the greatest icon the game has ever seen, weighed in at 120kg. That's 60 percent heavier than Wright, yet they played the same position only a couple of years apart. While a 100kg winger was unheard of prior to Jonah Lomu, they are closer to the norm nowadays. The average weight of Tier-1 international wingers debuting this century is 95kg.

It wasn't only Lomu who was much heavier than his predecessors. As we touched on before, the dawn of the Professional era, which kicked off in 1996, spurred a marked increase in player weights. The weight leap in the 1990s in most rugby positions is readily apparent in Figure 3.3 (and a bit more subtly back in Figures 3.1a and 3.1b). The average weight of the hooker, centre, scrum-half and fly-half positions have grown at a remarkable clip; players in these positions in the 1990s weighed almost ten percent more than their predecessors in the 1980s. All positions except locks greatly exceeded the weight growth of the general population during the 1990s, too.

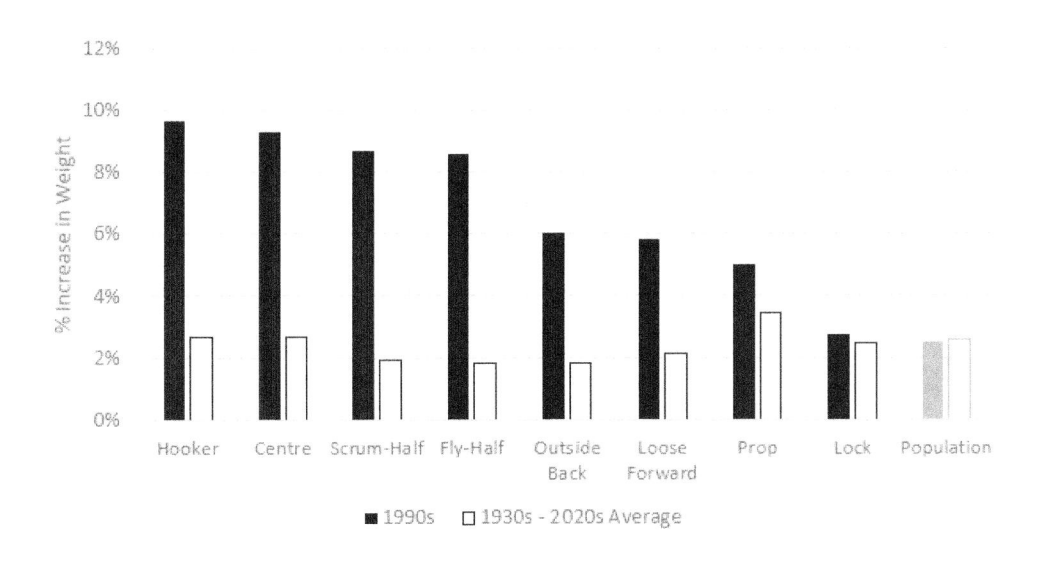

Figure 3.3. *Average decadal weight increase of Tier-1 rugby internationals. 'Population' represents the average male adult in OECD countries.*

3. Tackling Titans: The Rise of Rugby's Heavyweights and Their Sporting Rivals

There is evidence that some positions have perhaps reached 'peak size growth', at least for now. After all, greater bulk often means less speed, agility and fitness. Going back to Figures 3.1a and 3.1b, you can see a marked flattening out of the weight increase of most positions in recent years, with the weight of some positions even declining. The 2020s are obviously incomplete, and there's plenty of time for the numbers from this decade to change. However, even in the period from the 2000s into the 2010s, there was a slowdown in player weight increases across many positions. As you can see in Figure 3.4, the weight gain during that (recent) period was lower than the historical average across all positions, and even below that of the broader population.

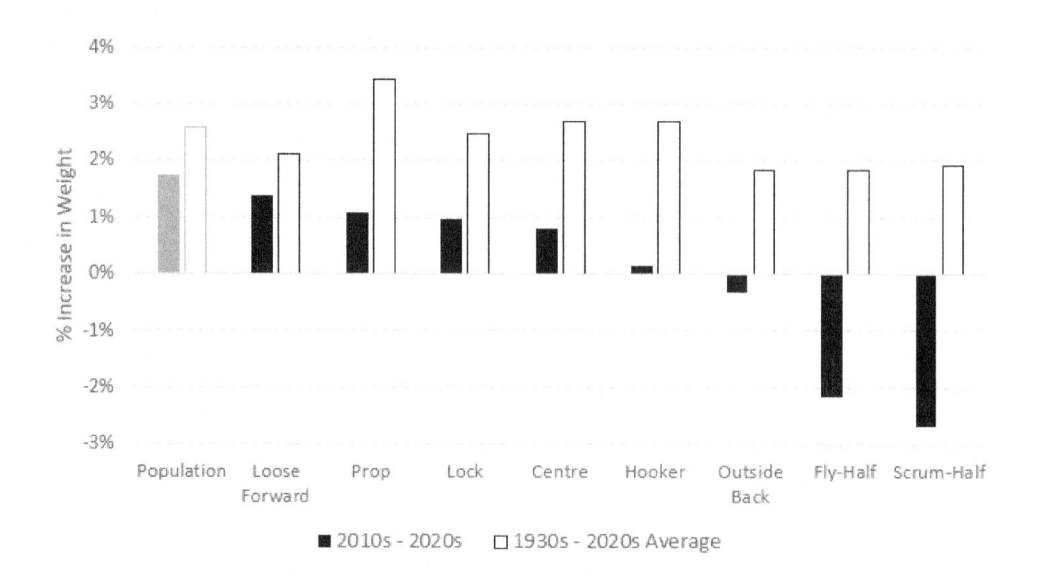

Figure 3.4. *Average decadal weight increase of Tier-1 rugby internationals. 'Population' represents the average male adult in OECD countries.*

One thing that's important to keep in mind when looking at the changing size of players is playing strategy, which has rapidly evolved as well. Much of this has been in reaction to rule changes, and arguably none have had a bigger impact than new substitution rules. It may be hard for some younger readers to believe, but back in the amateur days, the reserve bench was just that—reserve players to be called into action only in an emergency. Up until 1996, teams were only permitted to replace players who could no longer physically continue. As you might imagine, the stories of what players went through to remain on the field are legendary (and in some cases horrifying). The prevailing attitude back then was that you never walked off the field; if you were injured enough to require replacement, you had better be carried off on a stretcher!

Nowadays, the reserve bench is very much part of the match-day team and game strategy. Rugby today is really played by a 23-man team, rather than just the 15 who start the match. This change has no doubt driven the body-type evolution of certain positions, none more so than the front rowers. There is now a full set of replacement front rowers on the bench, and the starting props and hookers are generally replaced at around the 60-minute mark. Indeed, in the 2023 Six Nations, the starting front rowers lasted, on average, until the 59th minute.

It's therefore not surprising that front rowers' weight increased the most of any position through the 1990s and into the 2000s, as their role shifted from being a workhorse on the field for 80 minutes to strategically targeting only around 60 minutes of peak performance. With less playing time, their extra bulk became less of a fitness burden. Accordingly, props and hookers were the two positions with the greatest average weight gain over the last 100 years (Figure 3.2).

Another interesting trend that eagle-eyed readers may have picked up from Figures 3.1a and 3.1b is that there has been a slight divergence in size between backs and forwards over time. While forwards were still heavier than backs in the 1930s and 1940s, this separation became more pronounced from the 1960s onwards as the positions became even more specialised. In the 1930s–40s, forwards were 17 percent heavier than backs on average, whereas since 2000 they have been 23 percent heavier (Figure 3.5). It's also very interesting to see that the average back playing international rugby in the 2000s, at 92.1kg, is heavier than the average forward was in the 1930s–40s (90.8kg)!

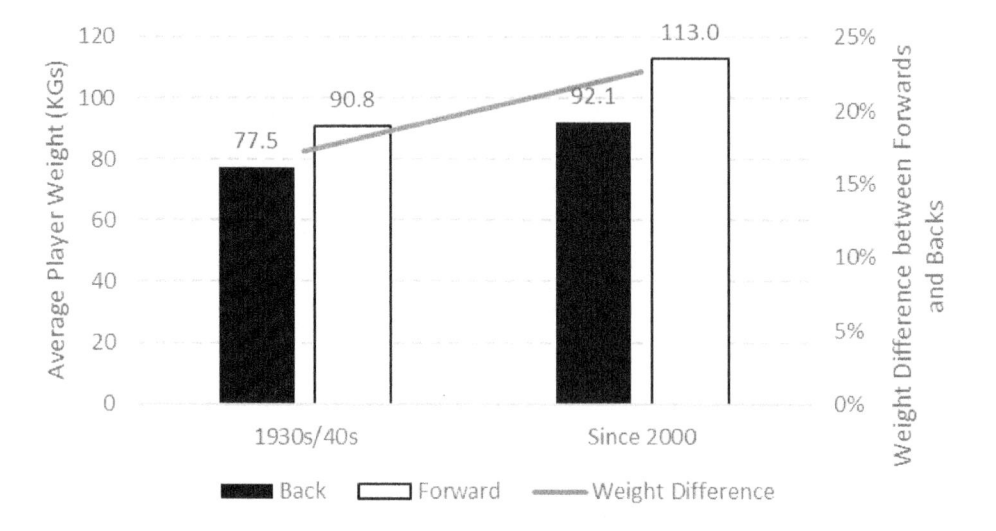

Figure 3.5. Average weight and weight difference between Tier-1 international forwards and backs, comparing the 1930s–40s to post-2000.

Player Height

Examining player height by position reveals some marked differences from what we saw with weight (Figures 3.6a and 3.6b). The locks and loose forwards separate themselves as the tallest players, while there is little to differentiate the front-row forwards (props and hookers) from the centres and outside backs. Predictably, scrum-halves are the only position that tend to be shorter than the broader population.

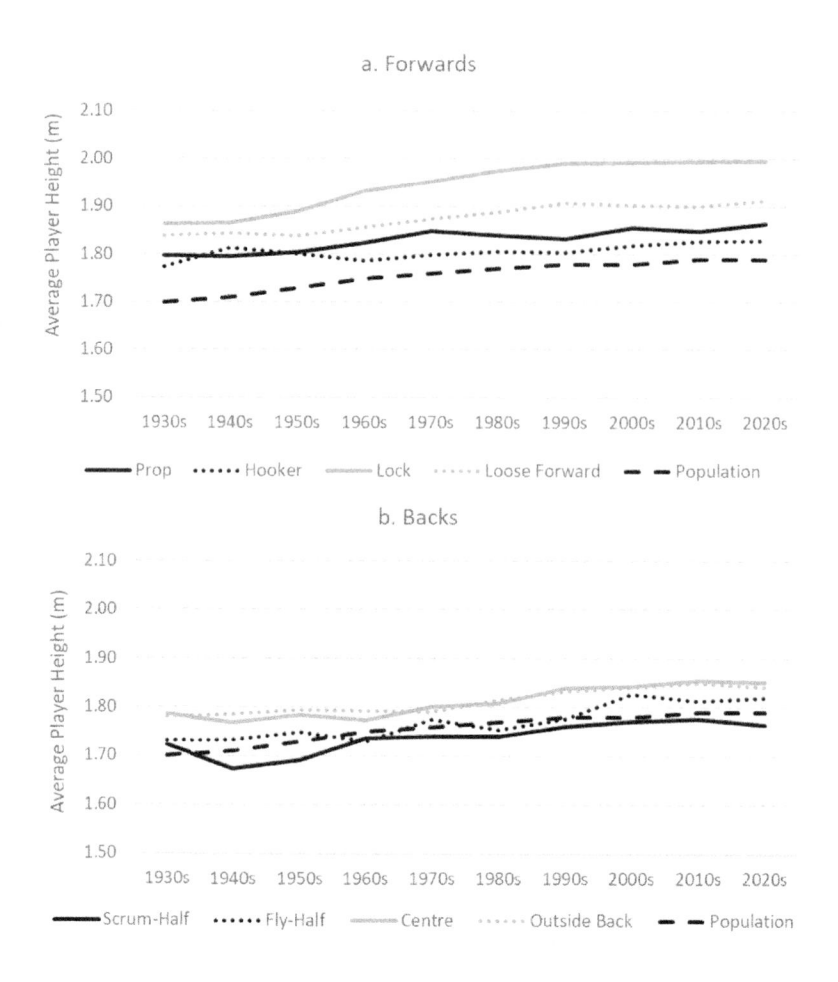

3. Tackling Titans: The Rise of Rugby's Heavyweights and Their Sporting Rivals

Figure 3.6. Average height of Tier-1 international players by position. 'Population' represents the average male adult in OECD countries. Figure 3.6a shows the forwards by position, and Figure 3.6b shows the backs.

I think it's fascinating that, except for locks, international rugby players have *under-indexed* in terms of their height increase versus the broader population over the last 100 years (Figure 3.7). The height of the average lock has increased 7 percent, from 1.86m in the 1930s to 2.00m today. But the other positions have not increased in height more than 5 percent, which is the overall population's average increase in OECD countries. This is quite surprising when you consider rugby's professionalisation during this time. You would think there'd be even more of an incentive for larger, taller, sports-minded males to apply themselves to the game. And yet, in the 1930s, the average Tier-1 international rugby player was 5.7 percent taller than the general population, while today they are 'only' 4.6 percent taller.

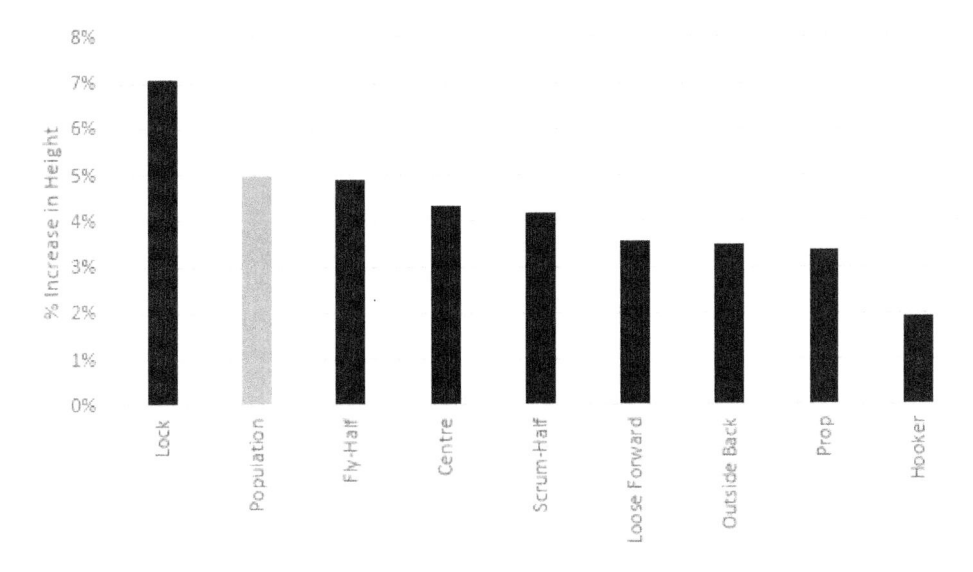

Figure 3.7. Average increase in height by Tier-1 rugby internationals from the 1930s–40s versus the 2010s–20s. 'Population' represents the average male adult in OECD countries.

While the locks have grown substantially taller and really separated themselves from the rest of the rugby pack and the general population (Figure

3. Tackling Titans: The Rise of Rugby's Heavyweights and Their Sporting Rivals

3.6), this increase was really only significant between the 1940s and 1990s. During this time, the average height of locks increased 12cm, from 1.87m 1.99m. This was a 6.8 percent increase, while the average height of males in the general population increased by just 4.1 percent. But since reaching the 1.99m figure in the '90s, the average height of locks has flatlined. It remained at 1.99m through the 2000s and 2010s, before inching up to 2.00m in the 2020s. Figure 3.8 shows the heights of all 352 locks used in this analysis by their debut year, with the trendline showing steep growth from 1940 to 1990 before flattening out.

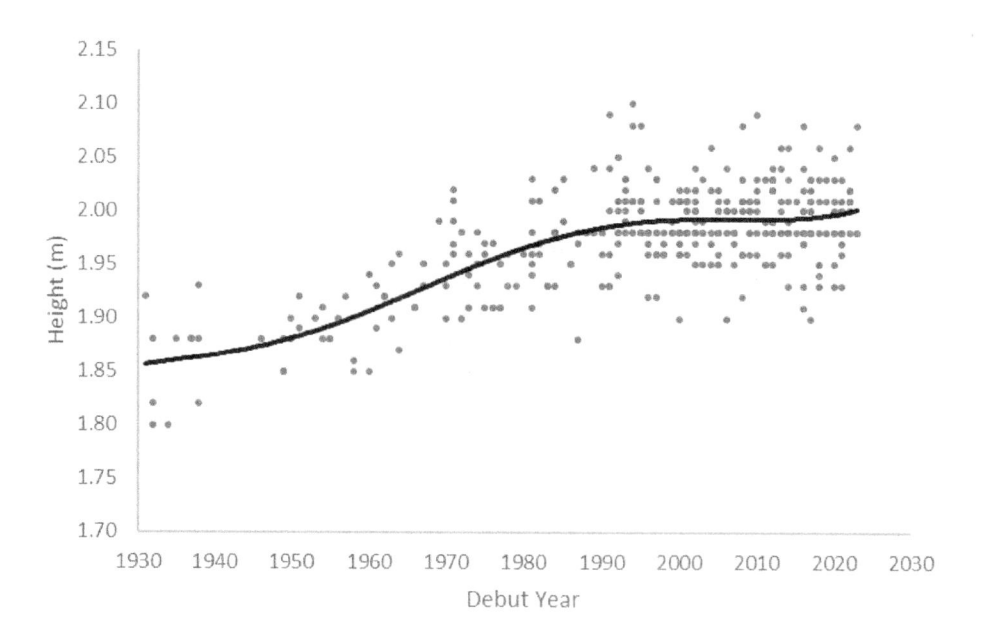

Figure 3.8. Height by debut year for Tier-1 international locks since 1930.

What caused this sudden halt in locks' height growth? Had all the tall people in rugby-playing countries already been snatched up to play? Highly unlikely. There is no doubt a number of reasons, but arguably the biggest one was a major law change that officially came into effect in 1999. The change allowed lifting in the lineouts, so suddenly extra height wasn't such a crucial requirement for the big fellas, as they could be thrown up there by their supporting players anyway. Since this law change (which, to be fair, many teams had been covertly doing for years anyway), the average height of locks hasn't really increased at all. It's a very similar trend with their weight (Figure 3.9), which is perhaps not surprising as even rugby forwards struggle to lift and support 140kg giants in the lineouts!

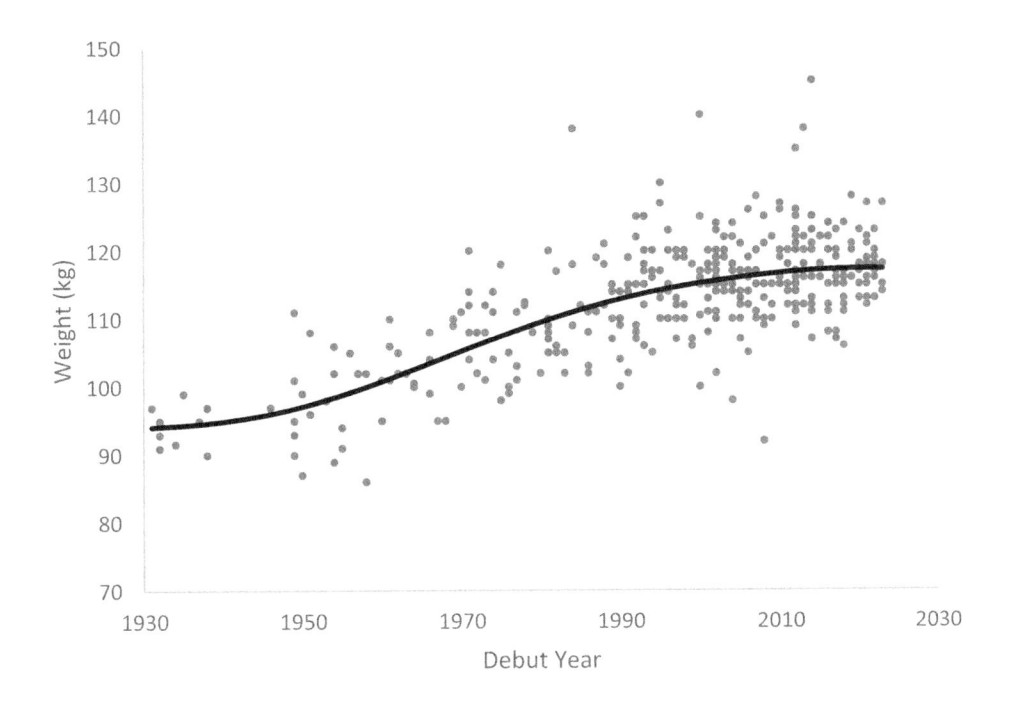

Figure 3.9. Weight by debut year for Tier-1 international locks since 1930.

3. Tackling Titans: The Rise of Rugby's Heavyweights and Their Sporting Rivals

Legalised lifting in the lineouts would not be the only factor, though. There is a natural limit to height and size that a lock can reach before their extra bulk starts to hurt other aspects of their game. After all, their job is not only to secure the lineout ball; they also need to hit rucks and mauls, tackle, carry the ball, and on occasion even show a bit of razzle-dazzle while running in open space. It takes a lot more effort to keep up with the fast pace of the modern game.

The 1990s and onwards also saw the growth of other sporting opportunities in traditional rugby strongholds. Basketball in particular exploded globally in the late 1980s and 1990s, and its popularity has not waned since. Even in rugby-mad New Zealand, one of the country's highest-profile athletes at the moment is National Basketball Association (NBA) centre Steven Adams. At 2.11m, he'd be right at the very upper end of international lock heights, and in another era, a Kiwi kid with that kind of size would have more than likely been ushered down the rugby pathway.

Basketball continues to draw a lot of tall talent. Between 2000 and 2020, rugby fell from first place to third in school-age sport participation in New Zealand, overtaken by football (soccer) and basketball. And the home of the All Blacks is hardly the only core rugby-playing nation confronting this trend.

Comparison to other sports

For context, we do see a similar levelling-off of player size in other power sports over a similar time period. American football is perhaps the most comparable major sport to rugby in terms of power, physicality and collisions. And it did in fact evolve from rugby (and football/soccer) some 150 years ago, although today it is a completely different sport.

The following data was taken from almost 9,000 NFL players. While there are no backs and forwards in the NFL like in rugby, there are some similarities in position categories. There are the big boys in the offensive and defensive lines, the 'skill positions' on both offense and defence, and the hybrid players such as tight ends and linebackers who shift between the line and the open field. Unlike rugby, however, the NFL was professional right from its founding, in 1920.

It's interesting to see that players in so-called skill positions haven't really increased in weight since then (Figure 3.10). The skill players that debuted in the 1930s averaged 87kg, which was 25 percent heavier than the adult male population average at the time. Today they average 91kg, just 4 percent heavier than the adult male population.

However, the big boys in the offensive and defensive line did grow A LOT from the 1930s to the 1990s—a 41 percent increase from 95kg to 134kg. But from the 1990s to the 2020s, they've only increased by 2kg on average, to 136kg today. What could have caused this sudden plateau? Well, the NFL began testing players for steroid use in 1987 and banning players in 1989, which would undoubtedly have contributed to this levelling off in size.

The hybrid players have had much slower weight growth since they were introduced to the game in the 1940s. Their average weight increased by 16

3. Tackling Titans: The Rise of Rugby's Heavyweights and Their Sporting Rivals

percent until the 1990s, before experiencing a similar plateau.

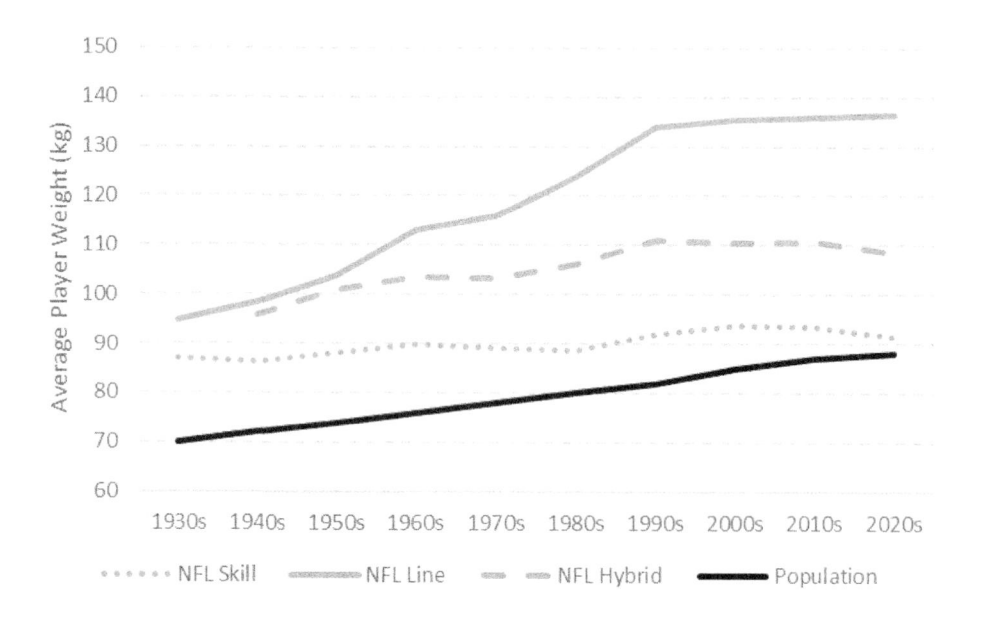

Figure 3.10. Average weight of NFL players by position category. 'Population' represents the average male adult in OECD countries.

The trends are similar but less pronounced when looking at NFL player height (Figure 3.11). There's been little increase among skill players, and a gradual increase among linemen and hybrid players, albeit even this has slowed down since the 1970s.

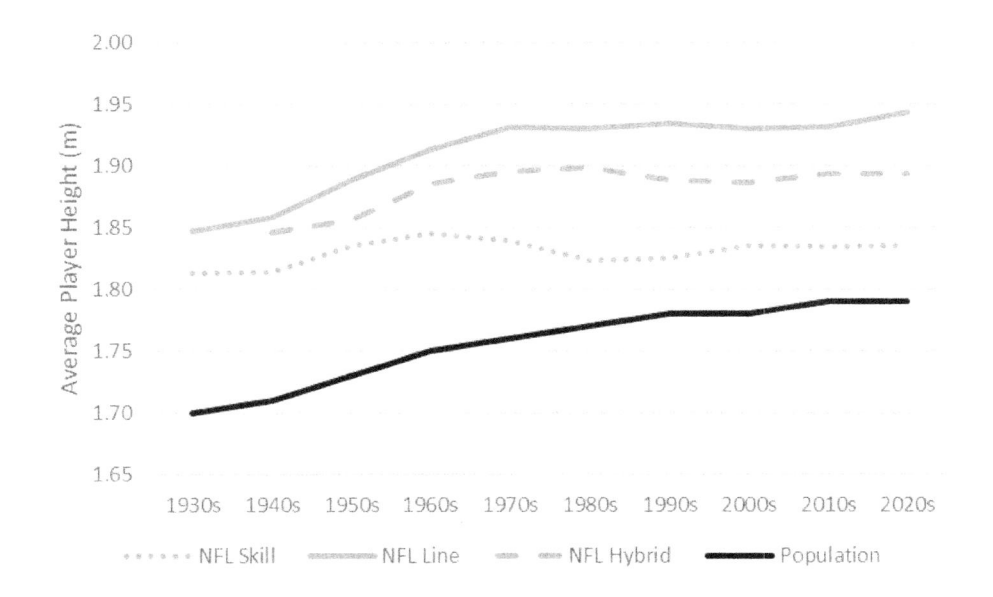

Figure 3.11. Average height of NFL players by position category. 'Population' represents the average male adult in OECD countries.

Of course, with data the devil is so often in the details. While the charts aggregate many different positions together, looking at individual positions tells a different story. For example, since the 1950s there's been a big divergence in height between two of the main skill positions, quarterbacks and running backs (Figure 3.12). Quarterbacks have become 5cm taller since the 1950s while on average running backs are 4cm *shorter*.

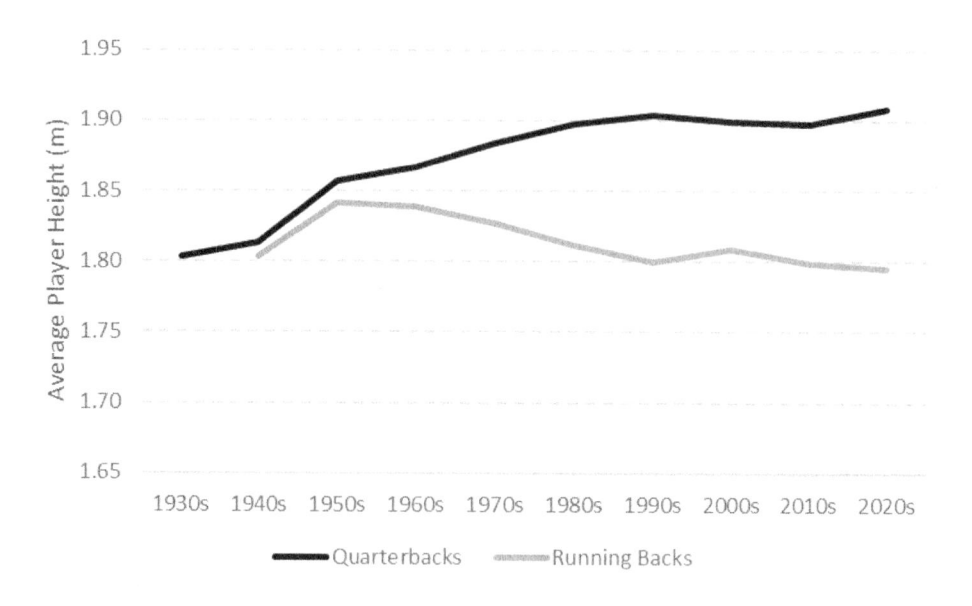

3. Tackling Titans: The Rise of Rugby's Heavyweights and Their Sporting Rivals

Figure 3.12. Average height of NFL quarterbacks and running backs since 1930.

So how do rugby players compare physically to NFL players? The first thing to note is that rugby backs have caught up to NFL skill-position players in both weight and height. As recently as the 1960s, Tier-1 international rugby backs were 12kg (15 percent) lighter and 7cm (4 percent) shorter than their NFL counterparts. Today they are the same weight—91kg—and almost the same height (1.84m vs 1.83m) on average (Figure 3.13).

Rugby forwards have undergone a similar transformation when compared to the NFL's hybrid players, overtaking them in both weight and height in the 1990s. However, rugby forwards are still dwarfed by the giants of the NFL line, who today are 22kg (20 percent) heavier and 3cm taller on average.

a. Player Weight

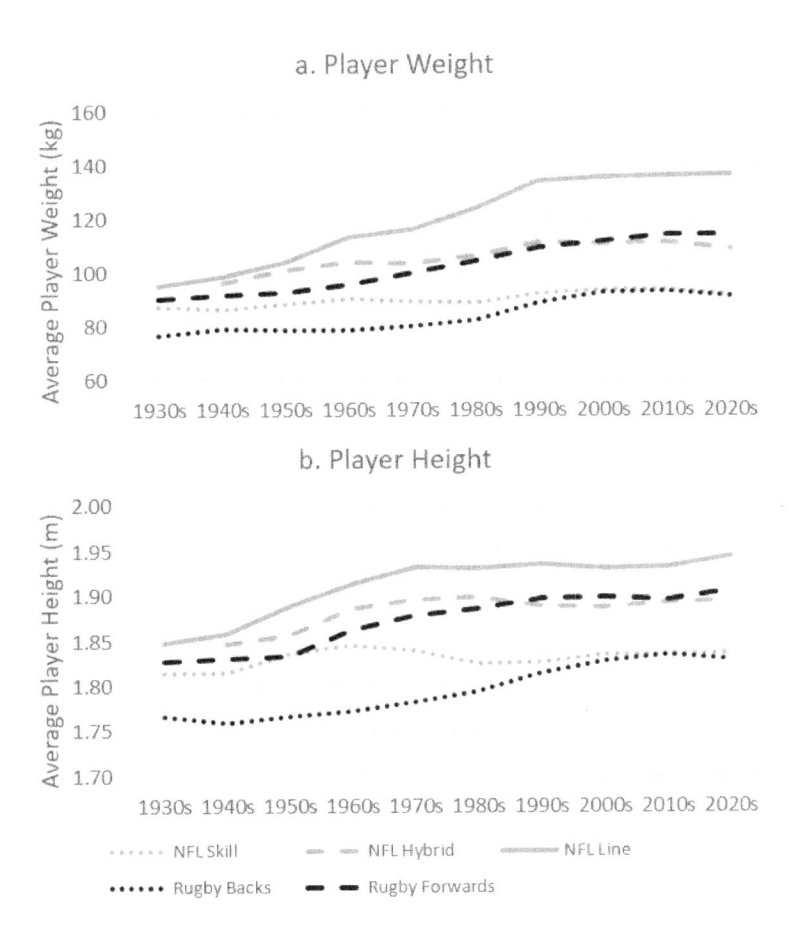

b. Player Height

Figure 3.13. Average weight and height of Tier-1 rugby internationals and NFL players by position category. Figure 3.13a shows player weight, and Figure 3.13b shows player height.

Even the heaviest rugby forward position—prop—is on average 16kg (14 percent) lighter than the NFL linemen today (Figure 3.14). However, the tall timber of the rugby forward pack, the locks, do currently edge the NFL linemen by 6cm in height.

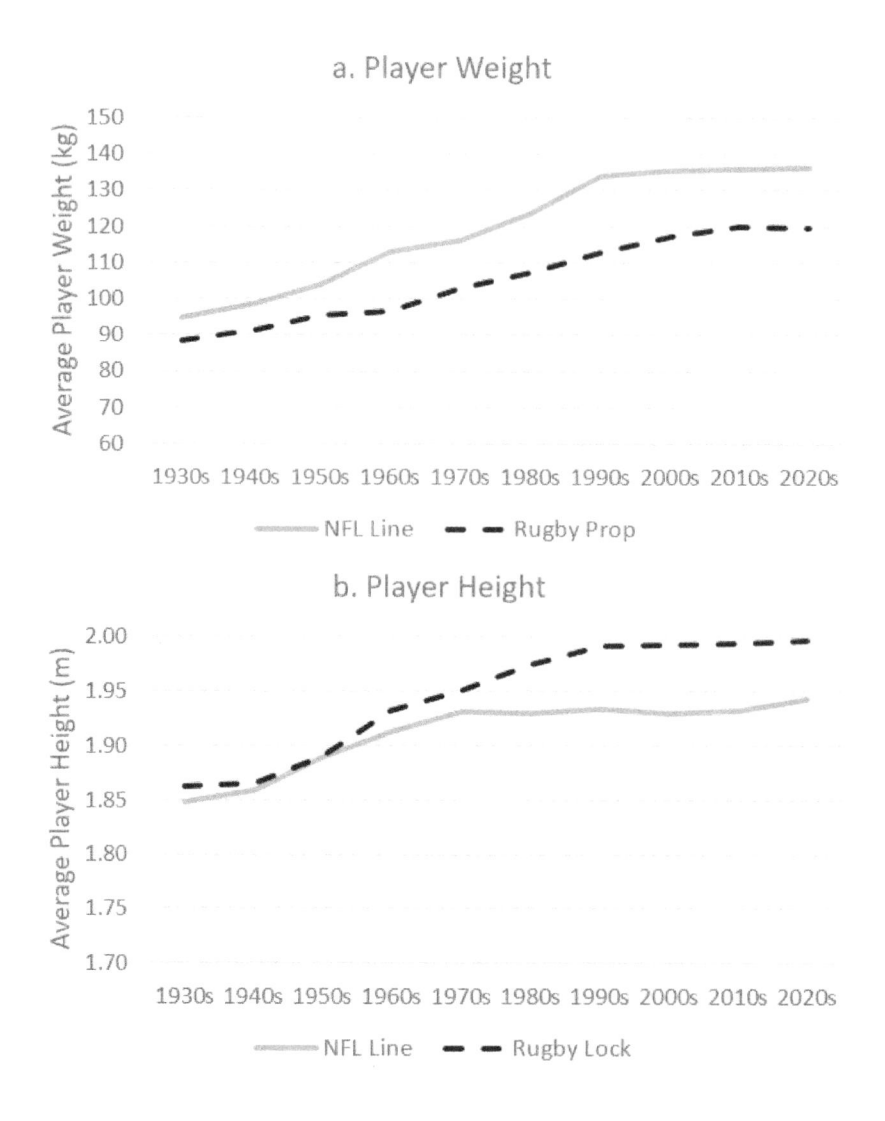

3. Tackling Titans: The Rise of Rugby's Heavyweights and Their Sporting Rivals

a. Player Weight

b. Player Height

Figure 3.14. Average weight and height of NFL linemen since 1930, compared to the heaviest and tallest rugby positions. Figure 3.14a shows player weight of NFL linemen and rugby props, and Figure 3.14b shows player height of NFL linemen and rugby locks.

If we want to compare rugby players with the truly tallest timber in American professional sports, however, we need to go to another league entirely, the NBA. You can see from Figure 3.15 that rugby locks are dwarfed by NBA centres, who are currently 12cm taller on average, at 2.12m. The perception of height is often warped when watching NBA basketball. It's easy to forget that the 'little' fast, speedy, and skilled guys (aka the guards) are usually over 1.90m tall! In fact, those 'little' guys average 1.94m in height, only 6cm shorter, on average, than the big 'lumbering locks' of rugby.

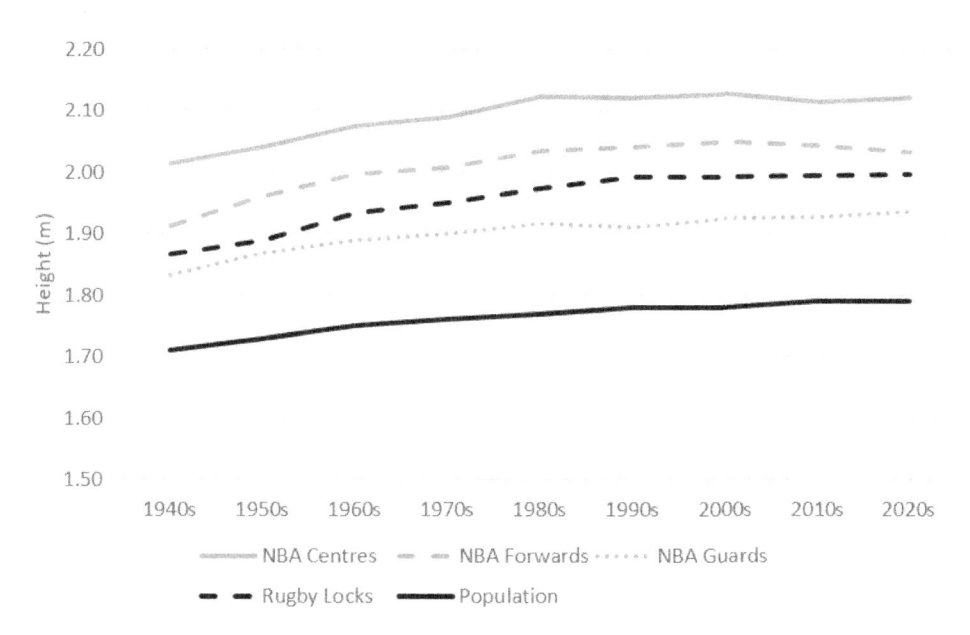

Figure 3.15. Average height of NBA players by position since the 1940s, compared to Tier-1 international rugby locks and the OECD male population.

Locks are ever so slowly catching up, and they have grown at a higher rate than all NBA positions over the last 80 years (Figure 3.16). However, even if

3. Tackling Titans: The Rise of Rugby's Heavyweights and Their Sporting Rivals

the growth rates in Figure 3.16 continued at the same pace (and we have seen that they are not), it would still take around 300 years for rugby locks to catch up to NBA centres!

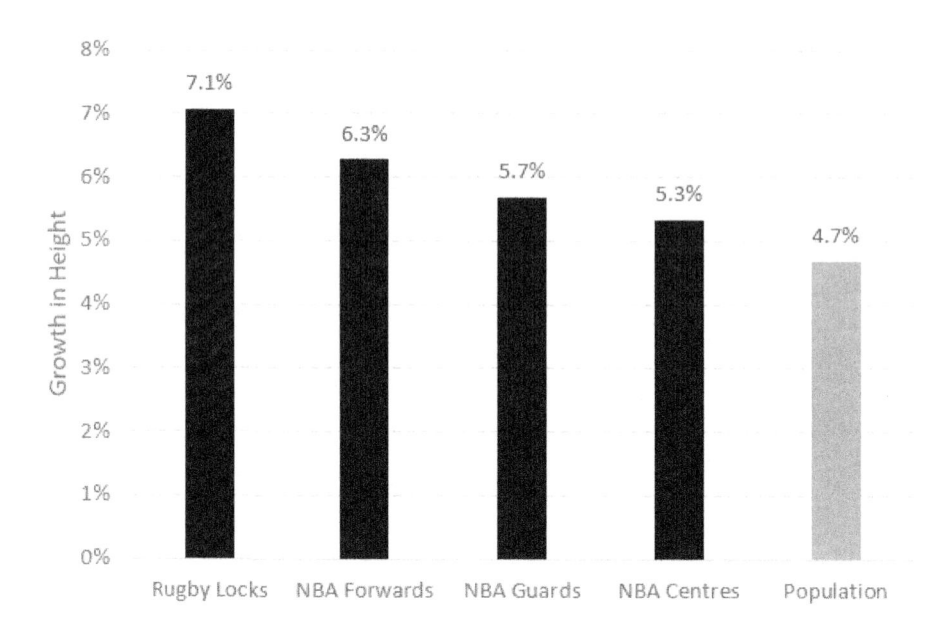

Figure 3.16. Average increase in height of NBA players by position and Tier-1 international rugby locks between the 1940s and the 2020s.

Of course, the body shapes of basketball players and rugby players are quite different. Basketball is not a full-contact sport (though try telling that to someone who has just courageously taken a charge from a centre at full speed!). But in terms of weight, rugby locks and NBA centres have been on a par over the past 80 years, with locks just edging the big men out (Figure 3.17).

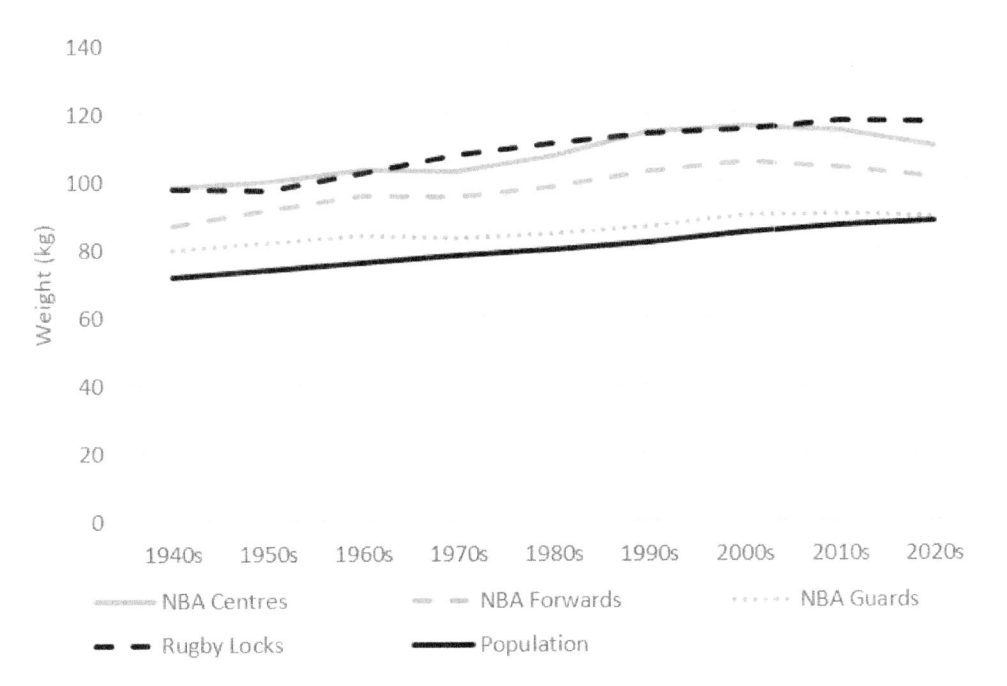

Figure 3.17. Average weight of NBA players by position since the 1940s, compared to Tier-1 international rugby locks and the OECD male population.

We saw in Figure 3.2 that locks have slightly under-indexed against the broader population in weight growth (in OECD countries) in the last 80 years. Well, as Figure 3.18 shows, NBA players have under-indexed even more.

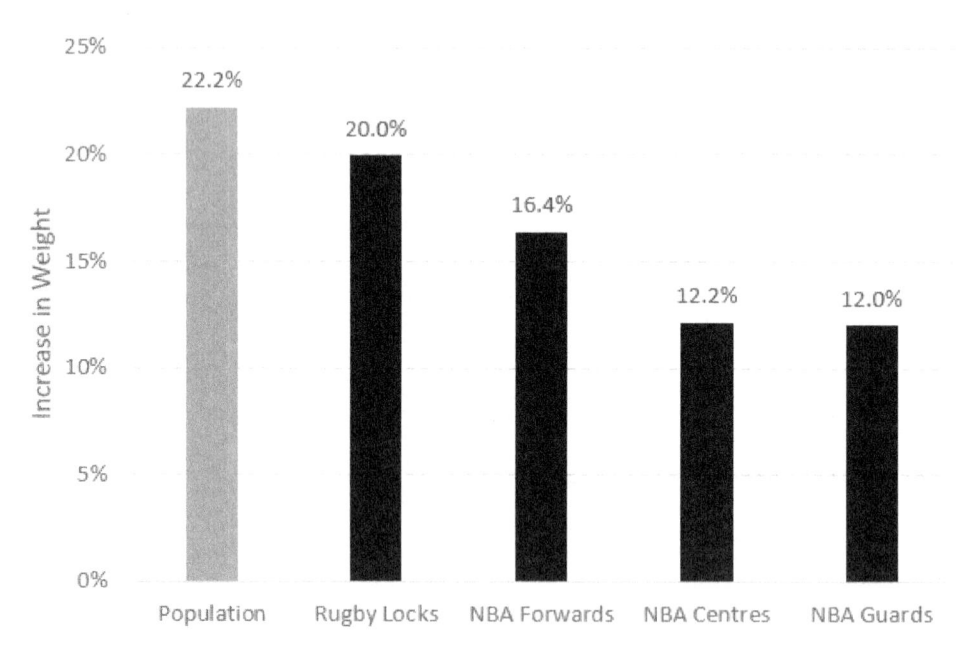

3. Tackling Titans: The Rise of Rugby's Heavyweights and Their Sporting Rivals

Figure 3.18. Average weight increase of NBA players by position since the 1940s, compared to Tier-1 international rugby locks and the OECD male population.

Comparing body mass index (or BMI) is a convenient way to visualise the difference and divergence in body shape between rugby locks and NBA players. Rugby locks are bulkier than NBA players—a difference that has intensified since the 1970s (Figure 3.19). NBA players of the 2020s actually have a very similar average BMI to players in the 1940s, whereas contemporary locks have an average BMI that's almost 5 percent higher than their counterparts did 80 years ago. That said, the BMI growth of these professional sportsmen is dwarfed by the 11.5 percent average BMI growth of the male population in OECD countries during this same time period (Figure 3.20).

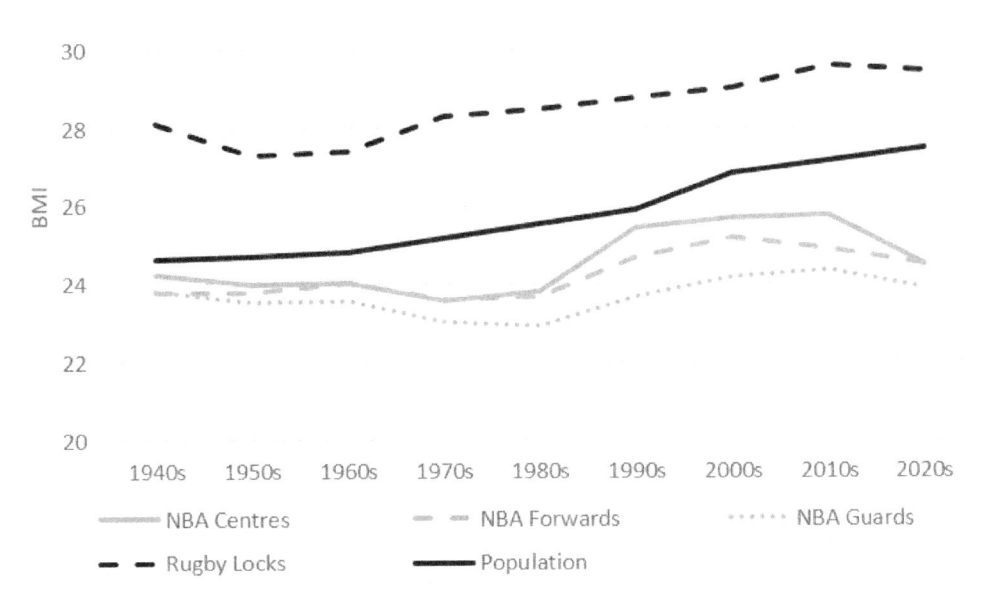

Figure 3.19. Average BMI of NBA players by position since the 1940s, compared to Tier-1 international rugby locks and the OECD male population.

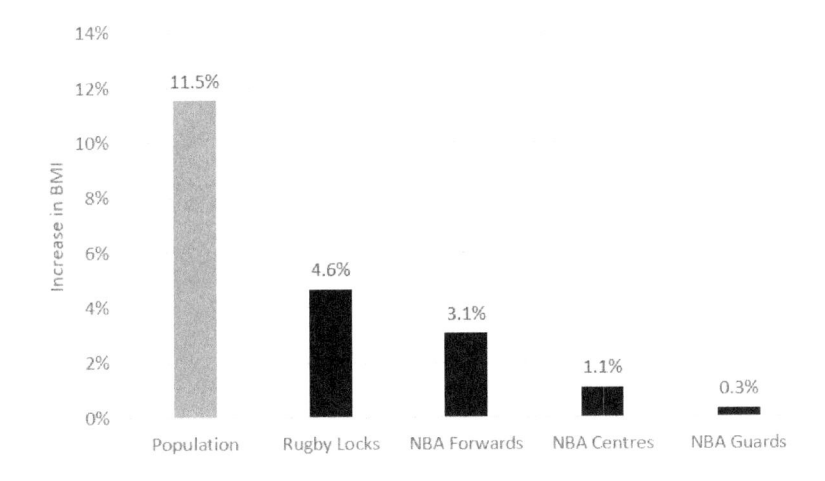

Figure 3.20. Average BMI increase of NBA players by position since the 1940s, compared to Tier-1 international rugby locks and the OECD male population.

3. Tackling Titans: The Rise of Rugby's Heavyweights and Their Sporting Rivals

If we want to visualise the differences and the changes in size of rugby players alongside NFL and NBA players, an XY plot showing height and weight is helpful (Figure 3.21).

A couple of things stand out from the following charts. First, there are fairly distinct groupings between the red NBA players and the blue NFL players; it's almost as if an imaginary diagonal line running from the lower left to the upper right separates them. The rugby players, in black, tend to straddle this imaginary line, but they also tend to overlap more with the lighter NFL players, especially in the 2020s (Figure 3.21c). The other thing that stands out is the general size growth across all the athletes. They form a fairly tight cluster near the lower left in the 1940's chart (Figure 3.21a), but really spread out both upwards and especially to the right (the weight axis) in the 2020's chart (Figure 3.21c).

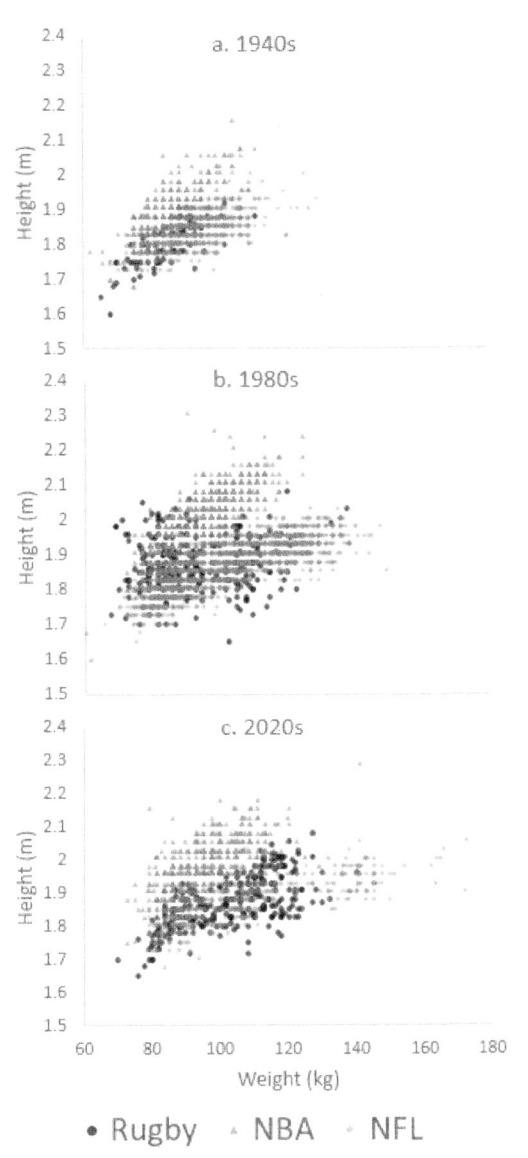

Figure 3.21. Comparison of player heights and weights for Tier-1 international rugby, NBA and NFL players during selected decades. Figure 3.21a shows player averages from the 1940s, Figure 3.21b the 1980s, and Figure 3.21c the 2020s.

3. Tackling Titans: The Rise of Rugby's Heavyweights and Their Sporting Rivals

If we use the same criteria to compare Tier-1 international rugby players between the Amateur era and the Professional era, we see that the main cluster also runs along a similar diagonal line (Figure 3.22). This pool of players moves slightly up (increased height) and to the right (heavier) in the Professional era. This is pretty predictable. What's really interesting is that another cluster starts to separate in the Professional era: a big group of players weighing 110–140kg and standing 1.8–1.9m in height. These are primarily the props of the modern era who have really separated themselves physically from the rest of the team.

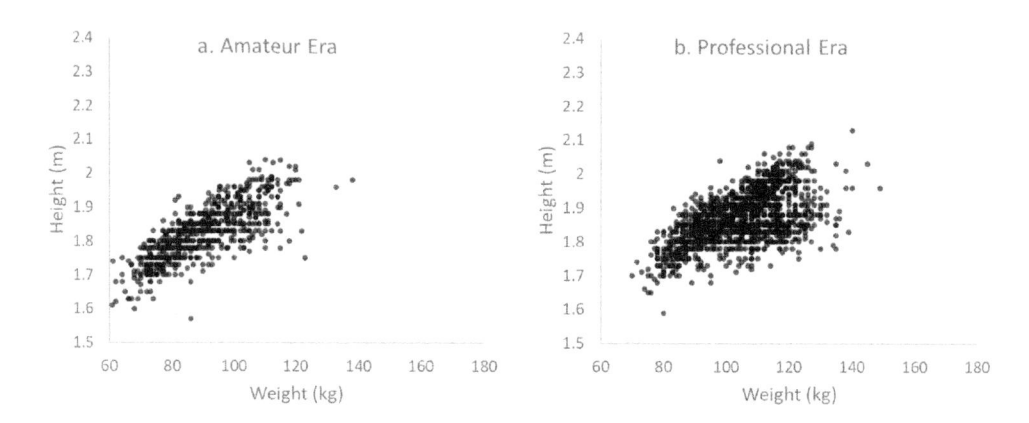

Figure 3.22. Comparison of player heights and weights for Tier-1 international rugby players during the Amateur and Professional eras. Figure 3.22a shows the player average from the Amateur era, spanning 1940–1995; Figure 3.22b shows the player averages from the Professional era, spanning 1996–2023.

The (literal) sleeping giants of world rugby

In this chapter we've explored how elite international rugby players compare in size to some of the biggest athletes in U.S. professional sport. While the physical demands and skills of the sports are completely different, I often wonder what some of these top U.S. athletes could do on a rugby field if they had focused on it from a young age. The ridiculous athleticism on display with some slam dunks you see in the NBA or touchdown catches in the NFL makes it hard to believe these players wouldn't be rugby superstars if they had grown up in a different country. No doubt when they look at their bank balance, they're probably very glad to have taken the path they have, as salaries in U.S. professional sports leagues are an order of magnitude higher than what top rugby players earn. And that's before we even consider the lucrative sponsorship deals on offer.

All of that said, it's fun to muse over what a U.S. rugby 'dream team' might look like. Here's my stab at such a team, drawn from U.S. athletes active in the early 2020s.

Prop: Trent Brown (NFL, offensive tackle)—2.03m, 168kg *(Tier-1 Rugby Average: 1.86m, 120kg)*

An absolute giant of a man, Brown would dwarf most current international props, exceeding their average weight by 40 percent! While playing a full 40 minutes may take a toll on his fitness, he's no slouch on the field, boasting a very respectable 40-yard (36.5m) dash time of 5.29s. To put that in perspective, it's the same time that quarterback Tom Brady ran at his NFL Combine.

3. Tackling Titans: The Rise of Rugby's Heavyweights and Their Sporting Rivals

Prop: Mekhi Becton (NFL, offensive tackle)—2.01m, 165kg *(Tier-1 Rugby Average: 1.86m, 120kg)*

The average modern forward pack weighs a total of approximately 900kg. In these two props, we've already reached 333kg and we still have six players left! While slightly smaller than Brown, Becton is even faster, with a 40-yard dash time of 5.10s.

Hooker: Zion Williamson (NBA, forward)—1.98m, 129kg *(Tier-1 Rugby Average: 1.83m, 108kg)*

With tall props either side of him, we can slot in a tall hooker as well to comfortably bind between them in the scrums. Staying on the field would probably be Williamson's biggest challenge, as his burgeoning NBA career has been struck by myriad injuries since the start. But his athleticism is legendary, even amongst the rarified company he keeps in the NBA. His free-throw percentage of just under 70 percent is not fantastic but would be good enough to throw accurately to his locks in the lineout, especially when they're soaring so high above their opponents.

Lock: Joel Embiid (NBA, centre)—2.13m, 127kg *(Tier-1 Rugby Average: 2.00m, 117kg)*

The 2023 NBA MVP may have been born in Cameroon, but he now plays basketball internationally for the U.S. At 2.13m tall with a 2.26m wingspan, not much lifting would be required in the lineout as he can jump through the gym ceiling on his own. Embiid is no beanpole either, tipping the scales at 127kg.

Lock: Bam Adebayo (NBA, centre)—2.06m, 116kg *(Tier-1 Rugby Average: 2.00m, 117kg)*

In terms of height and weight, Adebayo fits the mould of a modern international rugby lock. What would set him apart is a wingspan of 2.17m and an athleticism that has earned him multiple All-Star appearances and an Olympic gold medal. His unique playmaking ability for a big man would keep defences guessing any time they were unlucky enough to find him running at them.

Blindside flanker: Draymond Green (NBA, forward)—1.98m, 104kg *(Tier-1 Rugby Average: 1.91m, 109kg)*

Green would certainly bring the attack-dog ethos to the forward pack, as he's renowned for being a bit of a hothead and never taking a step back. He was a nightly triple-double threat in his basketball heyday and this versatility would serve him and his team well in rugby.

Openside flanker: LeBron James—Captain (NBA, forward)—2.06m, 113kg *(Tier-1 Rugby Average: 1.91m, 109kg)*

Sure, King James is getting on a bit now, but there aren't many professional athletes that look after their bodies better than he does. He would be a talismanic figure in the Number 7 shirt, with an immense size, skill and athleticism advantage over his opponents. Any concerns over his work rate should be allayed by the fact that he fronts up and plays in 55+ games a season in the physical NBA. Many might also say he's a master at manipulating the ref

3. Tackling Titans: The Rise of Rugby's Heavyweights and Their Sporting Rivals

to get the calls he wants, which is why the captaincy would fit well with him.

Number 8: Travis Kelce (NFL, tight end)—1.96m, 113kg *(Tier-1 Rugby Average: 1.91m, 109kg)*
Already considered one of the greatest tight ends in NFL history, Kelce is both big and physical but also highly skilled. He already holds numerous records for his position (to go with his three Super Bowl rings)—and is on track to possibly break them all. Not to mention, Kelce's current girlfriend Taylor Swift would certainly help bring some much-needed exposure to rugby in the U.S. (and the world)!

Kelce completes a forward pack weighing a staggering 1,035kg, smashing the previous record of 962kg set by France. An average height of 2.03m would dwarf modern rugby packs, who average 1.91m.

Scrum-Half: Steph Curry (NBA, guard)—1.88m, 84kg *(Tier-1 Rugby Average: 1.76m, 82kg)*
Curry is widely regarded as the greatest basketball shooter of all time, and helped to revolutionise the game by elevating the three-point shot as a primary attacking weapon. Accuracy of the pass would not be a problem, with Curry boasting a 43 percent three-point career shooting percentage and a 91 percent free-throw percentage. His depth of passing would be staggering too, as he pioneered the art of consistently draining shots from well beyond the three-point line.

Fly-Half: Jalen Hurts (NFL, quarterback)—1.81m, 101kg *(Tier-1 Rugby Average: 1.82m, 87kg)*

The dreaded 'dual pivots' are going to come into play here as I opt for Jalen Hurts at fly-half and Patrick Mahomes outside him. If Hurts's kicking is anything near as accurate as his passing—and there's no reason to suspect it wouldn't be—he'd be an unbelievable triple threat (run, pass, kick) at first receiver.

Inside Centre: Patrick Mahomes (NFL, quarterback)—1.88m, 102kg *(Tier-1 Rugby Average: 1.85m, 97kg)*

Mahomes's bigger size pushes him out one spot from fly-half, but he'd be equally comfortable stepping in when needed to run the cutter. After all, at just 28, he's already the owner of three Superbowl rings and two NFL MVP awards while playing in the NFL's marquee position.

Outside Centre: Christian McCaffrey (NFL, running back)—1.80m, 95kg *(Tier-1 Rugby Average: 1.85m, 97kg)*

You could slot any starting NFL running back in here and they would undoubtedly get the team over the gain line. But McCaffrey has stood out in recent seasons as a dual-threat (running and catching) RB. Against the super-tight and structured defences that make up the NFL, he's averaged 4.3 metres per carry over his career and, more importantly, 2.6 extra metres after contact. Just feed him the rock and watch him quickly get up to his top recorded in-game speed of 35kph.

Wing: Noah Lyles (Athletics)—1.80m, 70kg *(Tier-1 Rugby Average: 1.84m, 92kg)*

With a current 100m personal best (PB) of 9.83s, Lyles would be absolutely electric. To put this time in perspective, Bryan Habana is considered among the fastest ever rugby players, and his unofficial PB is 10.4s. While Lyles's slight stature could make him a defensive liability, this is surely a team that wouldn't have to do much defending!

Wing: Tyreek Hill (NFL, wide receiver)—1.78m, 84kg *(Tier-1 Rugby Average: 1.84m, 92kg)*

Although short in stature, Tyreek Hill is fast—insanely fast—his nickname isn't 'Cheetah' for nothing! He has a 100m time of 9.98s under his belt from his high school days and, like McCaffrey, has been measured during games reaching 35kph.

Fullback: Justin Jefferson (NFL, wide receiver)—1.85m, 88kg *(Tier-1 Rugby Average: 1.84m, 92kg)*

Like Tyreek Hill, Jefferson is considered one of the best wide receivers currently in the NFL. Jefferson gets the nod at fullback due to his height. If you have any concerns over how he might handle catching the high ball, Google his 2022 catch of the year to allay your fears.

The breakdown

The professional rugby player of today is almost unrecognisable in terms of stature relative to his peers from yesteryear. This has been driven by the professional expectations of the modern game, but also by changes to the rules that have led to further specialisation. While professional rugby players are catching up to their professional sporting counterparts in the U.S., they still have a way to go to match the dimensions of some of the athletic giants that ply their trades in the NFL and NBA.

Now that we've seen how the players' physiques have changed over time, in the next chapter we'll explore how the game itself has evolved.

4. Try and Triumph: The Constantly Shifting Strategies of Rugby

When you embark on a journey to Fenway Park in Boston, it can feel like a step into a bygone era. Built in 1912, Fenway is the oldest Major League Baseball (MLB) stadium still in use and a bastion of baseball's rich heritage. Strolling down Jersey Street (formerly Yawkey Way) amidst the charm of old-style street vendors gives the feeling of being whisked a century back in time.

Sure, this nostalgic reverie persists only about as long as it takes for someone glued to their cell phone to bump into you. But it's nevertheless a pleasant throwback to simpler times. Within the stadium's walls, a profound sense of tradition envelops you. Here, the essence of baseball endures, from the game's timeless dynamics right down to the still-classic design of the players' uniforms. It's a sport that firmly holds on to its traditions and hasn't changed much over the past 100-plus years.

Rugby could not be more opposite. It seems that, much to the chagrin of many fans, World Rugby tinkers with the rules (and interpretations of them) every single season. To watch a match from only 30 years ago is almost like watching a completely different sport. Nowadays, you'll frequently hear complaints that there are too many stoppages, not enough ball in play, and tries only scored via boring lineout mauls. As is so often the case when we look back at things through our rose-tinted, nostalgia-fogged glasses, the reality doesn't always match the perception.

The purpose of this chapter is to explore, via data, how the evolution in rugby's rules has *actually* changed the game. Spoiler alert: it reveals that current perceptions are often quite removed from reality. It also busts open some widely held myths about the sport, such as how stark the differences in playing style are between the Northern and Southern Hemispheres.

Table 4.1 offers a broad overview of how the game has changed over the years. Here I compare data from a study World Rugby did of 16 Tier-1 internationals in the early 1980s to data I've collated from the Six Nations and Tri-Nations/Rugby Championship games throughout the 2000s. This data comes from the annual reports that World Rugby produces (which can be found on their website). While the Six Nations reports are available through until 2022, it's worth noting that Rugby Championship data was only available up until the 2016 competition.

The overall picture is of a game that is far more entertaining now than it used to be. For example, the ball-in-play percentage was one of the biggest gripes pundits had about the recent 2023 Rugby World Cup. Believe it or not, but this 'issue' used to be far worse: the stat is actually *up* by 50 percent compared to the early 1980s. Why? One big reason is that there are far more phases put together in the modern game through rucks/mauls and passes.

4. Try and Triumph: The Constantly Shifting Strategies of Rugby

It's worth remembering that the player skill level of today's professional athletes, from the props to the fullbacks, is generally far superior to what it was back in the Amateur era, which facilitates much more sustained attacking forays. And the number of set pieces (scrums and lineouts) has been halved in the modern game.

Endless kicking duels is another frequent complaint of the modern rugby viewer, but general play kicks are also down by almost one-third. And the scoring is up, especially via the most crowd-pleasing element, the try.

Table 4.1. Comparison of key stats between a World Rugby selection of 1980's test matches, the Six Nations Championship and the Rugby Championship.

Game Elements	Early 1980s	Six Nations (2004-2022)	Rugby Championship (2004-2016)
Ball in play	30%	47%	43%
Rucks/Mauls per game	46	183	155
Passes per game	149	283	262
Kicks per game	76	52	51
Scrums per game	31	14	16
Lineouts per game	52	27	27
Tries per game	2.8	4.2	4.6
Penalty goals per game	4.3	4.8	5.3
Drop goals per game	0.9	0.3	0.3
Points scored per game*	33	42	46

* Modern scoring has been applied to the 1980s games (e.g., 5 points per try).

The Six Nations Championship (prior to 2000, the Five Nations Championship) provides a consistent barometer for showing how scoring patterns have changed over the years (Figure 4.1). The gradual increase in scoring prior to 1996 was largely driven by increased penalty goals. But immediately following professionalisation there was a jump in points scored, this time driven by tries. (The volume of tries was also responsible for the subsequent dip around 2013).

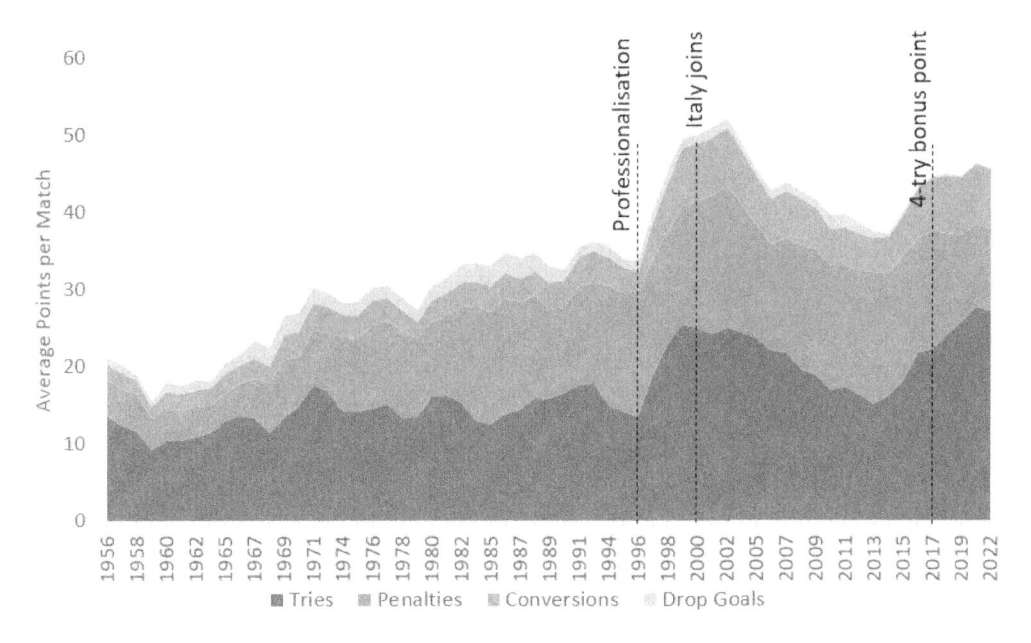

Figure 4.1. Average points per match (by scoring method) in the Six Nations (formerly Five Nations) tournaments. Points allocated using modern scoring (e.g., five points for a try).

And if we compare rugby (through the Six Nations) to the MLB and NFL, we can see just how much rugby scoring has changed relative to some other

4. Try and Triumph: The Constantly Shifting Strategies of Rugby

sports (Figure 4.2). Figure 4.2 shows that, to a large degree, the scoring in MLB and NFL games has remained relatively stable over the last 70 years. The MLB has barely deviated from an average of nine runs scored per game, while NFL scores have crept up slightly but largely remained between 40 and 45 points per game. Meanwhile, the points scored in rugby have more than doubled, rising from under 20 points per match in the 1950s to 45 points per match in the last ten seasons.

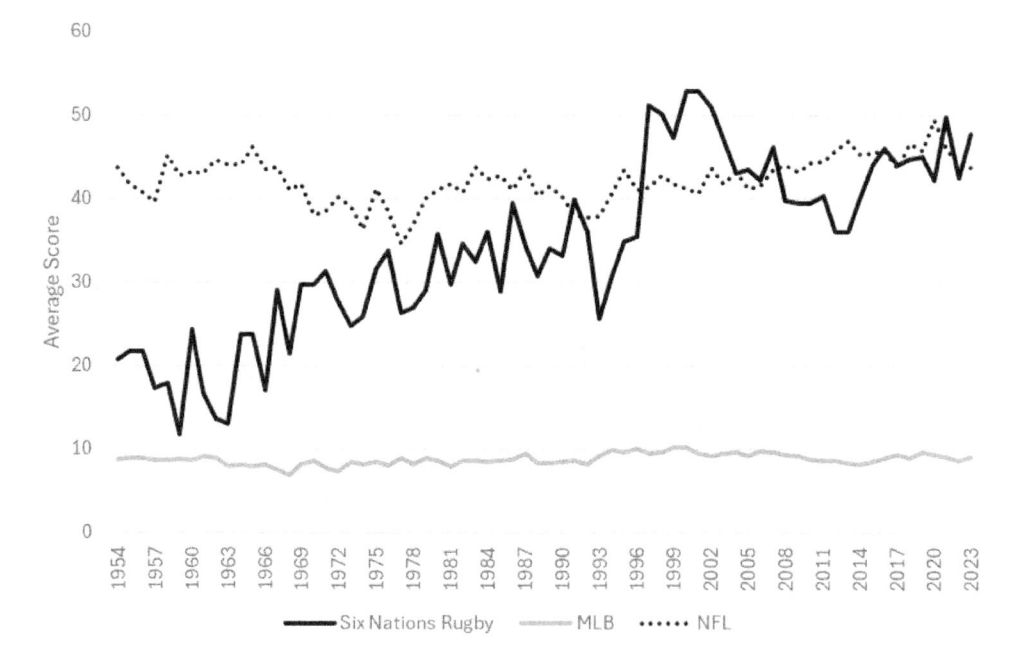

Figure 4.2. Comparison of the total score per game in Six Nations rugby, MLB baseball and NFL football over time. Six Nations points allocated using modern scoring (e.g., 5 points for a try).

Now that we can see the broad contours of how rugby has transformed over the years, let's dive in a bit deeper to break down a) how the various elements of the game have changed, and b) how the changes compare across hemispheres.

The Scrum

As always with anything data-related, there's the devil and the details and all that. While we see 50 percent fewer scrums these days, the time actually taken to set (and reset, and reset) the modern-day scrum is much longer than it used to be. In the amateur days, scrums took less than 30 seconds on average to complete, with relatively few sanctions or resets. Scrums today take an average of 70 seconds to complete!

In a 2017 Six Nations match between France and Wales, the 20 scrums in the match took up a total of 22 minutes of precious gametime; that was an incredible 27 percent of the total 80-minute playing time! The 13th scrum wasn't even awarded until the 78th minute, then seven more scrums were awarded to the attacking team (France) on the back of penalty after penalty. While scrum reset after scrum reset isn't necessarily everyone's cup of tea, it does provide a high degree of drama when (as in the case of France) a team is hot on attack, using their scrum as an offensive weapon to try to win the match. However, the time dedicated to scrums in the France-Wales match wasn't even an isolated occurrence in the 2017 Six Nations tournament, as six of the 15 matches had scrums that took up >20 percent of total playing time.

4. Try and Triumph: The Constantly Shifting Strategies of Rugby

This highlights how much the strategy behind scrums has fundamentally shifted in rugby. Scrums used to be simply a restart of play in which the teams struggled to gain quality possession. In today's game, scrums are increasingly seen as an essential way to induce penalties from the opposition. The percentage of scrums resulting in a penalty has doubled across both the Six Nations and Rugby Championship in the last 20 years, from approximately 15 percent to >30 percent (Figure 4.3). The Springboks took this penalty-seeking strategy to a whole new level in the 2023 Rugby World Cup, calling directly for a scrum from a mark inside their 22 during both their quarter-final and semi-final. This was an absolutely unheard-of strategy up to that point, and it had rugby pundits equally aghast and awestruck. Generally, you want to get away from your own defensive 22 zone as quickly as possible, and a kick downfield is considered the safest option. The Springboks backed their dominant scrum to earn them a penalty deep within their own territory, and it paid off on both occasions (in matches they won by a single point no less!).

While it doesn't perfectly coincide with the big rise in penalties in 2009, there was a major scrum law change in 2007. This was when the 'crouch, touch, pause, engage' process was introduced, primarily to minimise the initial gap between front rows. A further law adjustment in 2013 saw props being required to bind before the packs could start to push, to further minimise the initial impact.

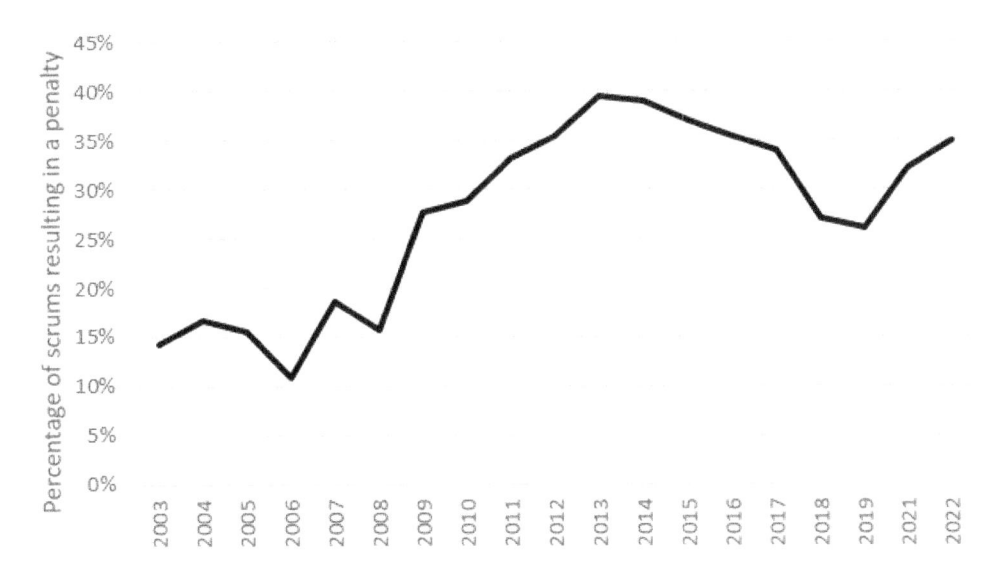

Figure 4.3. Percentage of scrums resulting in a penalty across Six Nations and Rugby Championship competitions between 2003 and 2022. Includes Rugby Championship data up until 2016 only.

Lineouts

The lineout is another distinct area of the game that has tactically changed. It is now seen as a major strategic source of tries via a lineout maul near an opponent's try line. This strategy has been so successful that kickable penalties are often now turned down in favour of booting the ball to the corner for the inevitable lineout maul that follows. It has led to a dramatic decrease in contested lineouts across both hemispheres (Figure 4.4a). Not surprisingly, less contesting in the lineouts has resulted in a greater lineout success percentage for the throwing team, up from approximately 80 percent to 90 percent today (Figure 4.4b).

4. Try and Triumph: The Constantly Shifting Strategies of Rugby

a. Percentage of lineouts contested

b. Lineout success rate

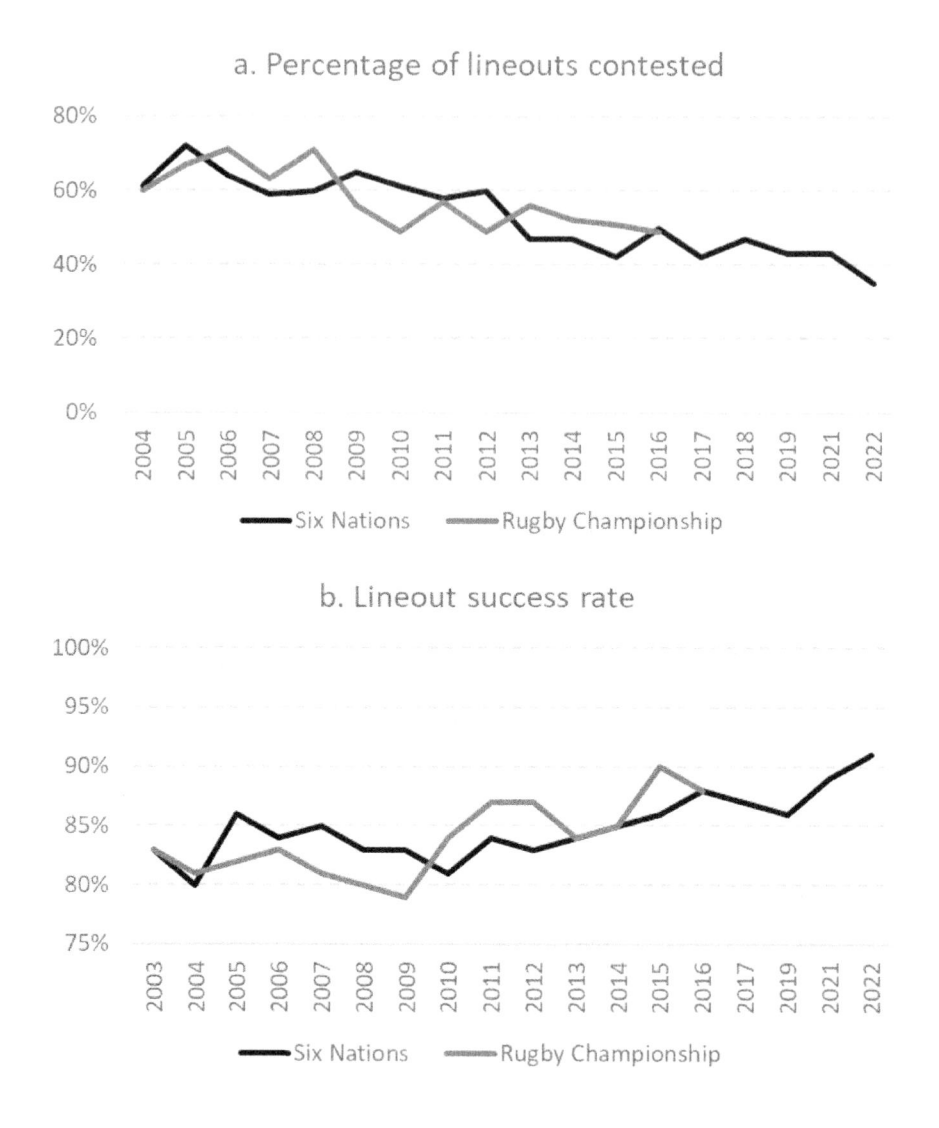

Figure 4.4. Lineout statistics across the Six Nations and Rugby Championship competitions between 2004 and 2022. Figure 4.4a shows the percentage of lineouts contested by the opposition. Figure 4.4b shows the lineout success rate of the team throwing into the lineout.

Interestingly, while it might seem that hookers are now the leading try-scoring threats due to the lineout maul, the percentage of tries scored by forwards versus backs hasn't actually shifted in the last 20 years. It has remained about a 70:30 split in favour of the backs, consistent across hemispheres (Figure 4.5). In fact, the Rugby Championship, that self-proclaimed bastion of free-flowing and attacking rugby, has a slightly *higher* percentage of tries scored by forwards (29 percent) than the Six Nations (25 percent).

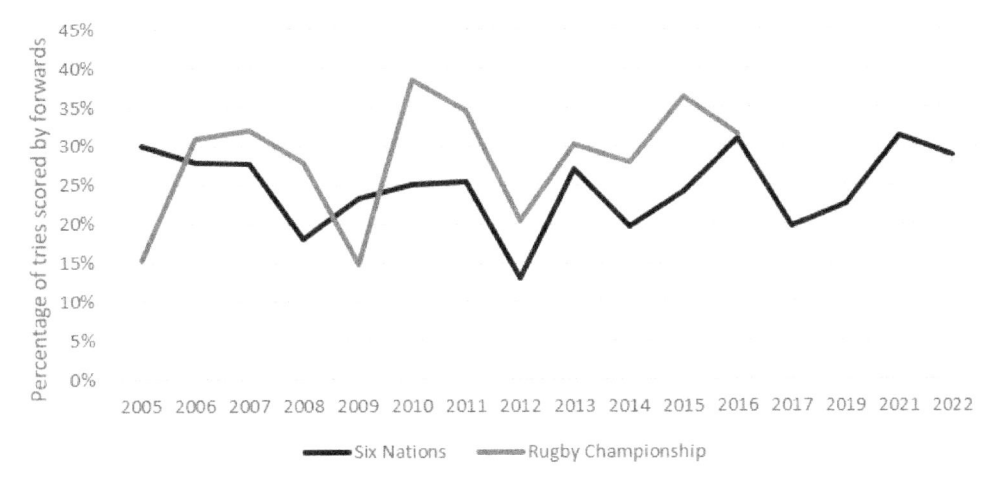

Figure 4.5. *Percentage of tries scored by forwards across the Six Nations and Rugby Championship competitions between 2004 and 2022.*

There's no doubt though that the lineout is a key source of try-scoring opportunities, and annual changes in the volume of total tries scored have largely been driven by the number of tries scored directly from lineouts (Figure 4.6).

4. Try and Triumph: The Constantly Shifting Strategies of Rugby

Six Nations

Rugby Championship

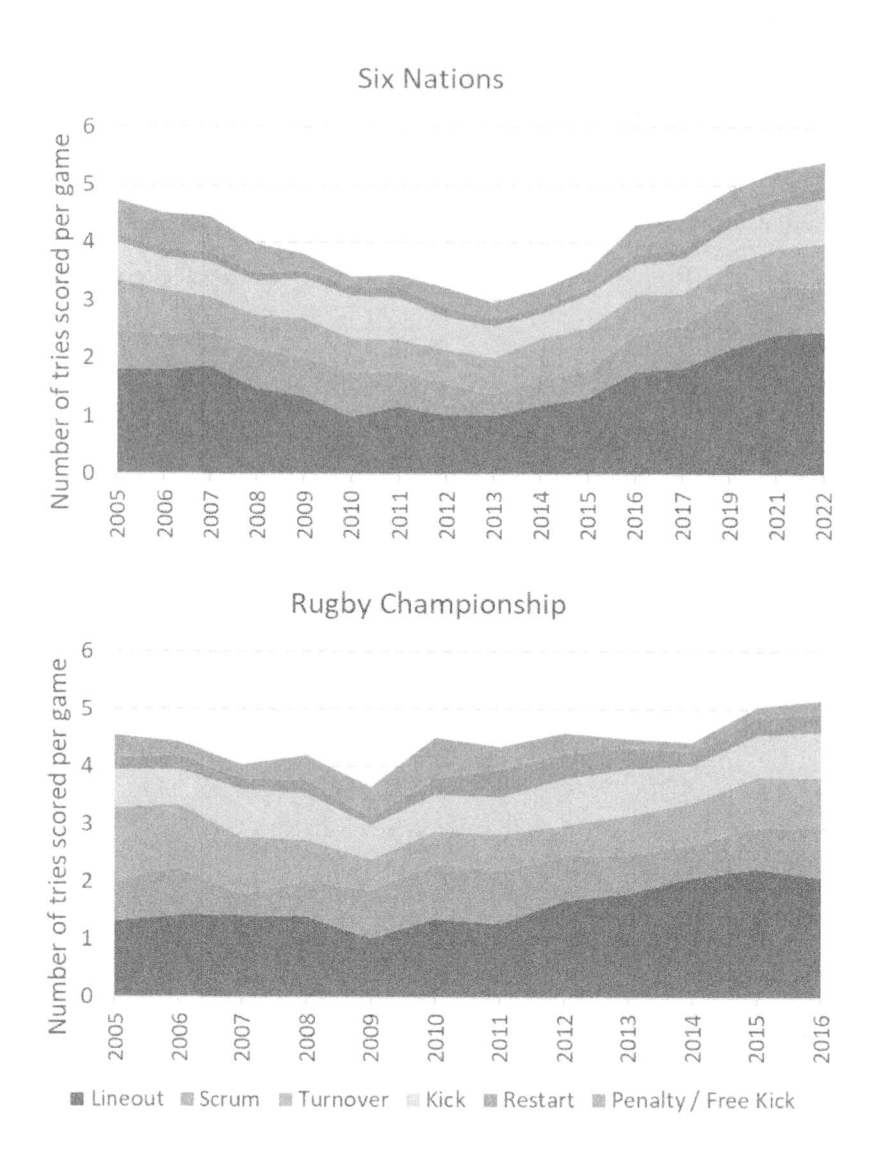

■ Lineout ■ Scrum ■ Turnover ■ Kick ■ Restart ■ Penalty / Free Kick

Figure 4.6. Average number of tries scored per game originating from various methods across the Six Nations and Rugby Championship competitions between 2005 and 2022.

What is intriguing is that, contrary to popular belief, this is not such a recent phenomenon. The lineout has been the primary source of tries almost every season in both the Six Nations and Rugby Championship since the early 2000s. Although the proportion has increased slightly, it's been a gradual shift rather than a dramatic change (Figure 4.7).

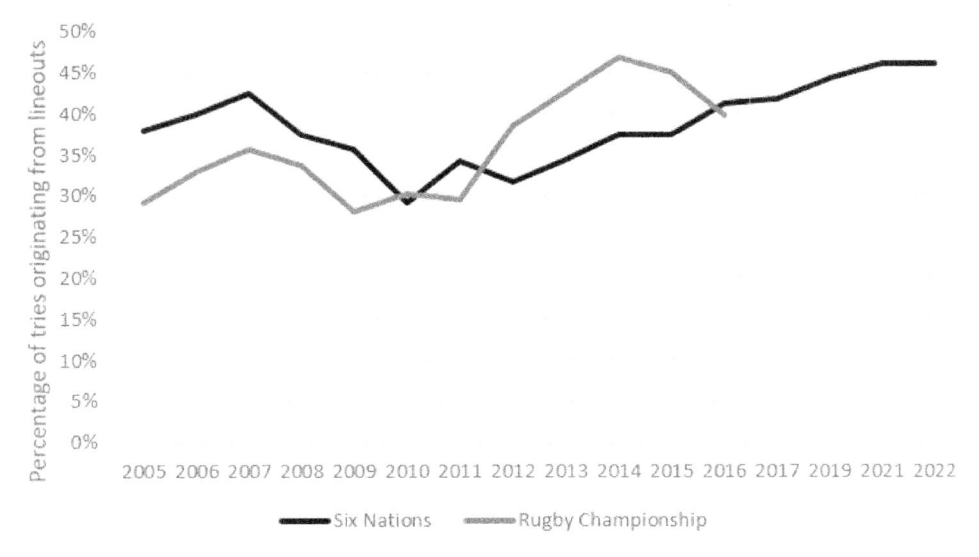

Figure 4.7. Percentage of total tries originating from the lineout across the Six Nations and Rugby Championship competitions between 2005 and 2022.

You can see from Figure 4.6 that the set piece (lineout and scrum) has been the major source of tries in both the Six Nations and Rugby Championship. What may surprise some is that as a percentage of total tries, this actually hasn't changed much over the last 20 years (Figure 4.8); consistently around half of tries have originated from lineouts and scrums during this period.

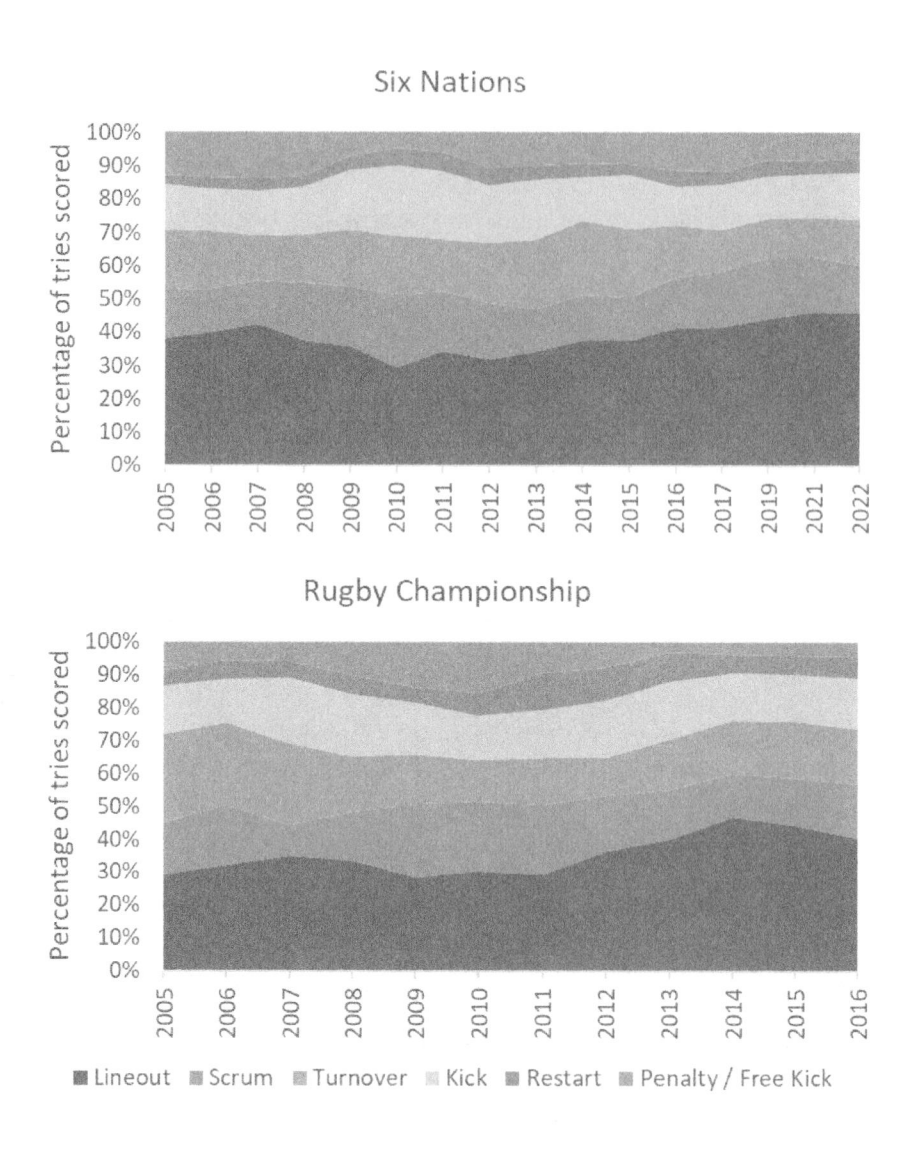

4. Try and Triumph: The Constantly Shifting Strategies of Rugby

Figure 4.8. Percentage of tries scored originating from various methods across the Six Nations and Rugby Championship competitions between 2005 and 2022.

The battle of the hemispheres

One thing that struck me when looking at this analysis was how similar the two hemispheres are when it comes to the trends I've outlined. This is especially fascinating given the preconception that there are vastly different playing styles between north and south, and because each hemisphere tends to look down their nose at the other. The Southern Hemisphere prides themselves on playing 'champagne rugby' and derides the perceived forward-dominated 'kickfests' of the north. The Northern Hemisphere tends to think of the south (Springboks excluded) as playing 'popcorn rugby', with minimal application of defence and the set piece—the very foundations of the game for the rugby purist.

However, Table 4.2 shows that the Six Nations and Rugby Championship have varied by less than ten percent across almost all key metrics between 2004 and 2016. The exceptions are points scored, which is driven by a higher number of tries in the Rugby Championship, and rucks and mauls. There have been ten percent more rucks and mauls in the Six Nations, which also helps drive up that competition's ball in play time to an average of 47 percent.

4. Try and Triumph: The Constantly Shifting Strategies of Rugby

Table 4.2. Comparison of key stats between the Six Nations and Rugby Championship between 2004 and 2016 (period of data availability for both competitions).

Average per Game	6 Nations	Rugby Championship	Difference
Points	41.3	46.0	10%
Tries	3.8	4.5	16%
Penalties	5.2	5.3	2%
Drop Goals	0.31	0.29	7%
Ball in Play	47%	43%	9%
Passes	273	262	4%
Rucks/Mauls	173	157	10%
Ruck/Maul Retention	95%	93%	2%
Kicks in play	53.3	50.1	6%
Lineouts	27.9	27.1	3%
Lineouts Contested	57%	58%	1%
Lineout Success	84%	84%	0%
Scrums	15.4	16.2	5%
Scrum Success	87%	90%	3%
Penalty and Free Kicks	21.5	22.1	2%

Even if we delve deeper into these metrics, there are striking similarities between the competitions which defy common (mis)perceptions about the strategies used in the two hemispheres. When it comes down to it, all the talk of hemispheric differences doesn't really stand up to scrutiny.

This data also helps provide a deeper understanding of how the modern international game flows in general. In both competitions, penalties are front-loaded into the first half at exactly the same rate (61 percent, Figure 4.9a). While the Rugby Championship is slightly more balanced with respect to tries, they are still more prevalent in the second half of both competitions (Figure 4.9b). So, strategies tend to be built around taking the points on offer early and reverting to pushing for tries later, when defences are tiring and the win or a 4-try bonus point are at stake. (The highly contentious debate around when to 'take the 3' and when to go for the try will be dissected further in the next chapter.)

a. Penalty Goals

	Six Nations	Rugby Championship
2nd Half	39%	39%
1st Half	61%	61%

b. Tries

	Six Nations	Rugby Championship
2nd Half	58%	54%
1st Half	42%	46%

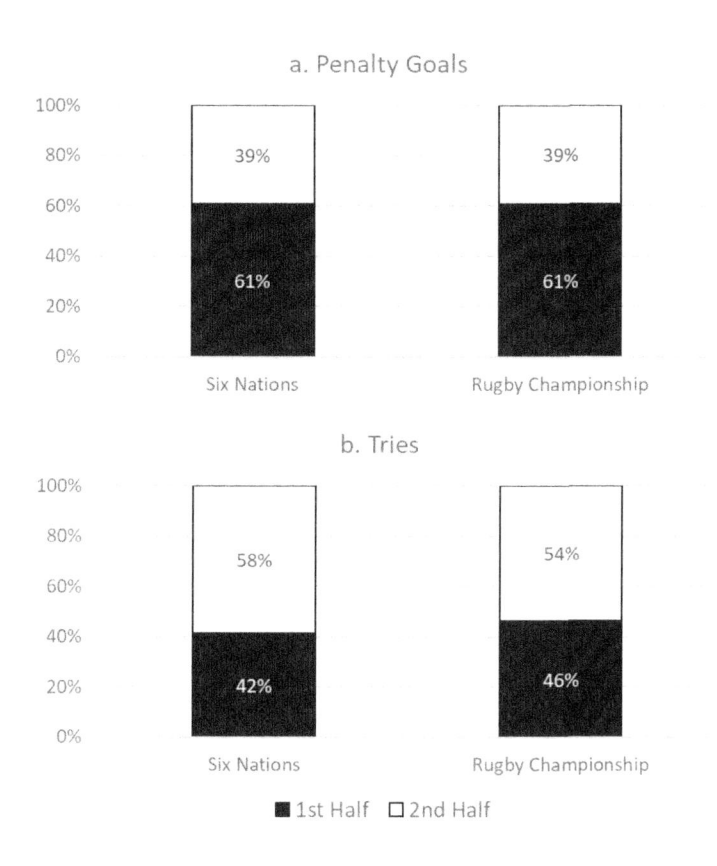

■ 1st Half   □ 2nd Half

Figure 4.9. Percentage of scoring plays by half across the Six Nations and Rugby Championship competitions between 2004 and 2016. Figure 4.9a shows a breakdown of penalty goals scored by half, Figure 4.9b shows tries scored by half.

4. Try and Triumph: The Constantly Shifting Strategies of Rugby

In both tournaments, the majority of tries are scored by backs, with the Six Nations (perhaps surprisingly) slightly more backs-centric (Figure 4.10).

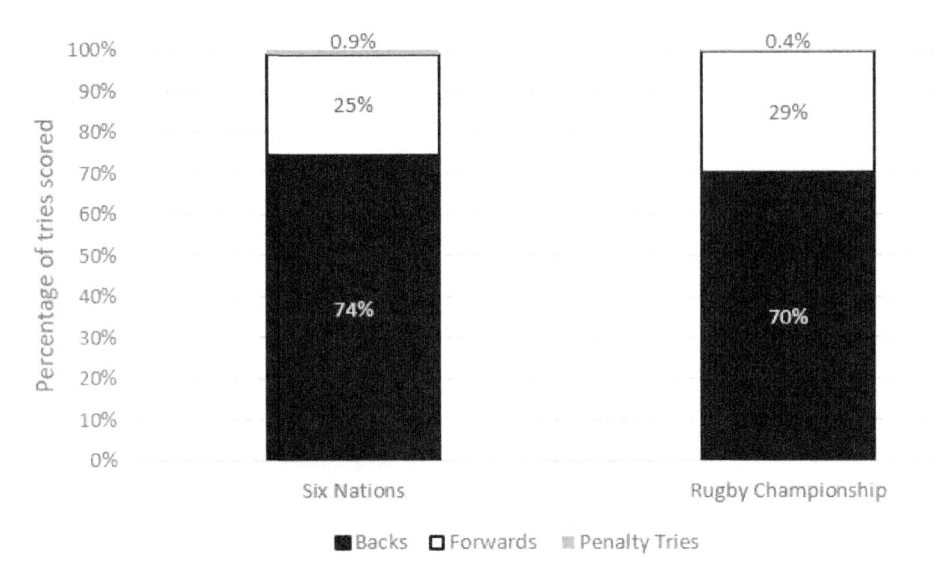

Figure 4.10. Percentage of tries scored by forwards, backs, and penalty tries across the Six Nations and Rugby Championship competitions between 2004 and 2016.

Tries originate from very similar positions on the field across the hemispheres, most commonly within an opponent's 22m line (not surprisingly, Figure 4.11). There's only a slight increase in tries originating from within a team's own half in the Rugby Championship.

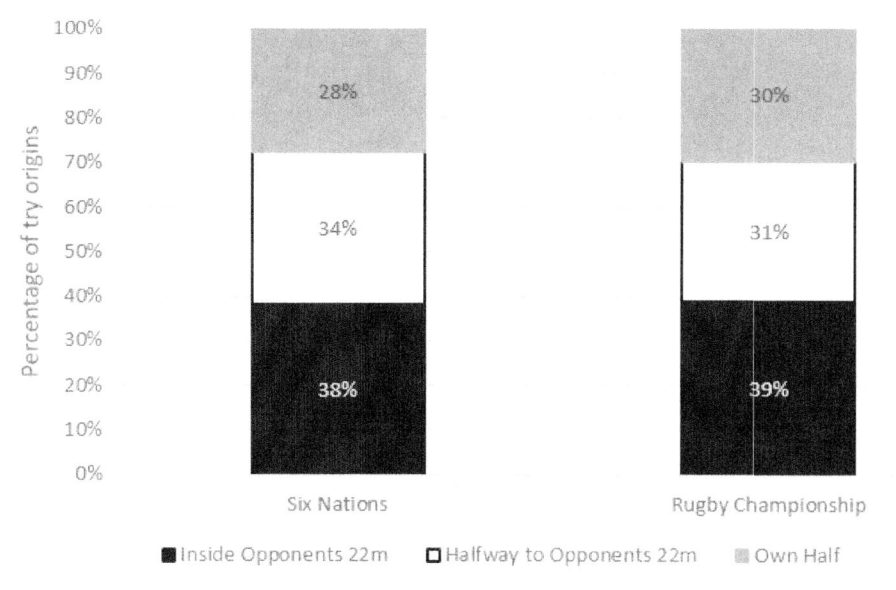

Figure 4.11. Origin of tries across the Six Nations and Rugby Championship competitions between 2004 and 2016.

When it comes to the passes strung together in the leadup to a try, there are almost identical profiles between the Six Nations and Rugby Championship; indeed, it's quite incredible how similar they are (Figure 4.12). This metric has been changing over time, with longer buildup required to break down modern defences. Tries originating from seven or more passes have almost doubled, from around 20 percent of the total in the mid-2000s to 35 percent in recent years (Figure 4.13).

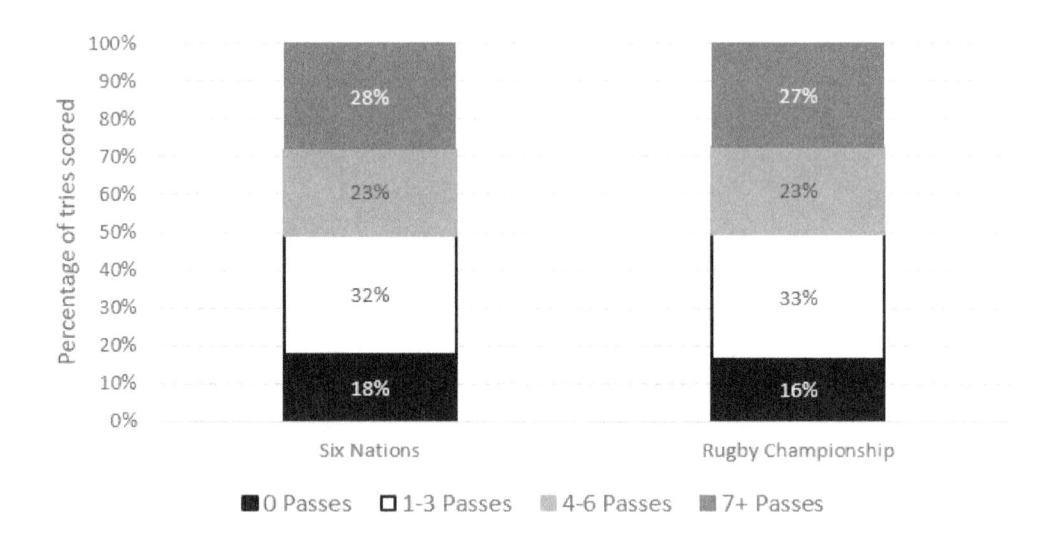

4. Try and Triumph: The Constantly Shifting Strategies of Rugby

Figure 4.12. Buildup of tries (by passes) across the Six Nations and Rugby Championship competitions between 2004 and 2016.

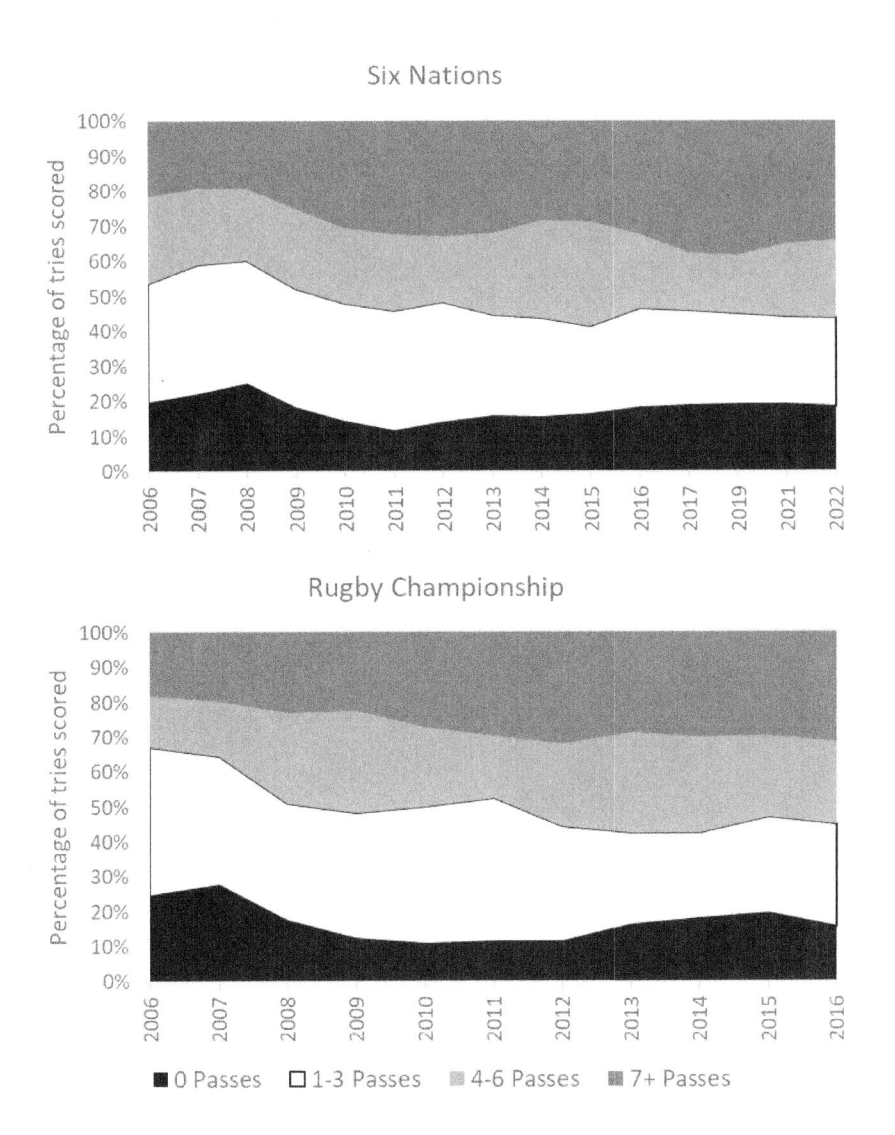

Figure 4.13. *Timeline of the buildup of tries (by passes) across the Six Nations and Rugby Championship competitions.*

4. Try and Triumph: The Constantly Shifting Strategies of Rugby

The buildup of tries in terms of phases is also very similar between the hemispheres (Figure 4.14). Slightly more phases are required in the Six Nations, which may be testament to the competition's defensive intensity. This is another metric that has been changing significantly, with three-plus phases going from comprising around 25 percent of tries in the mid-2000s to 50 percent in recent years (Figure 4.15). So, once again we see that in recent years a lot more sustained buildup has been required to break down increasingly stout defences.

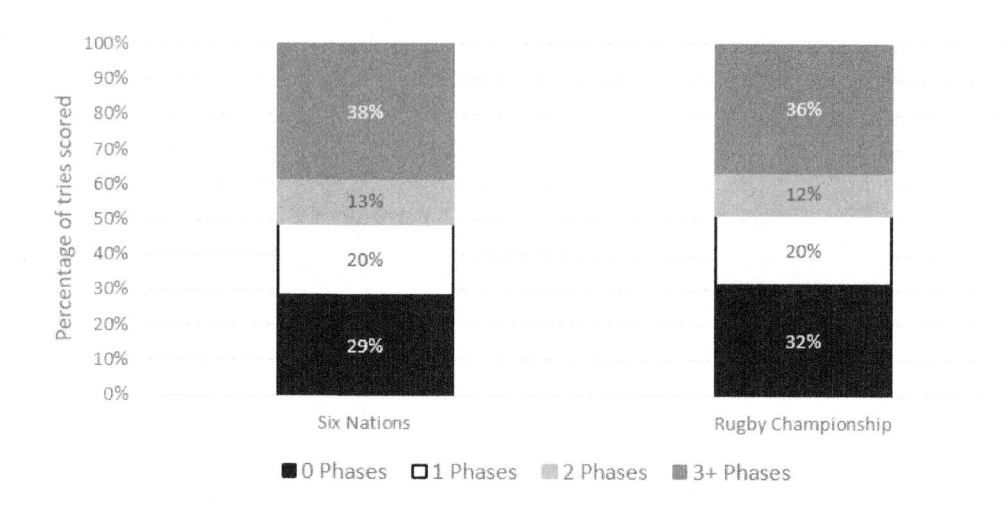

Figure 4.14. Buildup of tries (by phases) across the Six Nations and Rugby Championship competitions between 2004 and 2016.

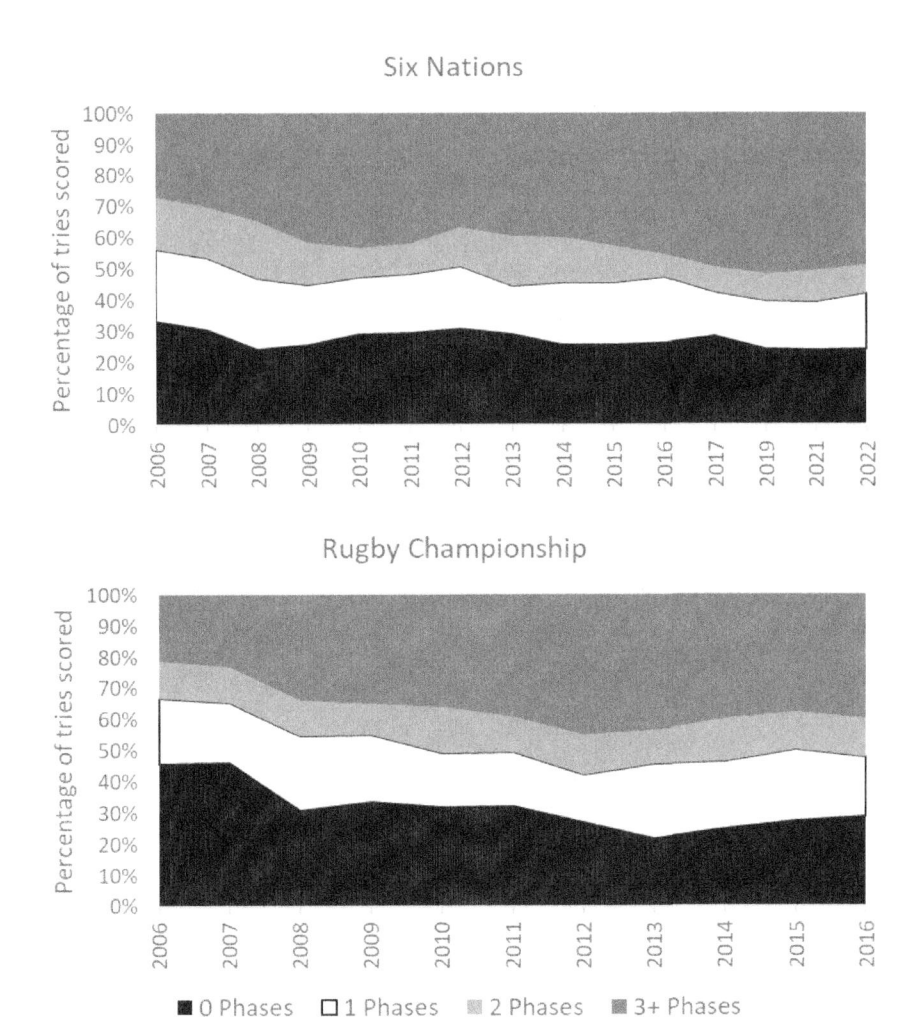

Figure 4.15. Timeline of the buildup of tries (by phases) across the Six Nations and Rugby Championship competitions.

4. Try and Triumph: The Constantly Shifting Strategies of Rugby

The passing profile is similar across the hemispheres, with (not surprisingly) the scrum-half's alone accounting for almost half of all passes thrown (Figure 4.16). In the Rugby Championship, there has been a marked increase in passes thrown by forwards compared to the Six Nations.

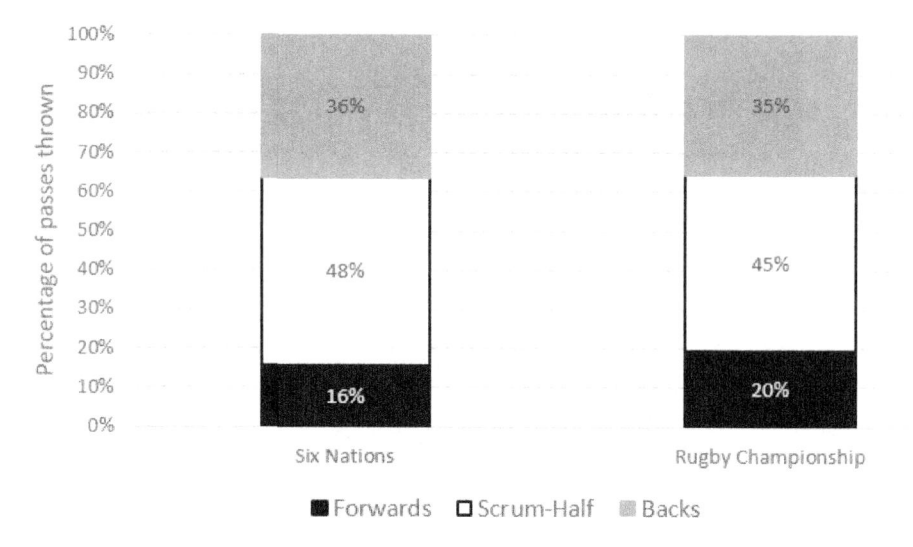

Figure 4.16. Percentage of total passes thrown by position, across the Six Nations and Rugby Championship competitions between 2004 and 2016.

One area where the Six Nations and the Rugby Championship have begun to diverge is in the number of rucks and mauls. While they had an equivalent number at the start of the 21st century, the Six Nations had almost 20 percent more by the mid-2010s and has continued to outpace the Rugby Championship since then (Figure 4.17a).

On the other hand, ruck and maul retention rate—which is extremely high in both competitions—not only doesn't vary much year to year (Figure 4.17b), but is very consistent even between the teams within a single competition.

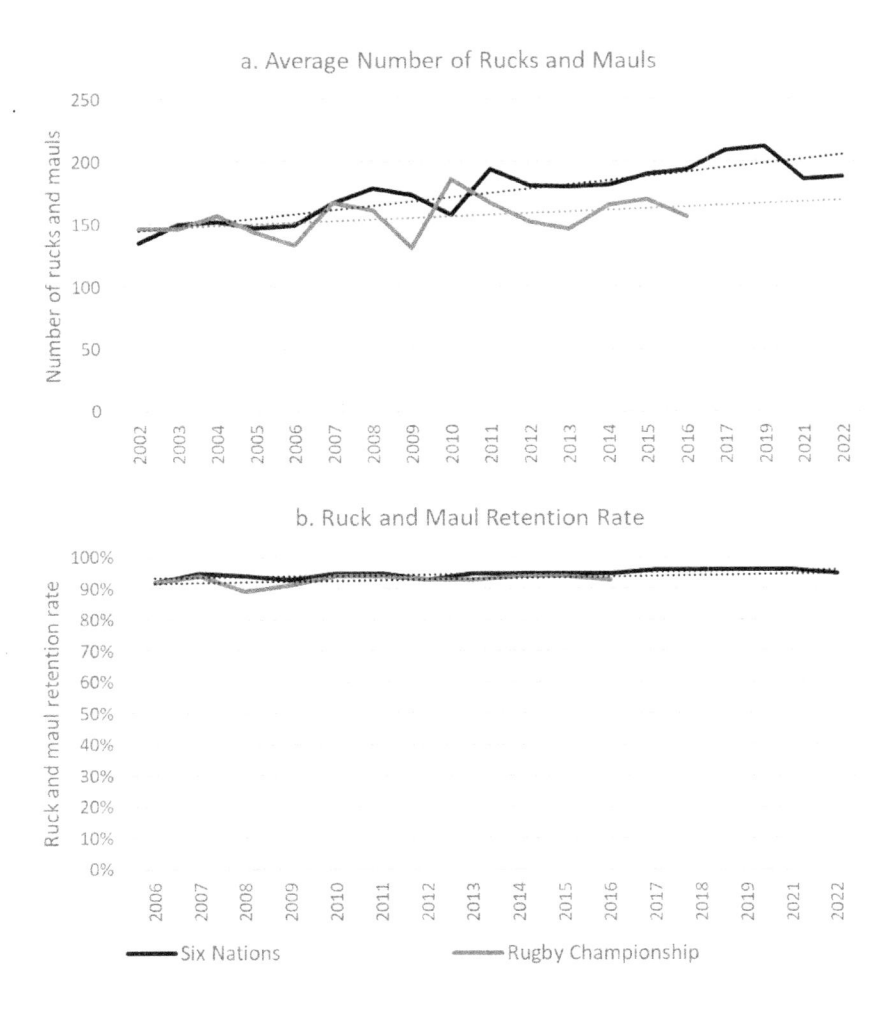

Figure 4.17. Comparison of ruck and maul statistics from the Six Nations and Rugby Championship competitions. Figure 4.17a shows the average number of rucks and mauls per match. Figure 4.17b shows the average ruck and maul retention rate.

4. Try and Triumph: The Constantly Shifting Strategies of Rugby

Data from recent Six Nations championships (Figure 4.18) clearly demonstrates this consistency: you can see that the black bars, indicating each team's success at retaining the ball at their own rucks, doesn't vary greatly. In fact, almost all teams retain their ball between 94 and 97 percent of the time in any given year. And while there is a relationship between successful ruck retention and winning (measured in Figure 4.18 in terms of competition points), it's not strong. Italy, for example, are retaining their ruck ball at an average of 95 percent, the same rate as England and France, but are seldom rewarded with many competition points.

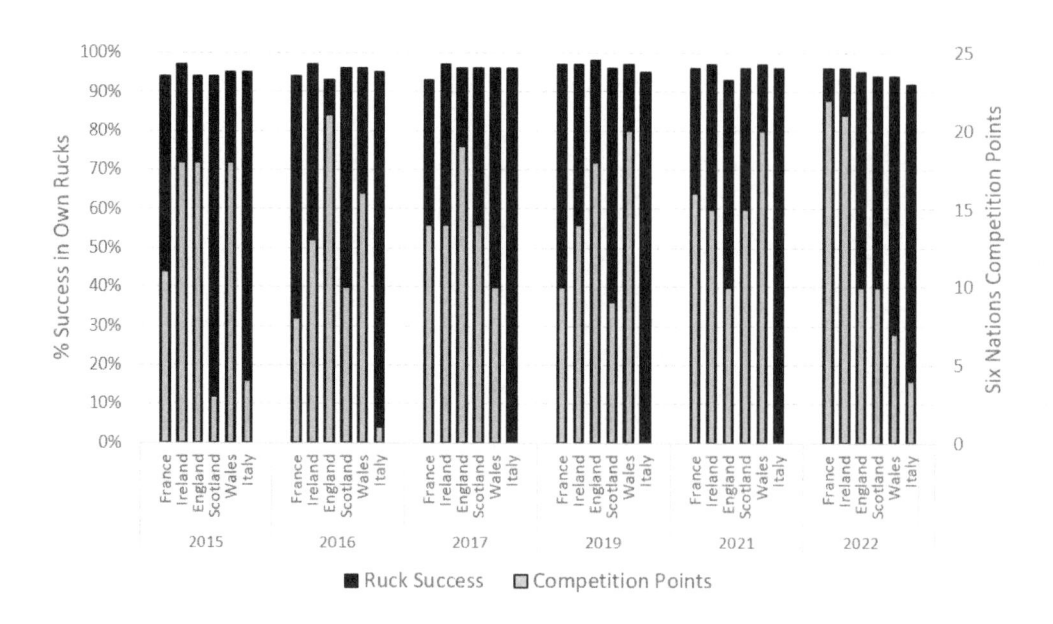

Figure 4.18. Ruck retention success versus competition points in the Six Nations between 2015 and 2022.

Competing in rucks is not only about winning or retaining the ball, though. A big part of it is about slowing down the opposition's ball and allowing your defence to reset. And on the offensive side, getting fast attacking ball is paramount to being able to open up defences. The publicly available data on this is patchy but, as you can see from Figure 4.19, the attacking ruck speed margins were razor-thin during the 2022 Six Nations. In recent seasons, Ireland has been considered the global benchmark for getting quick ruck ball. During the 2022 Six Nations, while on attack they averaged 2.6s compared to the 3.0s of Scotland and Wales. Yes, this is a difference of just 0.4 seconds, but in rugby, receiving attacking ball even 0.4 seconds faster is lightning in a bottle.

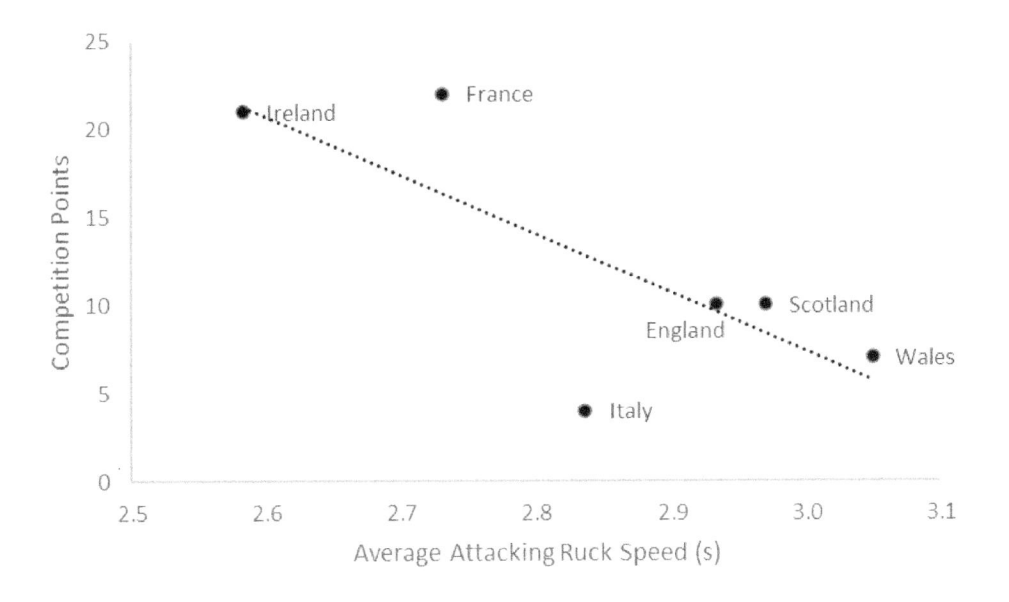

Figure 4.19. *Average attacking ruck speed versus competition points in the 2022 Six Nations.*

4. Try and Triumph: The Constantly Shifting Strategies of Rugby

General play kicking

If I had a dollar for every complaint I heard about All Blacks fullback Beauden Barrett and his 'aimless kicking' in 2023, I probably wouldn't have needed to go out and write this book to feed my family! This is an especially common gripe among those from the Southern Hemisphere where tactical kicking—which can often descend into a game of aerial ping-pong—is seldom applauded. However, the complaints steadily died down as the All Blacks made a somewhat surprising run all the way to the 2023 World Cup final. A clutch quarter-final victory over number 1-ranked Ireland was set up in part by a tactical kicking masterclass by, you guessed it, Beauden Barrett.

The groans about too much kicking are yet another example of perception not necessarily matching reality. In fact, the number of kicks in general play has been *decreasing*, especially in the Rugby Championship (Figure 4.20). Today they're down to under 50 per game, whereas as Table 4.1 showed, in the halcyon days of the 1980s we were 'treated' to over 75 kicks per game.

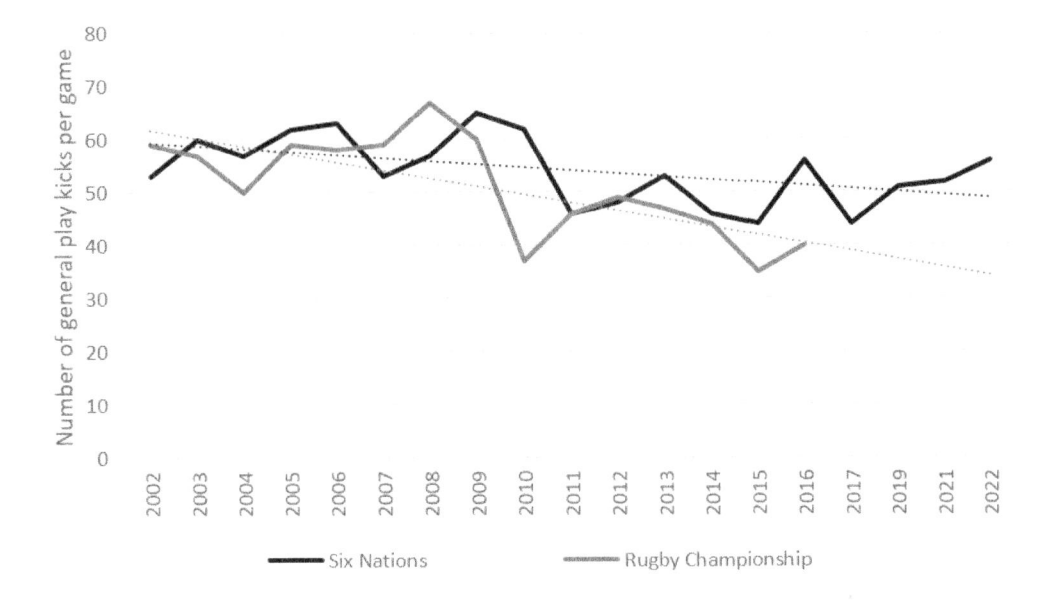

Figure 4.20. *Average number of kicks in general play across the Six Nations and Rugby Championship competitions.*

Kicking is also intrinsically linked to game situation and playing strategy. As defences have become harder to break down and ruck retention has become better, kicking has become a means of controlling territory and opening up defences. Keep in mind that sometimes the actual kick itself doesn't need to have a directly successful outcome to have a larger positive impact. Even if a dink over the top is regathered by the defensive team, it can plant a seed in their mind that next time they can't afford to rush up so quickly and potentially be exposed by a deft chip kick with a kinder bounce for the attacking team.

Tactical kicking has reached a point today where the number of kicks a team puts in is highly correlated to their success in a match. To help understand

4. Try and Triumph: The Constantly Shifting Strategies of Rugby

where kicking fits in alongside other facets of the game, I built a statistical model examining the relationship between 35 game metrics and the match result. This shows us which facets of the game are most predictive of the outcome. In Table 4.3, we can see what the most impactful facets were across several competitions during the latest World Cup cycle (2020 to 2023).

To help you make sense of the table, here's a brief explanation on some statistics terminology (don't be scared, it really is brief!): The larger the coefficient, the greater the impact on the result. A positive coefficient is positively associated with winning (e.g., more clean breaks equal a greater chance of winning), whereas a negative value is negatively associated with it (e.g., conceding more turnovers or yellow cards decrease the chance of winning). The model results account for the combined impact of all the metrics in determining the match winner. They aren't being evaluated in isolation from each other.

The first thing that stands out in Table 4.3 is how similar the metrics are across the various competitions. The next thing that stands out is that a few of the facets have a consistent and significant positive impact—one of them being the number of kicks from hand. Turns out it's one of the top four most important metrics across every competition. This shows just how important owning the tactical kicking battle is to winning rugby matches. So the next time you hear someone moan about all that 'aimless' kicking, you have the data now to argue back!

Table 4.3. *Results of a logistic regression model of 35 game metrics and their importance in determining the match winner, across various competitions.*

Six Nations 2020 - 23

Metric	Coefficient
Clean Breaks	1.20
Mauls Won #	0.52
Kicks From Hand	0.51
Meters Run	0.51
Tackle Success %	0.35
Yellow Cards	-0.41
Scrums Lost	-0.68
Passes	-0.82
Rucks Lost	-1.11
Turnovers Conceded	-1.47

Rugby Championship 2020 - 23

Metric	Coefficient
Clean Breaks	1.30
Rucks Won %	0.97
Possession 1st Half	0.66
Kicks From Hand	0.51
Territory 2nd Half	0.51
Possession 2nd Half	-0.07
Mauls Lost	-0.39
Yellow Cards	-0.54

Premiership Rugby 2021 - 23

Metric	Coefficient
Meters Run	1.12
Clean Breaks	0.54
Kicks From Hand	0.53
Rucks Won %	0.31
Offloads	0.26
Scrums Won	0.25
Goalkicking %	0.21
Mauls Won #	0.20
Possession 1st Half	0.14
Possession 2nd Half	-0.34
Red Cards	-0.38
Turnovers Conceded	-0.50
Penalties Conceded	-0.77
Passes	-0.94

Top 14 2021 - 23

Metric	Coefficient
Meters Run	1.52
Clean Breaks	1.04
Mauls Won #	0.84
Kicks From Hand	0.78
Goalkicking %	0.45
Scrums Won	0.40
Territory 2nd Half	0.28
Possession 2nd Half	-0.42
Turnovers Conceded	-0.46
Penalties Conceded	-0.48
Scrums Lost	-0.51
Rucks Lost	-0.85
Passes	-1.23

Super Rugby 2021 - 23

Metric	Coefficient
Meters Run	1.41
Tackles Made	1.05
Kicks From Hand	1.03
Clean Breaks	0.78
Rucks Won %	0.75
Scrum %	0.67
Lineouts Won	0.58
Territory 2nd Half	0.22
Free Kicks Conceded	-0.06
Lineouts Lost	-0.06
Turnovers Conceded	-0.39
Possession 2nd Half	-0.62

The model is robust in that it considers all the metrics when evaluating each metric's contribution towards wins. But another, simpler way to view things is to look at individual correlations (aka relationships) between each metric and wins. This shows us how closely related each metric is to match

4. Try and Triumph: The Constantly Shifting Strategies of Rugby

outcome, but in isolation and with no regard to any other metric. This is what's displayed in Table 4.4.

Here again we see a lot of similarities across all competitions, regardless of hemisphere and type of competition. Some especially key observations:

- Winning is negatively correlated with second-half possession in every competition. This means the team that wins tends to have *less* of the ball in the second half.
- General play metrics including kicks from hand, metres run, clean breaks and defenders beaten tend to have strong positive correlations with winning.
- However, the number of passes and runs are *not* associated with winning (except in the Rugby Championship).
- Losing rucks is very detrimental to winning, as are losing lineouts. This trend is exacerbated at the international level.
- Discipline through penalties and yellow cards is paramount, especially at the international level.

Table 4.4. Correlations between key metrics and match outcome across various competitions.

Competition Type		International		Club		
		Six Nations 2020-23	Rugby Championship 2020-23	Top 14 2021-23	English Premiership 2021-23	Super Rugby 2021-23
Category	Metric	North	South	North	North	South
Possession	Overall Possession	9%	40%	5%	9%	3%
	Possession 1st Half	12%	61%	9%	3%	15%
	Possession 2nd Half	-21%	5%	-6%	-11%	-16%
Territory	Overall Territory	6%	25%	2%	6%	9%
	Territory 1st Half	6%	13%	1%	-3%	17%
	Territory 2nd Half	2%	26%	1%	10%	-4%
General Play	Kicks From Hand	47%	43%	41%	37%	44%
	Passes	-22%	16%	-9%	-18%	-2%
	Runs	-8%	26%	-3%	-11%	-5%
	Meters Run	31%	50%	25%	13%	31%
	Clean Breaks	42%	60%	36%	31%	41%
	Defenders Beaten	17%	43%	13%	2%	18%
	Offloads	-6%	1%	5%	10%	11%
	Turnovers Conceded	-24%	-14%	-23%	-28%	-28%
Rucks	Rucks Won #	-13%	19%	-8%	-17%	-15%
	Rucks Lost	-41%	-38%	-24%	-21%	-30%
	Rucks Won %	30%	49%	16%	12%	20%
Mauls	Mauls Won #	21%	12%	15%	16%	24%
	Mauls Lost	2%	-6%	-10%	-10%	-2%
	Mauls Won %	0%	15%	8%	16%	6%
Tackling	Tackles Made	9%	-21%	8%	18%	20%
	Tackles Missed	-17%	-43%	-13%	-2%	-18%
	Tackle Success %	26%	31%	19%	17%	31%
Scrums	Scrums Won	-15%	33%	13%	29%	19%
	Scrums Lost	-15%	-3%	-8%	-4%	-5%
	Scrum %	0%	5%	9%	9%	19%
Lineouts	Lineouts Won	2%	30%	1%	5%	8%
	Lineouts Lost	-28%	-22%	-14%	-6%	-10%
	Lineout %	24%	37%	12%	8%	12%
Discipline	Penalties Conceded	-16%	-26%	-16%	-19%	-6%
	Total Free Kicks Conceded	21%	24%	2%	-8%	2%
	Yellow Cards	-31%	-42%	-15%	-7%	-3%
	Red Cards	-8%	-24%	10%	-14%	0%

4. Try and Triumph: The Constantly Shifting Strategies of Rugby

Who wants the ball at the end of the game?

Near the end of the titanic 'game for the ages' struggle between the All Blacks and Ireland in the 2023 Rugby World Cup quarter-final, scrum-half Aaron Smith made an interesting decision that got many All Blacks fans' blood boiling at the time. With just two minutes left on the clock, the All Blacks were up by four points and in possession at the halfway line. Rather than try to keep possession and wind down the clock, Smith put up a kick that essentially handed the ball back to the Irish, seemingly inviting them to go 80 metres and score the match-winning try (which they nearly did!). There was much yelling at their TVs by All Blacks fans wondering why in the world the team would surrender possession so close to the end. This approach resulted in the Irish putting together phase after phase of relentless attack (37 in total) and almost stealing the game in added time.

Table 4.4 offers some support for the All Blacks' strategy, as it shows (and as I pointed out earlier) that across all five competitions, winning teams have tended to have more possession than their opponents in the first half but less in the second. But they have also tended to control the territory in the second half.

Of course, every game has its own specific context so it's difficult to generalise, but it seems that in modern rugby, teams are comfortable closing out games by playing for territory, typically via kicking the ball deep and backing their defence. This was exactly what Aaron Smith was doing in the 2023 quarter-final: playing for territory rather than risk conceding a ruck penalty near halfway which would have resulted in an inevitable and dangerous Irish lineout maul drive.

The second-half possession deficit of winning teams can also explain why the number of passes is negatively associated with winning. For one, the team that strikes quickly and easily is the one that will be scoring points, as opposed to the team labouring through pass after pass, phase after phase, when trying to crack the opposition's defence. In addition, sometimes playing without the ball and backing your defence and then striking quickly off turnovers is a successful strategy. It was on full display at the 2023 Rugby World Cup, where the winners of six of the eight knockout games had less total possession than their opposition.

(In)discipline

Nobody suffers more vitriol in rugby than the poor old man in the middle holding the whistle. Being a referee is often a thankless job, though without them we wouldn't have a game. A big part of the controversies surrounding rugby refereeing is that calls are seldom completely black and white. The referee's interpretation is required in almost every circumstance. Former Irish fullback Rob Kearney has said, probably only partly in jest, that every single breakdown could have 19 different infringements whistled. It's the referee's job to walk that fine line between punishing infractions that are giving a team a clear advantage and letting the players play and the game flow.

4. Try and Triumph: The Constantly Shifting Strategies of Rugby

It's the players job to play the game with sufficient discipline that they avoid the notice, and potential ire, of the referee. Tables 4.3 and 4.4 earlier in this chapter show how vital discipline is to winning. Unsurprisingly, penalties and yellow cards conceded are strongly negatively correlated with match outcome.

The number of penalties and free kicks awarded in recent years has been extremely stable and similar across hemispheres at between 20 and 25 per game (Figure 4.21). However, the composition of the penalised offences began changing around 2011, with the scrum subsequently assuming a greater proportion of them, primarily at the expense of offsides (Figure 4.22). Why? Well, recall that the scrum has evolved from being an opportunity to restart to being a search for penalties.

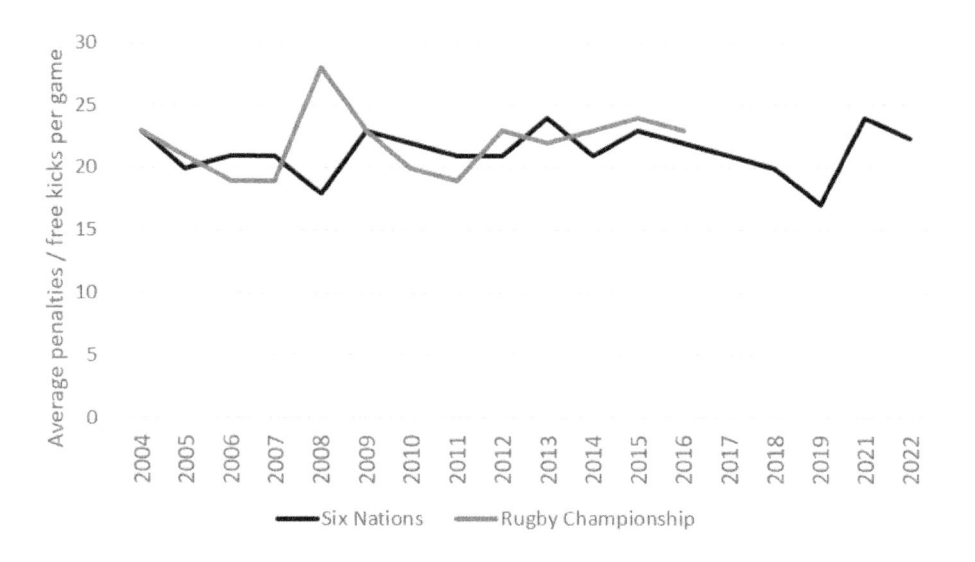

Figure 4.21. Average number of penalties/free kicks across the Six Nations and Rugby Championship competitions.

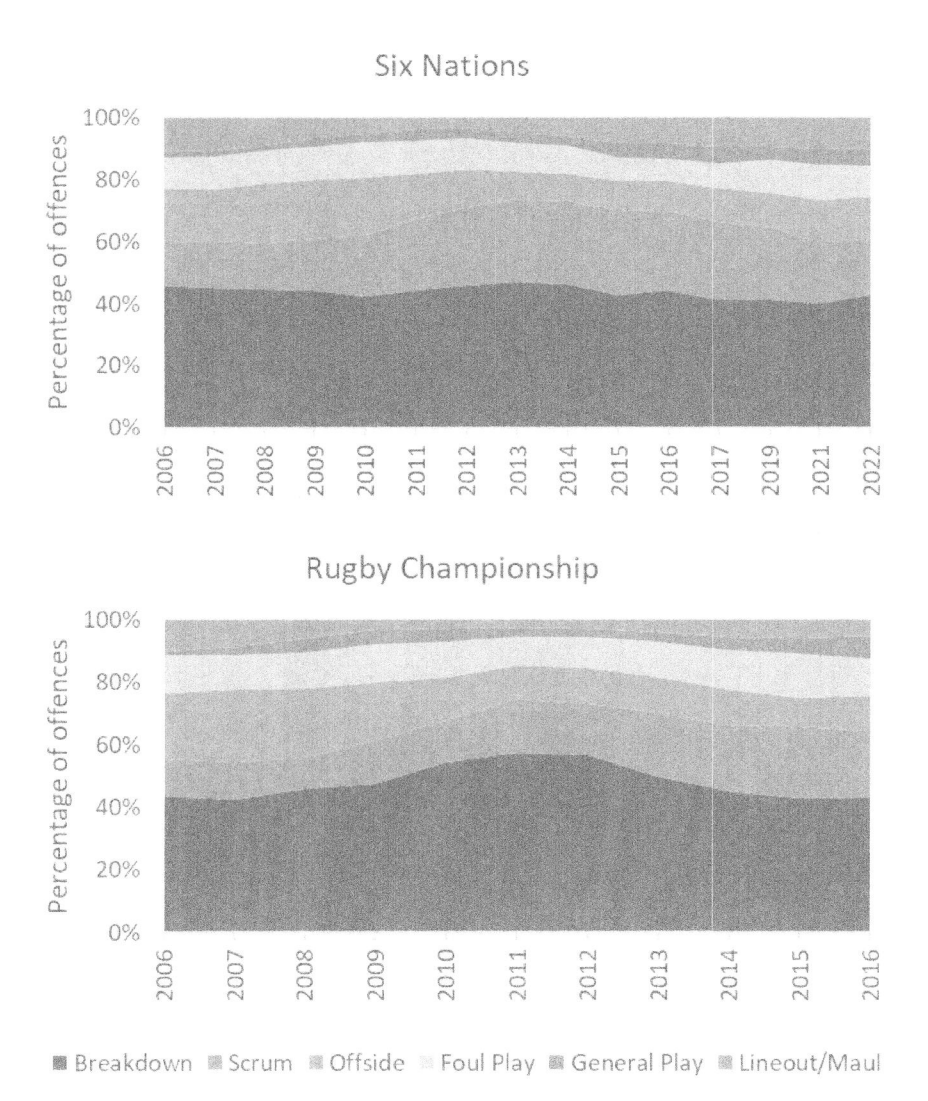

Figure 4.22. Composition of penalties/free kicks across the Six Nations and Rugby Championship competitions.

4. Try and Triumph: The Constantly Shifting Strategies of Rugby

Much to the fury of many a rugby fan, yellow and red cards are now dished out far more than they used to be. To put this into perspective, consider the 2023 Rugby World Cup final, World Rugby's showpiece event. Going into the final between the All Blacks and Springboks, there were huge concerns from the rugby punditry that a card could decide where the coveted Webb Ellis trophy would go.

Well, those fears were realised on the cold and wet Parisian night of October 28. In the nine World Cup finals preceding the 2023 event, a period spanning 760 minutes (including two extra time periods), only a single, solitary yellow card had been dished out (to All Black Ben Smith in 2015). The 2023 match was only two minutes old before that record was matched; by the time the referee blew the final whistle, he had shown the players a total of three yellow cards and the final's first-ever red card. The All Blacks were forced to play more than three-quarters of the match with just 14 men.

Across the Six Nations and Rugby Championship, there is a lot of variability year to year in terms of cards (Figure 4.23). The general trend has been a gradual increase in cards from 2004 until 2013, after which there was a decline until the 2018–2019 seasons. The 2021–2023 seasons then saw some of the highest number of cards dished out across both competitions. Overall, the Rugby Championship has seen 50 percent more yellow cards dished out (0.9 per game) compared to the Six Nations (0.6 per game), although red cards are equally rare in both competitions, at a rate of around one in every 20 games.

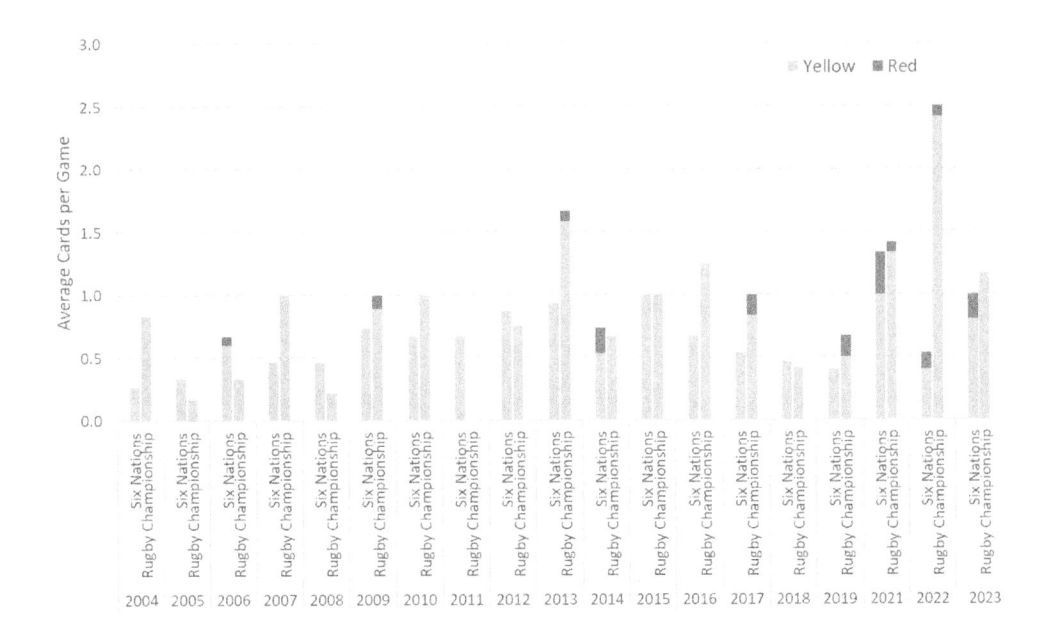

Figure 4.23. Number of yellow and red cards handed out across the Six Nations and Rugby Championship competitions from 2004 to 2023.

There aren't any clear trends over time in terms of which offences are leading to more cards, due to the relative scarcity of cards and the inconsistency of offence categorisation in World Rugby reports across different years. Since 2004, the overall proportion of offences has been similar between the Six Nations and Rugby Championship (Figure 4.24). The two notable exceptions are that there have been a) far more dangerous tackles in the Rugby Championship and b) more set piece (lineout/maul/scrum) offences in the Six Nations.

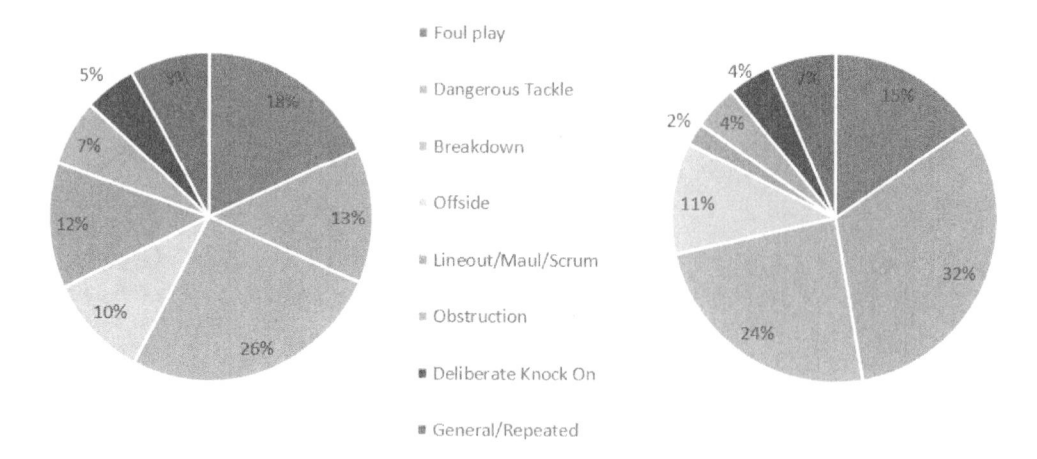

4. Try and Triumph: The Constantly Shifting Strategies of Rugby

Figure 4.24. Categories of yellow and red card offences across the Six Nations and Rugby Championship competitions since 2004.

The breakdown

I think there are three important takeaways from the data presented in this chapter. Each was somewhat of a surprise to me, and I'm sure they will be to many readers.

The first surprise I found is that while the game of rugby has undeniably changed since the advent of professionalisation and continues to change on a yearly basis, these changes aren't as bad as commentators and complaining fans like to make out. Next time you get nostalgic about a return to the 'good old amateur days' when the players played purely for the love of the game, refer back to Table 4.1 to refresh yourself on what a trip back to those days would entail, i.e., more kicks and set pieces, and less running and passing, try-scoring and ball in play.

Second, the difference between the hemispheres is in reality quite subtle. Whenever the heavyweights of the two hemispheres meet, it's often portrayed as a test of who plays the game the 'right way'. But just as when competing groups of humans unite to fight for a common cause in alien invasion movies, we can see from the rugby data that what unites the two hemispheres is far stronger than what divides them.

Third—and perhaps most painfully—we may need to accept that professional rugby teams, with all the resources, experience and analytic tools at their disposal, actually know what they're doing on occasion! Strategies such as doing lots of tactical kicking and playing without the ball in the second half do appear to be winning strategies.

Speaking of strategies: we'll examine what the evidence has to say about kicking a penalty versus going for a try in the next chapter.

Ready? Let's keep marching down the field.

5. Winning Time: Where Matches are Won or Lost

As you've probably gathered from all the stats and tables I've thrown at you so far, rugby has become a much more strategic game in the Professional era. Teams are now using data and analytics to determine what their best option for winning is at each decision juncture. There is more on the line now than simply outscoring the opposition, too. In most competitions there are four-try bonus points on offer, as well as 'losing' bonus points for getting within seven points of the opponent. And yes, as much as some quarters deride it, there is a bigger focus on providing an entertaining product. In the current era, rugby is competing against a much larger array of entertainment options. Fans only have so much leisure time at their disposal.

With enhanced data and analytics available, the days of teams automatically 'taking the points on offer' (i.e., kicking for goal at every given opportunity) are over. The decisions around what teams should do when awarded a kickable penalty generate a lot of animated discussion, so in this chapter we'll dive into that. But before we do, I want to delve a little deeper into the scoring patterns during matches. To that end I've broken up hundreds of matches into five-minute intervals from the Six Nations, Rugby Championship, Rugby World Cup knockout rounds, English Premiership, Top 14 and Super Rugby, and then averaged them. The result of this data-crunching is far greater detail on how scoring patterns tend to transpire. All the data presented in this chapter is from matches played between 2019 and 2023, except for the Rugby World Cup knockout rounds, which for sample size reasons was extended to include the 2011, 2015, 2019 and 2023 tournaments.

Let's start with penalty kicks. Chapter 4 showed us that penalty goals are more prevalent in the first half than the second. Our detailed data confirms this: it's immediately apparent that more penalties are kicked in the first half than the second (Figure 5.1). But within the first half, penalties peak between the sixth and 20th minutes, and again at the very end of the first half (which includes added time). In the second half, there's a consistent level of penalties kicked from the 41st to the 65th minute, before they tail away for the last 15 minutes of the match.

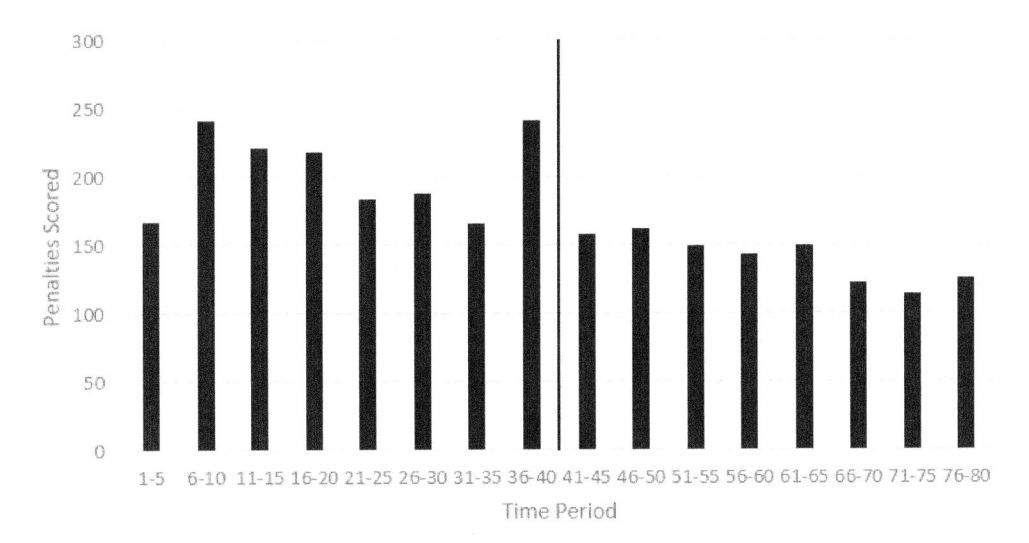

Figure 5.1. *The number of successful penalty goals kicked throughout matches across the Six Nations, Rugby Championship, Rugby World Cup knockout rounds, English Premiership, Top 14 and Super Rugby.*

5. Winning Time: Where Matches are Won or Lost

Contrasting this with tries gives a completely different picture (Figure 5.2). Tries are more prevalent in the second half, although as with penalties they peak in the last five minutes before halftime. Try-scoring rates are quite consistent throughout the second half, until a big increase in the last five minutes of the match.

Notably, the number of conversions follow tries almost exactly, and there is no difference in the conversion rate of tries between the first half and the second half. Across all these competitions, the conversion success rate during both halves has averaged 73 percent, with no evidence of goal kicker fatigue later in matches impacting the rate.

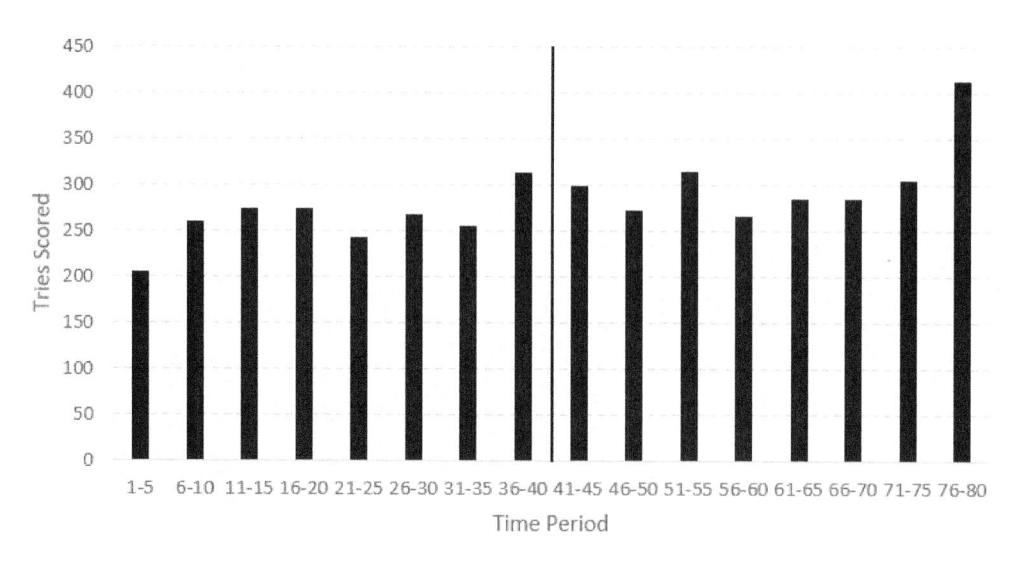

Figure 5.2. The number of tries scored throughout matches across the Six Nations, Rugby Championship, Rugby World Cup knockout rounds, English Premiership, Top 14 and Super Rugby.

The eagle-eyed among you may have noticed that Figures 5.1 and 5.2 were graphed using different vertical scales. If we combine penalties and tries on the same vertical scale (Figure 5.3), you can see that tries greatly outnumber penalties throughout matches. This will be a relief to those who enjoy watching attacking rugby. Even at the peak of penalty kicking—between the sixth and tenth minute of games—you are still slightly more likely to see a try being scored, on average.

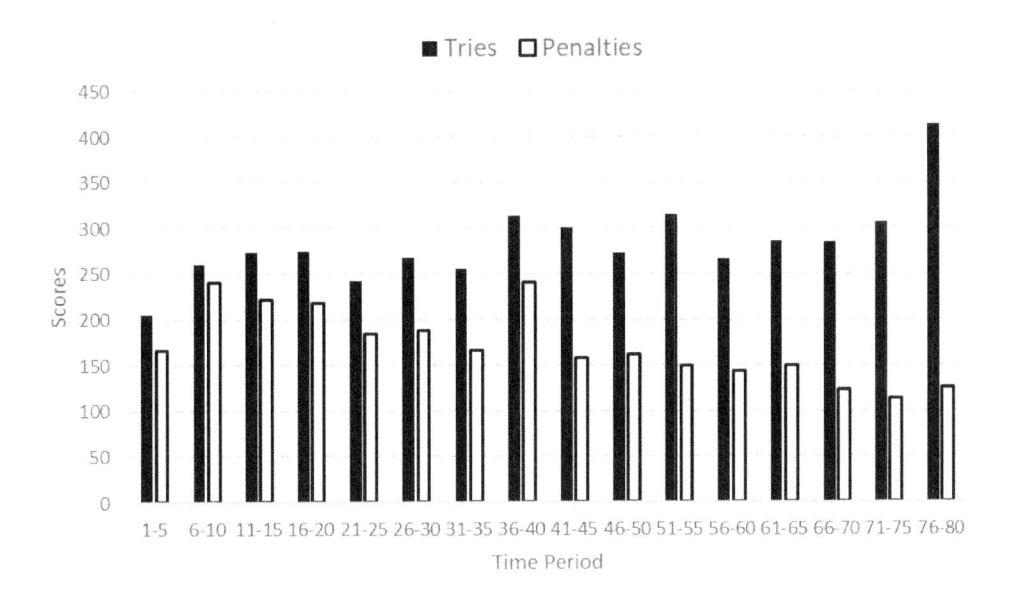

Figure 5.3. The number of tries and penalties scored throughout matches across the Six Nations, Rugby Championship, Rugby World Cup knockout rounds, English Premiership, Top 14 and Super Rugby.

In Chapter 4, I mentioned how remarkably similar competitions across the world were in terms of their playing and scoring patterns, contrary to popular

5. Winning Time: Where Matches are Won or Lost

belief. This is also true here. Figure 5.4 shows the penalty and try-scoring patterns across the six competitions that made up this analysis. Some, such as the Rugby World Cup knockout matches, have a limited sample size and are therefore subject to 'noise' (i.e., fluctuations) in the trends. But the general patterns persist: namely, that tries outnumber penalties, they tend to be scored in different halves, and there are peaks in scoring immediately before the end of each half.

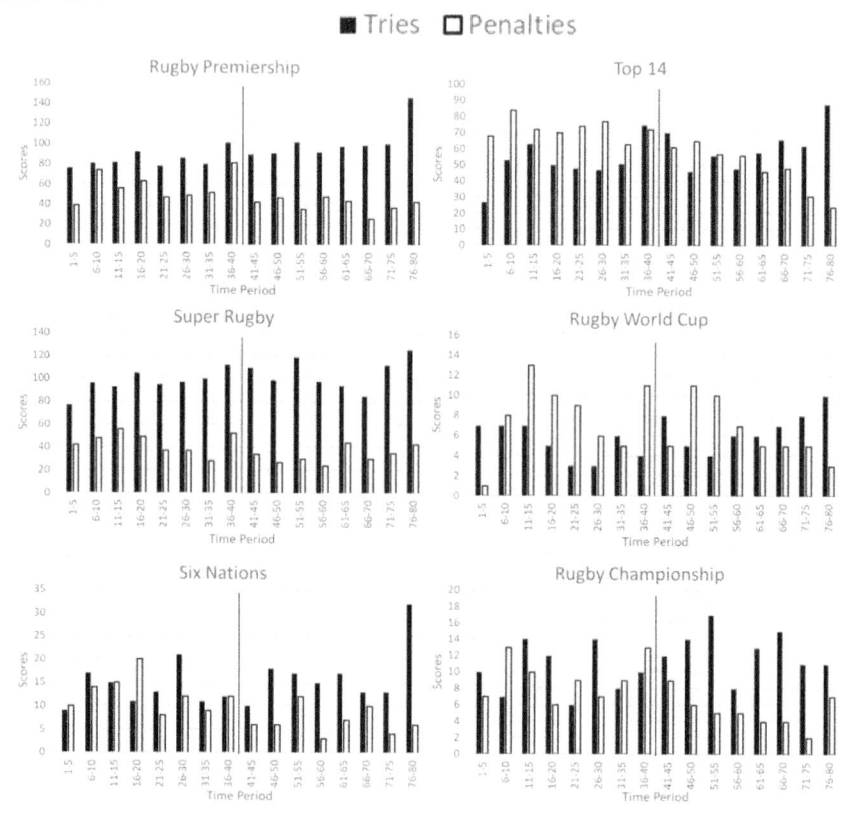

Figure 5.4. The number of tries and penalties scored throughout matches by competition, across the Six Nations, Rugby Championship, Rugby World Cup knockout rounds, English Premiership, Top 14 and Super Rugby.

There are some important differences between the various competitions, however. At the international level, where the stakes are higher, the ratio of tries to penalties decreases (Table 5.1); in fact, in the Rugby World Cup knockout matches, penalties outnumber tries by almost 20 percent. Interestingly, despite the 'French flair' we're used to hearing about, the French Top 14 league sees slightly fewer tries than penalties. But, as Table 5.1 shows, the distribution of tries and penalties across the first and second halves of games is very similar across all the competitions examined.

Table 5.1. Try-to-penalty ratio and distribution of scores by half, across the Six Nations, Rugby Championship, Rugby World Cup knockout rounds, English Premiership, Top 14 and Super Rugby.

Level	Competition	Try to Penalty Ratio	% Tries Scored in 1st Half	% Penalties Scored in 1st Half
Domestic	Rugby Premiership	1.9 : 1	45%	59%
Domestic	Super Rugby	2.6 : 1	48%	57%
Domestic	Top 14	0.9 : 1	46%	60%
International	Rugby World Cup	0.8 : 1	44%	55%
International	Six Nations	1.6 : 1	45%	65%
International	Rugby Championship	1.6 : 1	45%	64%

What happened to the good old 'droppie'?

There's one other scoring mechanism in rugby that we haven't touched upon yet in this chapter: drop goals. They were always fairly rare, but in the modern game seem to have gone out of fashion faster than the VHS tape. Between 1955 and 1985 in the old Five Nations, drop goals accounted for 7 percent of total

5. Winning Time: Where Matches are Won or Lost

points scored. In both the Six Nations and Rugby Championship (known as the Tri Nations prior to 2012), this fell to 4 percent between 2005 and 2010. And since 2011, they've accounted for only 1 percent of points scored in both competitions.

Be that as it may, the drop goal still has its time and place. As recently as 2023, England's George Ford gave us a reminder of the power of the drop goal during a vital Rugby World Cup pool game against Argentina. When English flanker Tom Curry was shown a red card after just three minutes, Argentina became odds-on favourites to win what at the outset had seemed an evenly poised contest. Up stepped Ford, who was only starting because English captain Owen Farrell had been suspended. He calmly banged over three drop goals to propel the undermanned England to a 12-3 lead at halftime—one that the stunned Pumas couldn't overturn in the second half.

But that game was very much the exception to the modern-day rule. So why are drop goals so rare today? One of the reasons is undoubtedly that, despite Ford's three-from-three masterclass, they're extremely difficult to execute. The low success rate of drop goals may surprise, but in the Six Nations and Rugby Championship. it's been just 32 percent and 30 percent, respectively, between 2004 and 2022. One caveat is that some drop-goal attempts are 'throwaway' efforts undertaken when a team already has a penalty advantage. But even so, this is a very low-percentage play—and teams have reacted accordingly. Although the success rate hasn't fundamentally changed over time, the number of attempts has (Figure 5.5). In both the Six Nations and Rugby

Championship, the average number of drop-goal attempts has more than halved over the past decade and a half, from 1.2 per game between 2005 and 2012 to 0.5 per game since 2013.

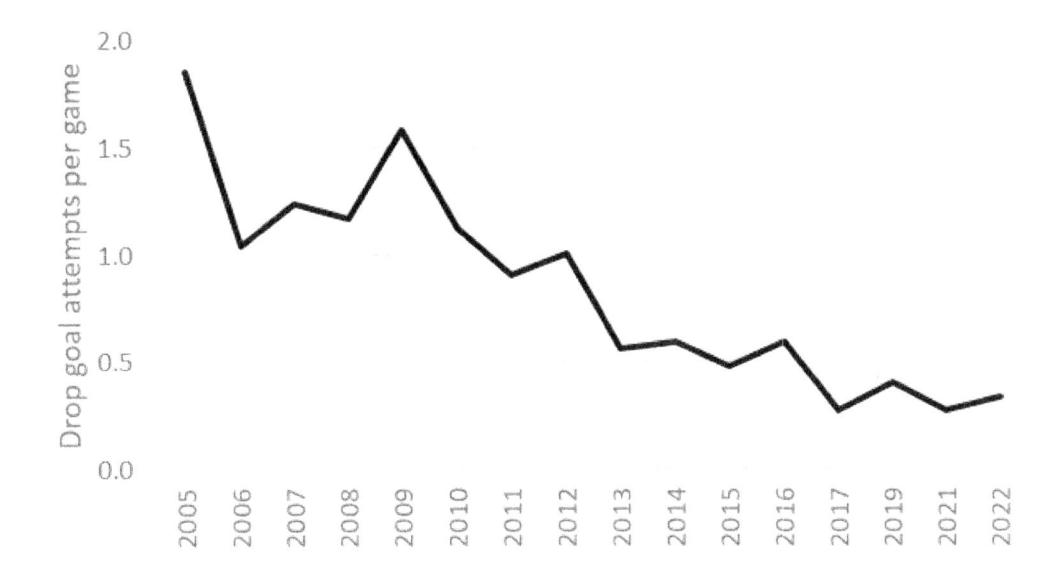

Figure 5.5. Average drop-goal attempts per game in the Six Nations and Rugby Championship combined.

It's difficult to infer too much about the timing of drop goals because there are so few of them, so even aggregating the data across multiple competitions only gives a handful per five-minute time period (and lots of fluctuations). But from the limited data we have, we can see they're only slightly more common in the second half (58 percent). There also appears to be a slight bump in drop goals in the last five minutes of each half if we ignore a lot of 'noisy' data (the 'peak' between 21 and 25 minutes is likely just an anomaly, Figure 5.6).

5. Winning Time: Where Matches are Won or Lost

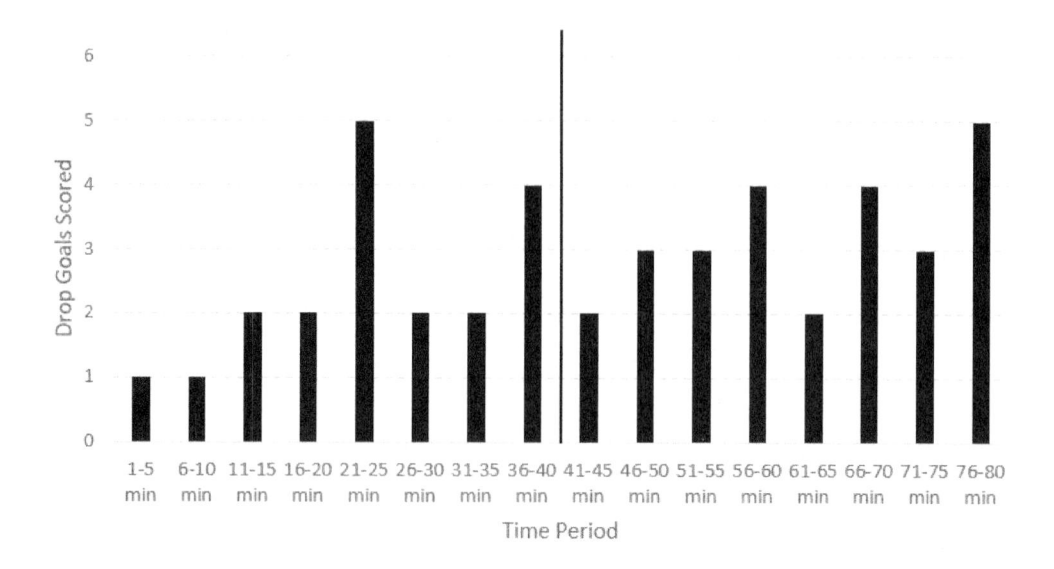

Figure 5.6. The number of drop goals scored throughout matches across the Six Nations, Rugby Championship, Rugby World Cup knockout rounds, English Premiership, Top 14 and Super Rugby.

Deciding the match

Now that we understand how scoring patterns tend to unfold during matches, this is a good time to move on to a related topic: lead changes. Specifically, when does the decisive lead change tend to occur in games, after which the leading team never relinquishes their winning position for the rest of the match?

I'm sure you have your theories. In fact, I decided that before I dove into the stats, I'd first survey some rugby-loving friends to see how fan beliefs match the data. The verdict among my completely unscientific straw poll was that this decisive lead change would occur in the last ten to 15 minutes of most matches.

Unfortunately for my rugby-loving friends, this is dead wrong. Analysis taken from almost 1,000 games reveals that, on the contrary, the definitive lead in rugby games is often reached very early in games (Figure 5.7). In 41 percent of matches, the final definitive lead change occurred in the *first 20 minutes* of the match. However, there is a spike in matches decided in the last ten minutes, with 18 percent of matches decided then. But counter to what most people would probably guess, almost 60 percent of matches don't see a lead change at all in the second half!

This doesn't necessarily mean that these games are boring and one-sided. A couple of recent examples can illustrate how even the tensest, tightest matches don't require the lead to change hands right to the end. The 2023 Rugby World Cup quarter-final between the All Blacks and Ireland, hailed at the time as one of the greatest games in history, is a good example. The All Blacks prevailed 28-24, withstanding a 37-phase Irish attack in added time at the end. In that match, the All Blacks took the initial lead in the eighth minute and were never bested on the scoreboard from that stage on, despite Ireland narrowing the gap to a single point at various stages.

Only a couple of weeks later, the All Blacks and South Africa battled out an extremely tense and tight final which South Africa won by a single, solitary point—12-11. The Springboks hit the front with a penalty in the *third minute* and were never caught on the scoreboard by the All Blacks from that point on. No lead change for 77 whole minutes, but definitely not boring!

5. Winning Time: Where Matches are Won or Lost

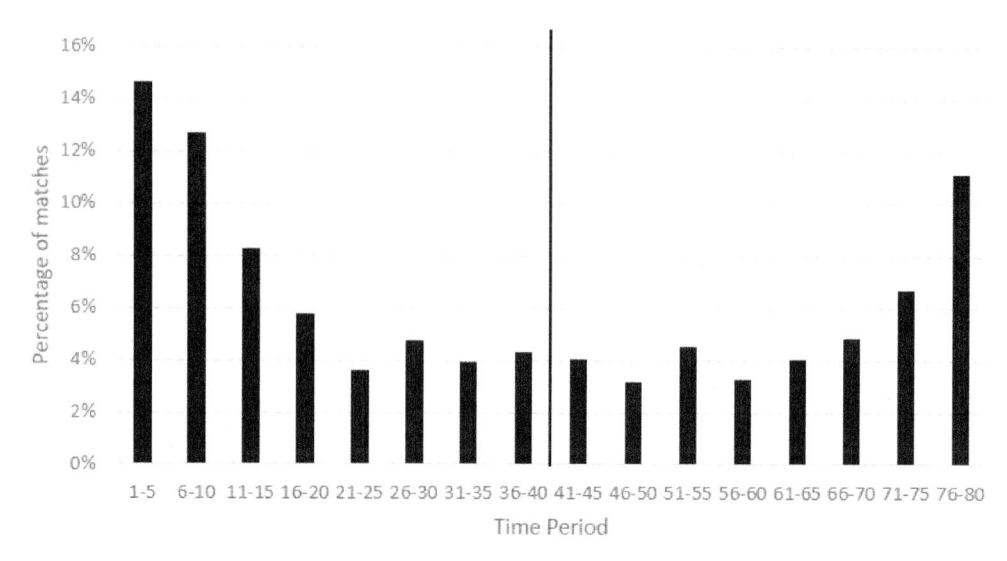

Figure 5.7. The time when the final lead change occurs in matches across the Six Nations, Rugby Championship, Rugby World Cup knockout rounds, English Premiership, Top 14 and Super Rugby.

I created the images in Figure 5.8 to help you better visualise this pattern across the different competitions. Think of each graphic—one drawing from the domestic competitions, the other from the international ones—as a kind of clock, with the 80 minutes of the matches unfolding in a clockwise direction. The further you are from the centre, the higher the proportion of definitive lead changes there are per five-minute segment. For both the domestic and the international competitions, there is a clear peak at the beginning of matches and, to a lesser extent, at the end. You can see how closely the different competitions follow each other, although with a smaller sample size there is some 'noise' in the international data. That caveat aside, it's interesting to note that the internationals are even more skewed towards early definitive leads. Final lead changes occurred in the first 20 minutes in no less than *half* of their games.

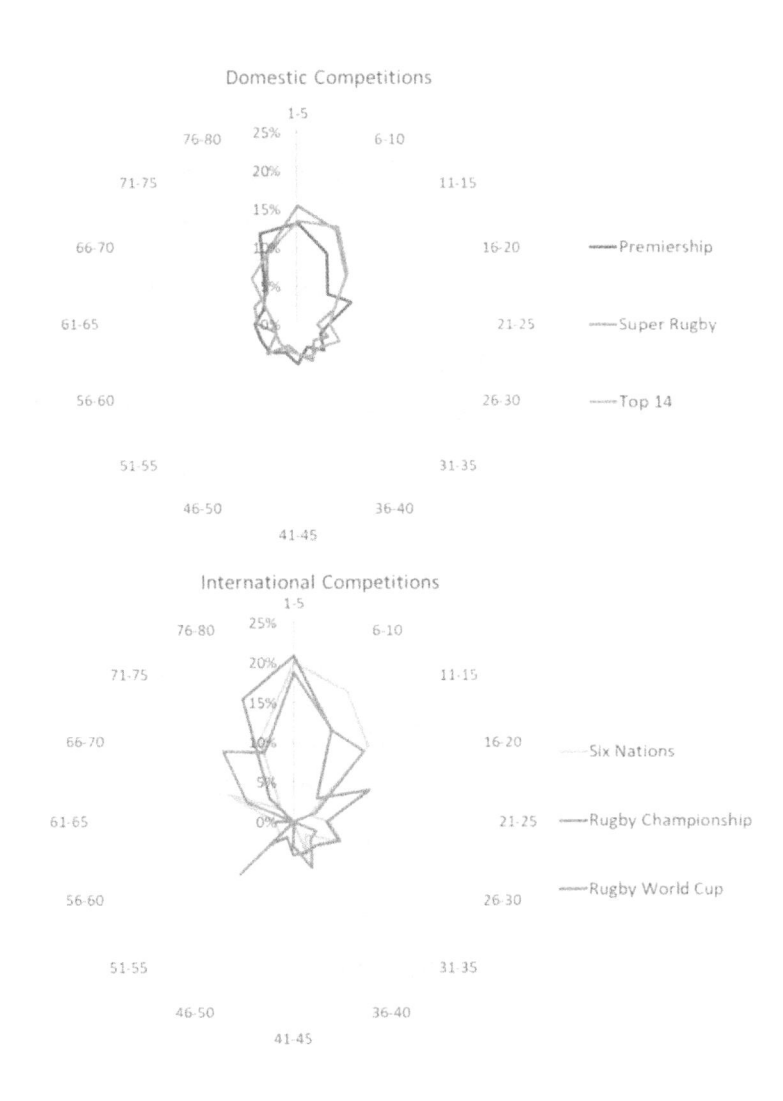

Figure 5.8. *The time when the final lead change occurs by competition, across the Six Nations, Rugby Championship, Rugby World Cup knockout rounds, English Premiership, Top 14 and Super Rugby.*

5. Winning Time: Where Matches are Won or Lost

It should come as no surprise that the closeness of the final score has a big bearing on when the definitive lead change occurs. After all, it's almost impossible in a blowout win for the winning team to take the lead within the last five minutes. Figure 5.9 shows that 'close wins' (decided by seven points or less) and 'comfortable wins' (decided by more than seven points) are at the opposite ends of the spectrum when it comes to the definitive lead change. For comfortable wins, the definitive lead change occurs in the first half in 78 percent of matches, whereas for close wins it's only 28 percent of matches.

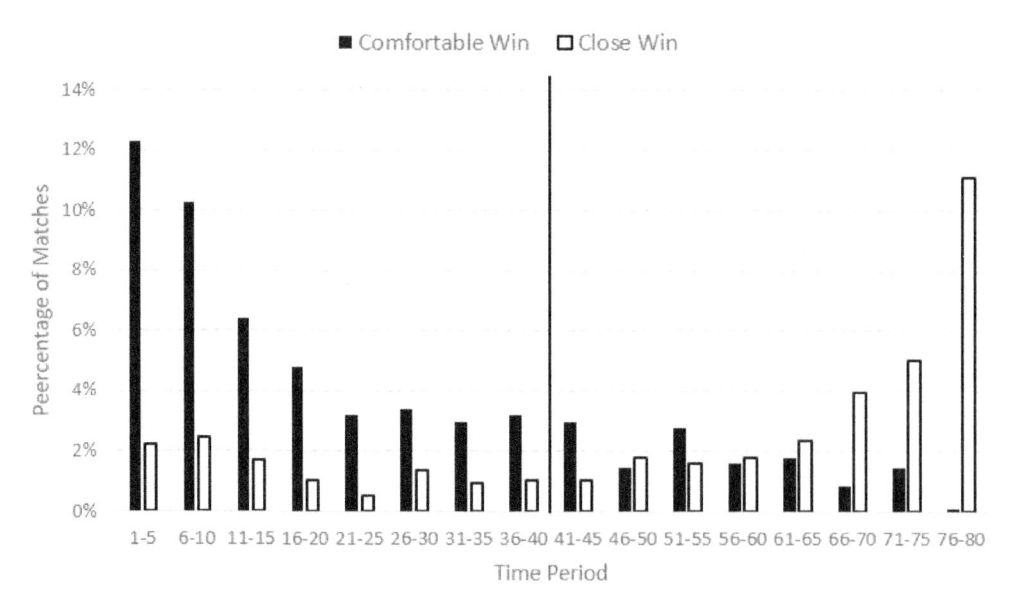

Figure 5.9. Comparison of the time when the final lead change occurs between 'comfortable wins' (matches decided by more than seven points) and 'close wins' (matches decided by seven points or less). Data taken from matches across the Six Nations, Rugby Championship, Rugby World Cup knockout rounds, English Premiership, Top 14 and Super Rugby.

The most important finding remains in force, however: across all rugby matches, the definitive lead change tends to occur relatively early in the match.

First score wins?

If the definitive lead change is occurring so early in matches, does that mean it's essential to score first? Let's find out the way we always do—through the data.

Figure 5.10 shows that teams which score first go on to win more often than not, and that this effect is intensified in the international game where scoring opportunities tend to be fewer. It peaks in the Rugby World Cup knockout stages, where three out of four teams that score first go on to win the match.

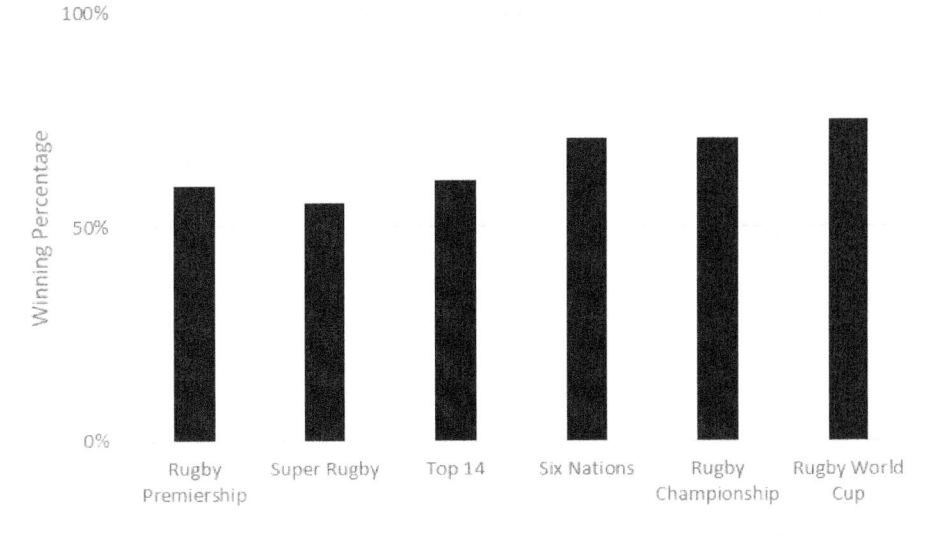

Figure 5.10. A team's match-winning percentage when scoring first across the Six Nations, Rugby Championship, Rugby World Cup knockout rounds, English Premiership, Top 14 and Super Rugby.

5. Winning Time: Where Matches are Won or Lost

If we compare the effect of scoring first versus scoring last, there's a marked difference between domestic and international rugby (Figure 5.11). In domestic rugby, teams scoring first win on average 59 percent of games, whereas the team that scores last wins 67 percent. But at the international level, it pays to put points on the board first. The teams scoring first in internationals win 72 percent of games, eclipsing the teams which score last by four percentage points.

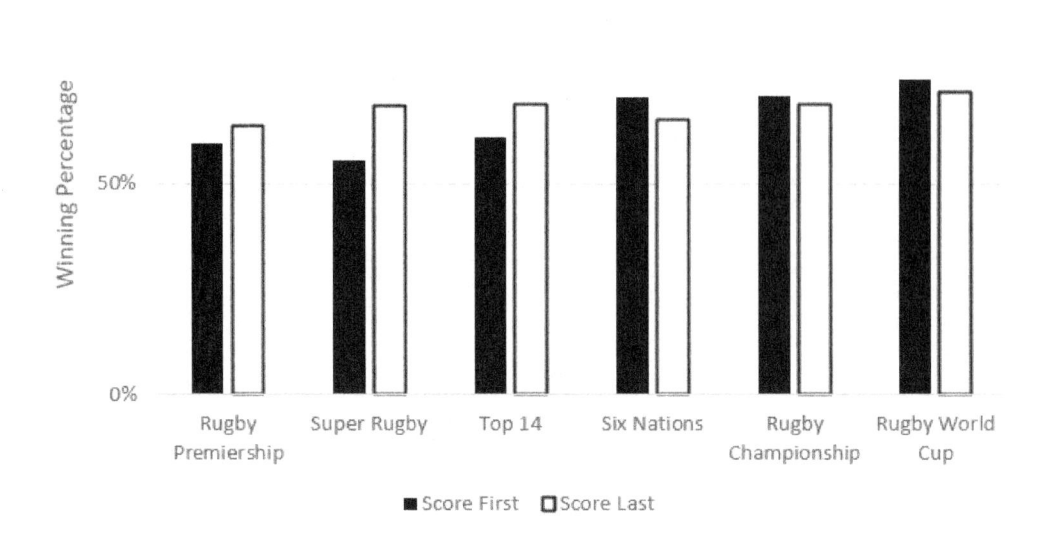

Figure 5.11. A team's match-winning percentage when scoring first versus last across the Six Nations, Rugby Championship, Rugby World Cup knockout rounds, English Premiership, Top 14 and Super Rugby.

What's even more interesting, at least in my mind, is the impact of different scoring methods. When a team scores first, penalties just don't cut it, especially at the domestic level. As Figure 5.12 shows, the winning percentage is far higher in all competitions when the opening score is a try rather than a penalty. This may sound obvious, since a try is worth more points, so of course it increases your chance of holding on for a victory. But the effect is so stark that in both the Rugby Premiership and Super Rugby competitions, you are actually *less likely* to win the match if you open the scoring with a penalty! This is quite an incredible statistic, and probably speaks to the high-scoring nature of those matches and the opportunity cost of 'settling' for just the three points while on attack (rather than getting five or seven through a try). The try effect is highest at the international level, where teams who open the scoring with a try go on to win 81 percent of matches (versus 63 percent when opening with a penalty score).

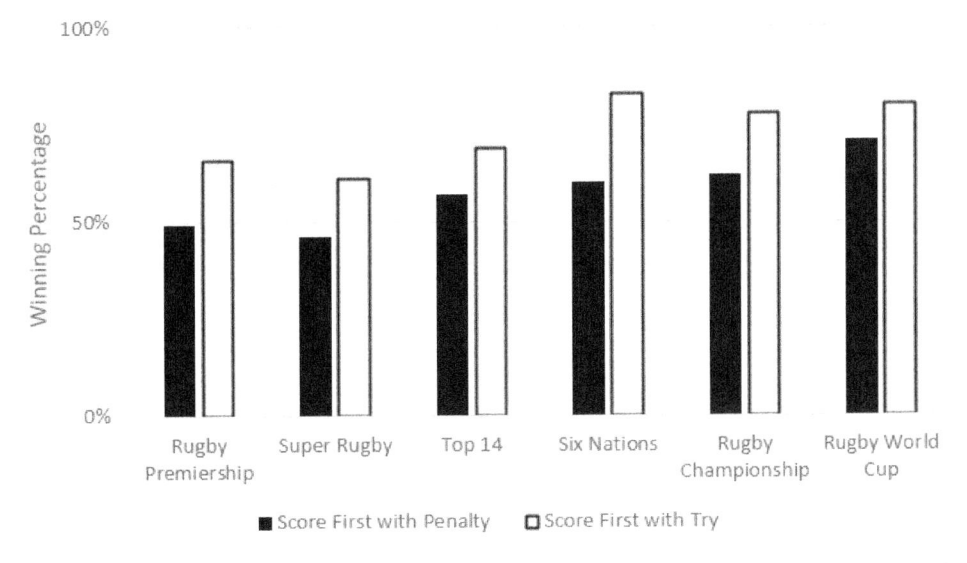

Figure 5.12. A team's match-winning percentage when scoring first through a penalty versus a try, across the Six Nations, Rugby Championship, Rugby World Cup knockout rounds, English Premiership, Top 14 and Super Rugby.

5. Winning Time: Where Matches are Won or Lost

For the last scoring play, the trend is reversed (Figure 5.13). Teams that score last via a penalty win more matches than those who score last via a try. This is the case across all competitions except for the Six Nations (where the winning split is almost even). This makes sense intuitively, as games where teams are taking penalties towards the end are likely to be close. So in those situations, the penalty may be to take the lead or to seal the game. However, it should be noted that a try (or subsequent conversion) is the final scoring play in the vast majority (75 percent) of games.

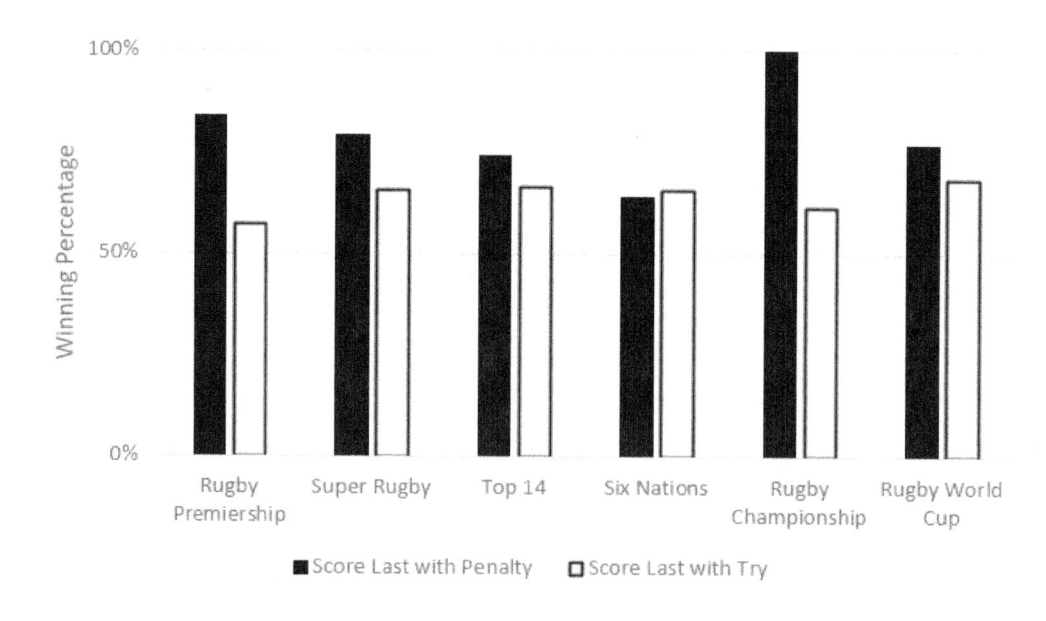

Figure 5.13. A team's match-winning percentage when scoring first through a penalty versus a try, across the Six Nations, Rugby Championship, Rugby World Cup knockout rounds, English Premiership, Top 14 and Super Rugby.

These results suggest that, strategically speaking, teams should try to reverse the scoring patterns documented earlier in the chapter in Figures 5.1 and 5.2, which showed that 60 percent of penalties are kicked in the first half, while 55 percent of tries are scored in the second half. Teams tend to start conservatively, try to accumulate points via the penalty to build a lead, and eventually open up and attack more through tries in the second half (and especially towards the end).

One-day cricket underwent a revolution in strategy in the 1990s. The first 15 overs transformed from a conservative period of scoring slowly and saving wickets to a period of unbridled aggression while fielding restrictions were in place. The data suggests that rugby should follow a similar trajectory, with teams starting aggressively to deliver the potential knockout blow through early tries. Then, if the game is tight towards the end, the team can revert to the penalty goal to eke out the win.

To add further fuel to the 'penalty fire' here, let's look at the overall relationship between scoring types and match wins. Table 5.2 outlines the correlations between the number of scores (whether through tries, conversions, penalties or drop goals) and winning across the six competitions. You can see that across all competitions, scoring tries is far more correlated with winning than penalties; in Super Rugby, the difference is a whopping 71 percent versus 12 percent. The 12 percent correlation means that there is practically no relationship between kicking penalties and winning matches in Super Rugby, and indeed scoring penalties is far less correlated with winning than metrics

5. Winning Time: Where Matches are Won or Lost

such as kicks from hand, tackles made and scrums won. The scoring-type gap is closest in the tightly contested Rugby World Cup knockout stage, where tries have a 58 percent correlation with winning versus 44 percent for penalties.

Table 5.2. The correlation between the various scoring types and winning across the Six Nations, Rugby Championship, Rugby World Cup knockout rounds, English Premiership, Top 14 and Super Rugby.

Level	Competition	Tries	Conversions	Penalty Goals	Drop Goals
Domestic	Rugby Premiership	64%	56%	25%	17%
Domestic	Super Rugby	71%	67%	12%	3%
Domestic	Top 14	60%	58%	22%	8%
International	Rugby World Cup	58%	43%	44%	13%
International	Six Nations	72%	62%	20%	0%
International	Rugby Championship	73%	64%	46%	22%

Table 5.3 further emphasises how important try-scoring is to winning. Across the competitions, teams who score more tries than their opponents but either the same amount or fewer penalties go on to win around 70 to 90 percent of matches. The teams that score more penalties but not more tries, on the other hand, tend to win fewer than half their matches.

Table 5.3. *The percentage of matches won under various scoring scenarios across the Six Nations, Rugby Championship, Rugby World Cup knockout rounds, English Premiership, Top 14 and Super Rugby.*

Level	Competition	Score More Tries but Same or Less Penalties	Score More Penalties but Same or Less Tries
Domestic	Rugby Premiership	86%	45%
Domestic	Super Rugby	90%	35%
Domestic	Top 14	85%	44%
International	Rugby World Cup	71%	60%
International	Six Nations	90%	34%
International	Rugby Championship	72%	43%

Again, the only competition where the balance between penalties and tries is relatively even is during the Rugby World Cup's knockout stages. This highlights why it's so important to examine different levels and competitions of rugby when looking for takeaways. There's no 'one size fits all'.

We can see this clearly in a 2015 study that the *Economist* published on the merits of passing up kickable penalties to attempt to score tries, exclusively centred around the 2015 Rugby World Cup. They had access to a wealth of data (which I unfortunately don't): the location on the pitch where each penalty was awarded, where the resulting lineouts or scrums were taken from, and if they successfully led to a try within the next two minutes. Their conclusion was that in almost all scenarios, a kickable penalty should be taken over a lineout or scrum. Their analysis showed that Tier-1 sides only conceded tries from attacking lineouts and scrums ten percent and 12.5 percent of the time, respectively.

5. Winning Time: Where Matches are Won or Lost

On closer inspection, though, I found this study to be less illuminating than promised. For one, their analysis was restricted to the 2015 Rugby World Cup pool stages only (and we've seen how competitions vary). They also included potentially lopsided Tier-1 versus Tier-2 contests. Most tellingly of all, they included all attacking scrums and lineouts within the 22m line to measure their attacking success rates. If a team turns down a kickable penalty, the onus is on the kicker to put the ball in to touch as close to the opponent's tryline as possible. No one would contemplate trading a shot at goal from 40m out only to end up with a lineout from 22m out! A more realistic data set to use for this analysis would have been lineouts within 10m of the tryline, which undoubtedly would have yielded much higher attacking success rates. All of which is to say, I'm not convinced of the conclusion that the penalty kick should be attempted almost every time from within the opponents half.

The value of the restart

There's another factor that needs to be considered when evaluating the overall impact of different scoring plays in rugby: the restart. After all, the team that just conceded points is the team that controls this next passage of play.

Think of a game of roulette. If you're about to start betting on a colour and you see that the last three spins were red, what would you put your money on? Most people would be tempted by black as it seems to be 'due'. But this is a fallacy. In roulette, the next spin is completely independent of what has just happened, so even if there have been ten consecutive reds, the chance of the next spin coming up red actually hasn't changed at all.

Rugby is not roulette. It's not a game of chance; it's a game of skill between two teams where one is usually superior to the other. If you're given money and told you must use it to bet on which team will score next, you would likely put your money on the more dominant, better team. They *should* score more often than the inferior team. Therefore, the expectation in rugby is that, on balance, the superior team was the most recent team to score, and will also be the next team to score.

In the real world, though, games don't actually flow like that. In fact, the data shows that it's slightly more likely that the team which just conceded points, and will be restarting the game from halfway, will be the next team to score. In Super Rugby, the team that just conceded a score is not only the next team to score 56 percent of the time, but outscores their opponent by an average of 0.61 points in the next scoring play (Table 5.4). Why? Because the team that just conceded gets to kick-off from halfway and control the restart. This gives them immediate field position in the opponent's half. And this restart control is powerful enough to overcome the effect of superior team's scoring dominance. The effect is most pronounced at the domestic level, where it equates to a 0.4-point advantage for the team restarting play.

Table 5.4. The net difference in average next points scored by the restarting team (over the receiving team), and the percentage of time that the restarting team scores next. Data compiled from matches in the Six Nations, Rugby Championship, Rugby World Cup knockout rounds, English Premiership, Top 14 and Super Rugby.

Competition	Net Difference in Next Points Scored by Restarting Team	Percentage of Time Restarting Team Scores Next
Rugby Premiership	0.35	54%
Super Rugby	0.61	56%
Top 14	0.26	54%
Domestic	**0.40**	**55%**
Rugby World Cup	0.34	55%
6 Nations	0.07	52%
Rugby Championship	0.18	53%
International	**0.16**	**53%**

The most important consequence of this effect is that it erodes the relative value of a penalty compared to a try. Shaving off 0.4 points from a penalty (the domestic competition average from Table 5.4) is a substantial proportion of the points that you've just earned. If you're successful with your penalty you get three points, but you're swapping an attacking position on the field for a defensive one once your opponent restarts. They are now the more likely team to score next.

'Take the points' or go for the try?

This discussion inevitably brings me to yet another common misconception in rugby circles. Whenever a kickable penalty is on offer, both commentators and armchair experts will insist the kicker 'take the points', as if kicking it through the posts is a fait accompli. Taking these points to be automatic, though, couldn't be more wrong. Here's why.

The kicker still needs to slot it over, and often under a fair bit of pressure. Figure 5.14 shows kicking percentages from various locations on the field, which I took from World Rugby's analysis of the 2003 World Cup. We can use this to estimate the 'expected value' of a penalty on offer, i.e., if a kicker was given 100 attempts at the same kick, how many points they can expect to walk away with on average. Unless the penalty occurs right under the posts, the expected value is actually less than three points.

Consider, for example, that a penalty awarded just to the left of the uprights, between the 22m and 40m lines, has an 80 percent chance of success. This means that an international kicker could expect to achieve an average of just 2.4 points when going for goal from this position. Most rugby pundits would assume a kick from here is a 'gimme' and would be imploring their team to 'take the three', but instead they should be shouting at the TV screen for their team to 'take the 2.4'!

5. Winning Time: Where Matches are Won or Lost

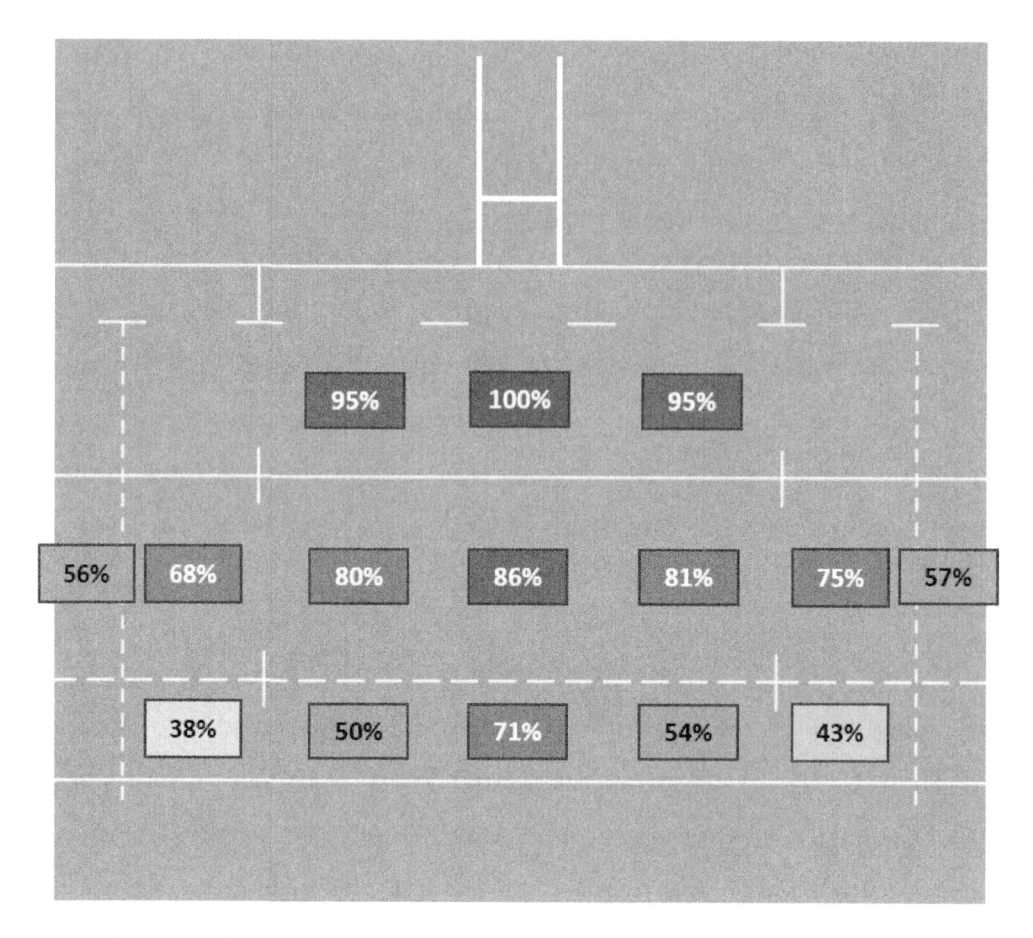

Figure 5.14. *Goalkicking success from various areas of the field during the 2003 Rugby World Cup.*

If the team opts for an attacking lineout to attempt to score a try instead, they only need to convert this into a try on 40 percent of occasions (four out of every ten attempts) for it to be a more profitable decision in the long term.[6] This strategy would net 2.5 points per attempt on average, versus the 2.4 points

---
[6] Calculation assumes the resulting conversion is kicked 65% of times.

for attempting the penalty kick. And a team that can convert 5 out of every 10 attacking lineouts would be scoring an average of 3.15 points per attempt.

So if you think you can convert an attacking lineout maul into a try at least four out of every ten attempts, forsaking the penalty kick for the try in this scenario becomes the long-term better option.

Give your kicker a break!

There's almost nothing in rugby that 'grinds my gears' more than seeing a player dot down a try completely unopposed without making any effort to score closer to the posts. I get it: securing the five points is paramount and there's no need to risk messing that up in any way. But how many times have you seen a player stroll over the tryline, with no opposing player in sight, and just place the ball down without striving to get as close as possible to the posts?

Why is this so important? Because in rugby the conversion is taken from the lateral point that the try scorer touches down on. And an extra two points can be crucial to a team's success. Just ask the All Blacks, whose missed conversion in the 2023 Rugby World Cup final ended up being the difference between a victory and a loss.

Figure 5.15 draws from data compiled across almost 750 conversion attempts from the Rugby World Cup, Six Nations and Rugby Championship.[7] Breaking the rugby field into seven lateral sections, it offers an illuminating

---

[7] Compiled from the World Rugby website reports.

5. Winning Time: Where Matches are Won or Lost

perspective on goalkickers' conversion accuracy as they are pushed further out towards the sidelines.

Let's begin our analysis by examining where tries tend to be scored, represented by the heatmap in the in-goal area. You can see that there's a slight left-hand skew to where this happens, with 12 percent scored in the left-hand corner versus 9 percent in the right-hand one. This is due to the right-hand dominance of most players, which enables them to move the ball from right to left with more accuracy and speed.

In terms of conversion success, there's a marked drop off from 100 percent in front of the posts to approximately 40 percent from the sidelines. Being pushed out from the 15m channel to the sideline drops the expected conversion success by 25 percent. And it goes down by roughly 25 percent between the regions immediately adjacent to the posts and the 15m channels. Now, these are obviously averages, so there isn't going to be a sudden 25 percent drop off in accuracy one metre either side of the 15-metre line! But it gives an idea of how crucial it is to conversion success for the try scorers to get as close as possible to the posts.

One way to quantify this is to look at conversion attempts from the section of field between the goal post and the 5-metre line (in from touch), which is approximately 27m in width. Within this section, goalkicking success drops by 60 percent (from 100 percent to 40 percent) the further away from the goalposts you get. On average, every metre towards the sideline corresponds to a 2.2 percent decrease in the goalkicker's chance of converting the try. So, if the try scorer can just dive an extra 5m closer to the posts, he gives his kicker an 11 percent higher chance of success. In a close game, that can easily be the difference between a victory and a defeat.

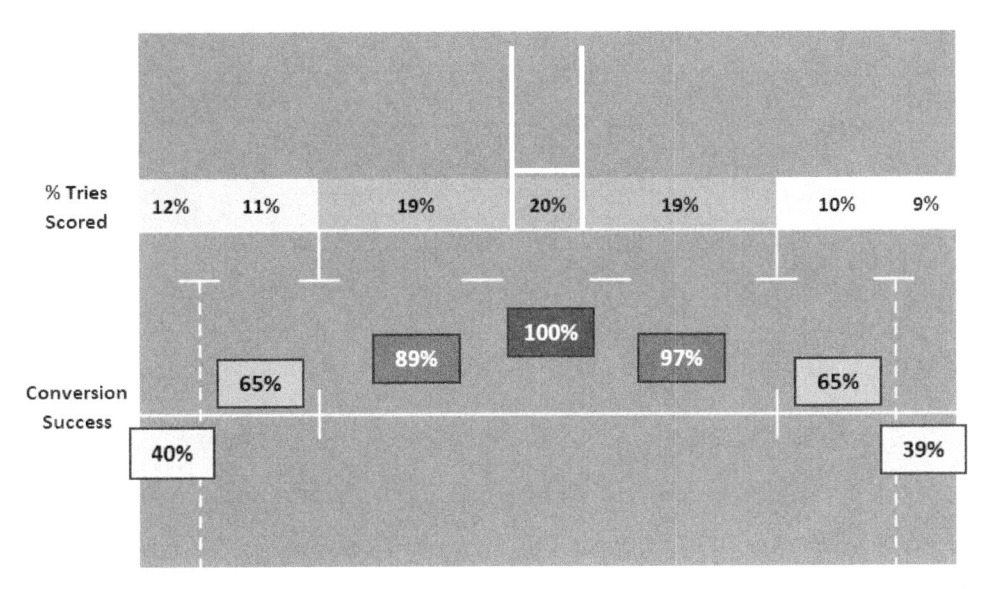

Figure 5.15. Conversion kicking success by area of the field across the Rugby World Cup, Six Nations and Rugby Championship.

The breakdown

Every match, and every decision within that match, will be context dependent based on the strengths of the teams playing and the current match dynamics. There's no 'one-size-fits-all' template as far as how to attack to secure the win. But in this chapter, we've drilled deep into the scoring data to reveal some fascinating patterns associated with winning:

5. Winning Time: Where Matches are Won or Lost

- Scoring first is very important, but especially scoring first via a try.
- The definitive lead change occurs much earlier in matches than most would assume, further underlining the need to put early points on the board.
- After your team scores, it is more likely than not that the opposition will score next, which exacerbates the opportunity cost of only scoring three points rather than five or seven.
- Unless a penalty is directly in front of the posts inside the 22m line (i.e., something that even I might be able to kick), it is less than 100 percent certain that the kicker will slot it.

All this data points to the long-term probabilistic advantage of going for the try rather than 'settling' for a penalty in most circumstances. However, each match has its own game situation and nuances to consider. Rugby matches aren't simply formulaic and predictable. In fact, in the next chapter we'll examine just how unpredictable rugby results are.

6. Underdogs Unleashed: A Comparative Look into Upsets

So much of the allure of sports is rooted in its unpredictability. Unlike a scripted Hollywood story, sports offer genuine suspense and surprise. The regularity of upsets—those fairytale moments of David triumphing over Goliath—fuel our fascination. These underdog victories and even honourable defeats create narratives that captivate fans worldwide, and the possibility of witnessing an historic upset or a dominant team's fall adds an element of suspense that keeps us hooked. If the outcome were predetermined, the magic of sports would truly be lost.

Consider some of the sports world's most legendary tales. Leicester City's 2016 Premier League victory, overcoming 5000–1 odds, wasn't just a one-match fluke; it was a triumph earned through a gruelling 38-match season. Emily Raducanu, ranked 150th, defied 500–1 odds to win the 2021 U.S. Open. The 'Miracle on Ice' in 1980, when the U.S. men's ice hockey team won Olympic gold at 1000–1 pre-tournament odds, is yet another enduring example of sporting greatness.

Sports thrive on finding the right balance between parity and dominance. On the one hand, fans need to believe in their own team's potential for success. On the other, the allure of dominant, dynastic teams like the 1980's Lakers

6. Underdogs Unleashed: A Comparative Look into Upsets

(NBA) or the 2000's Patriots (NFL) helps to draw in a broader audience. These teams become icons—admired or reviled, but always central to their sport's mythology. While a level of parity is crucial, striving for absolute equality in a competition isn't the goal. The mix of unpredictability and potential dominance, after all, is what keeps us watching.

This brings us back to rugby. How competitive and prone to upsets is it compared to other professional sports?

I've approached this question in two ways. One is to look at the parity of competitions as a measure of how competitive they are. Does the same team win year in and year out, or is there a lot of movement and variation in the final standings? The second way is to compare the actual results of rugby matches against the betting odds. Bookmakers have a vested interest in accurately predicting and setting their odds based on who is likely to win. It's their livelihood after all, and they're very good at it; there's a reason why the house almost always wins.

Competition parity and movement

In researching this topic, I found a number of existing methods used to quantify the competitiveness of sporting leagues, such as the Gini index, concentration ratio and rank variation. My aim here is to provide a simple comparison metric among leagues that is easy to communicate to you, so I've come up with my own version of rank variation that I call the Percent of Maximum Movement (or PMM).

The PMM is exactly as it sounds: the percent of the maximum possible shift in league standings teams in a league undergo from season to season. If the league standings are completely reversed from one season to the next, with the top team finishing last, the second team finishing second to last, and so on, right down to the last team finishing first, then we get a PMM of 100 percent, indicating the league has a maximum amount of possible movement (Figure 6.1).

Conversely, if there is no change in league standings and the same teams occupy the exact same positions year upon year, the league's PMM would be 0 percent. Because we're comparing the percentage of *maximum* league movement, we can make relevant comparisons across leagues of different sizes. It doesn't matter that teams in the Rugby Championship can only move a maximum of three places (from first to fourth), whereas in English Premier League football teams can theoretically drop from first all the way down to 20th. PMM provides a relevant comparison between sporting leagues of all different sizes.

For the technically minded who want to understand this calculation further, note that there is a subtle difference in PMM calculations for individual teams versus calculations for a league overall. For individual teams, average PMM is based on the maximum movement they could theoretically achieve in any given season. For example, in the Six Nations, a team that finished first the previous season can change a maximum of five places, down to last place this season. A team that finished third last season can only potentially change a

6. Underdogs Unleashed: A Comparative Look into Upsets

maximum of three places, down to last place. This is accounted for in each team's individual calculation.

When it comes to an entire sports league, however, not all teams can move to a position that matches their maximum potential. As shown in Figure 6.1, only one team can occupy first position. So even though the maximum movement for Team E would be to position one in the second season, that position has been taken by Team F. Team E therefore has to 'settle' for second place in Season 2 and a move of three places up the table. Because of this enforced constraint of maximum moves across an entire sporting league, the overall league maximum is lower than the maximum movement each individual team could undertake. Therefore, the overall league PMM is generally higher than it is for individual teams.

PMM of 100% (maximum movement possible)

Season 1			Season 2	
Pos.	Team		Pos.	Team
1	Team A		1	Team F
2	Team B		2	Team E
3	Team C		3	Team D
4	Team D		4	Team C
5	Team E		5	Team B
6	Team F		6	Team A

PMM of 0% (minimum movement possible)

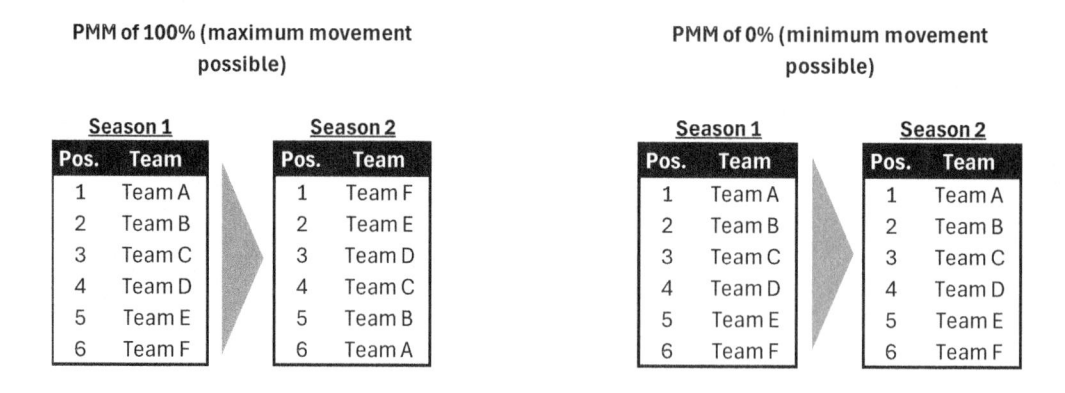

Season 1			Season 2	
Pos.	Team		Pos.	Team
1	Team A		1	Team A
2	Team B		2	Team B
3	Team C		3	Team C
4	Team D		4	Team D
5	Team E		5	Team E
6	Team F		6	Team F

Figure 6.1. Example of maximum movement in league standings (PMM of 100%) and minimum movement (PMM of 0%).

With that out the way, let's start our investigation with the dominant international rugby competitions of the Northern and Southern Hemispheres, the Six Nations and the Rugby Championship, respectively. The Six Nations competition was formed in 2000 when Italy was added to the old Five Nations. The 24 titles decided since then have been relatively evenly shared across four teams: England, France, Wales and Ireland (Figure 6.2).

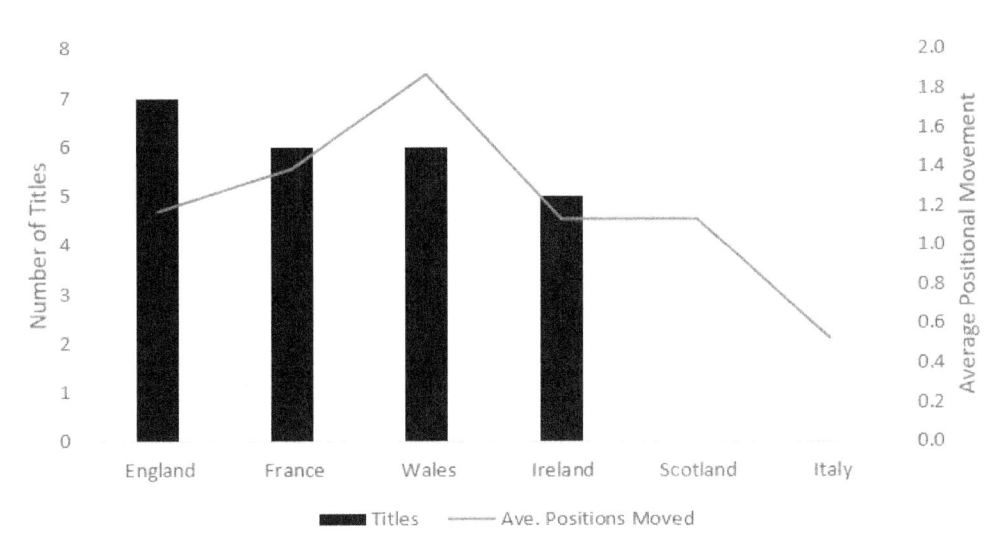

Figure 6.2. Number of titles won and average movement in the standings among Six Nations teams between 2000 and 2023.

Six Nations teams have moved an average of 1.2 positions either up or down the table each season (Table 6.1). But degrees of movement vary considerably among the teams, with poor old Italy (the frequent 'wooden spooners') only moving 0.5 places on average, while in contrast Wales has bounced around the table with regularity, moving almost two places each season on average.

6. Underdogs Unleashed: A Comparative Look into Upsets

Table 6.1. *Number of titles, average positions moved and PMM in the Six Nations between 2000 and 2023.*

Team	Titles	Ave. Positions Moved	PMM
England	7	1.2	29%
France	6	1.4	36%
Wales	6	1.9	46%
Ireland	5	1.1	31%
Scotland	0	1.1	31%
Italy	0	0.5	13%
OVERALL	**24**	**1.2**	**40%**

By contrast, the Rugby Championship has been dominated by New Zealand, which has won nine of the 11 editions to date (Figure 6.3).

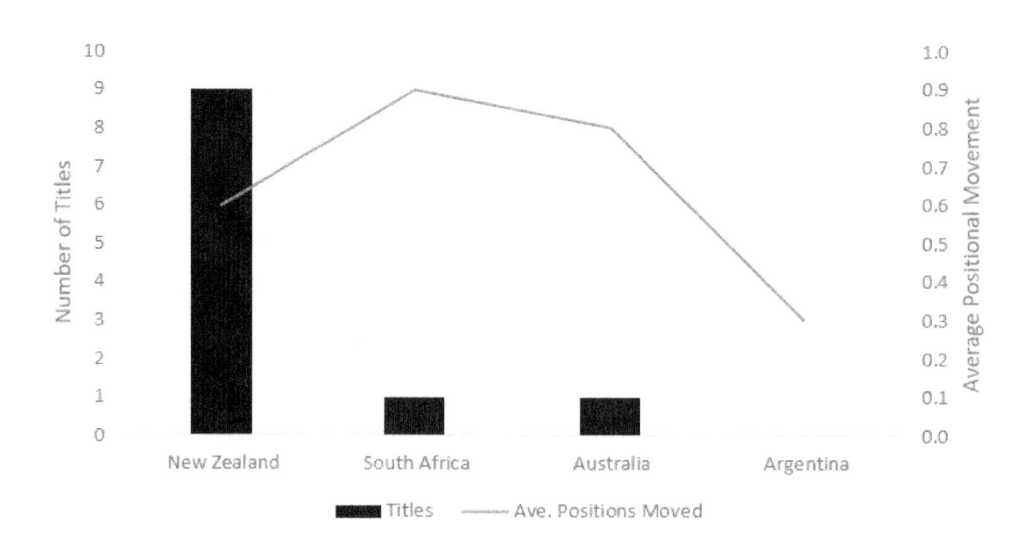

Figure 6.3. *Number of titles won and average movement in the standings among Rugby Championship teams between 2012 and 2023.*

Due to New Zealand's dominance, movement has been much more limited in this competition, with each team in it moving less than one position (0.7) on the table each season, on average (Table 6.2). However, it is a smaller competition, so indexed against the competition size, the teams are moving 33 percent of the maximum amount (versus 40 percent in the Six Nations).

Table 6.2. Number of titles, average positions moved and PMM in the Rugby Championship between 2012 and 2023.

Team	Titles	Ave. Positions Moved	PMM
New Zealand	9	0.6	25%
South Africa	1	0.9	40%
Australia	1	0.8	38%
Argentina	0	0.3	12%
OVERALL	**11**	**0.7**	**33%**

If we look at the five leading domestic rugby competitions around the world over the past ten years, they tell a similar story in terms of the ability of teams to move up and down their competition table. With the exception of Japan's League One (where movement is fairly limited), the other four major domestic competitions have seen movement between 36 and 44 percent of the maximum. Titles are consistently shared, with each league crowning between five and seven different champions over the past ten seasons.

6. Underdogs Unleashed: A Comparative Look into Upsets

Table 6.3. Number of different champions, most successful teams, PMM and highest- and lowest- moving teams in the five leading domestic rugby competitions over the past ten completed seasons.

League	Different Champions	Most Titles	PMM
French Top 14	7	3 - Toulouse	44%
English Premiership	5	5 - Saracens	42%
Super Rugby	6	5 - Crusaders	41%
United Rugby Championship	6	5 - Leinster	36%
Japan League One	4	5 - Wild Knights	31%

Also, when we look at the range of finishes of the teams that regularly compete in these leagues (Figure 6.4), we can see that the majority have spanned the table from near the top to close to the bottom. There is very little hegemony, so fans of most teams can hold out hope that *their* year is just around the corner.

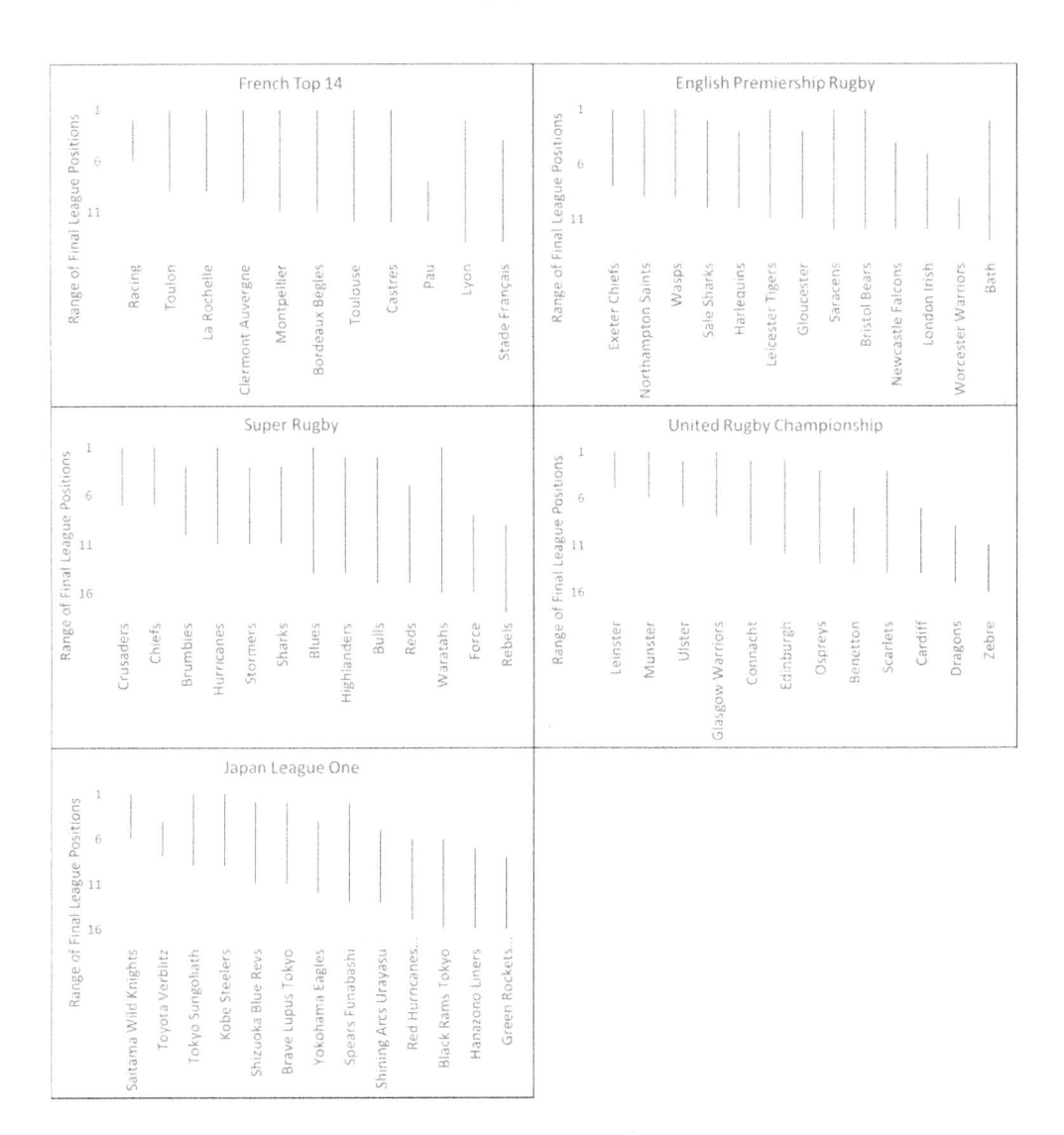

Figure 6.4. Range of final league positions of regularly competing teams in the five leading domestic rugby competitions across the past ten completed seasons.

6. Underdogs Unleashed: A Comparative Look into Upsets

Contrast this state of affairs to European football and you get a very different story. The top domestic football leagues in Europe are totally dominated year in and year out by a select few clubs. There is very little mobility, and the range of movement in the standings is much more limited. Each of the top five European football leagues have had four or fewer different champions over the past ten seasons, and the league PMM is in the 30s (Table 6.4).

Table 6.4. Number of different champions, most successful teams, PMM and highest- and lowest- moving teams from the leading domestic European football leagues over the past ten completed seasons.

League	Different Champions	Most Titles	PMM
Ligue 1	3	8 - Paris St Germain	38%
Bundesliga	1	10 - Bayern Munich	36%
Serie A	4	7 - Juventus	33%
English Premier League	4	6 - Manchester City	31%
La Liga	3	5 - Barcelona	30%

The teams that move the least are the dominant teams that stay rooted near the top of the table (Figure 6.5). The most extreme case is Bayern Munich, who have won each of the last ten Bundesliga titles.

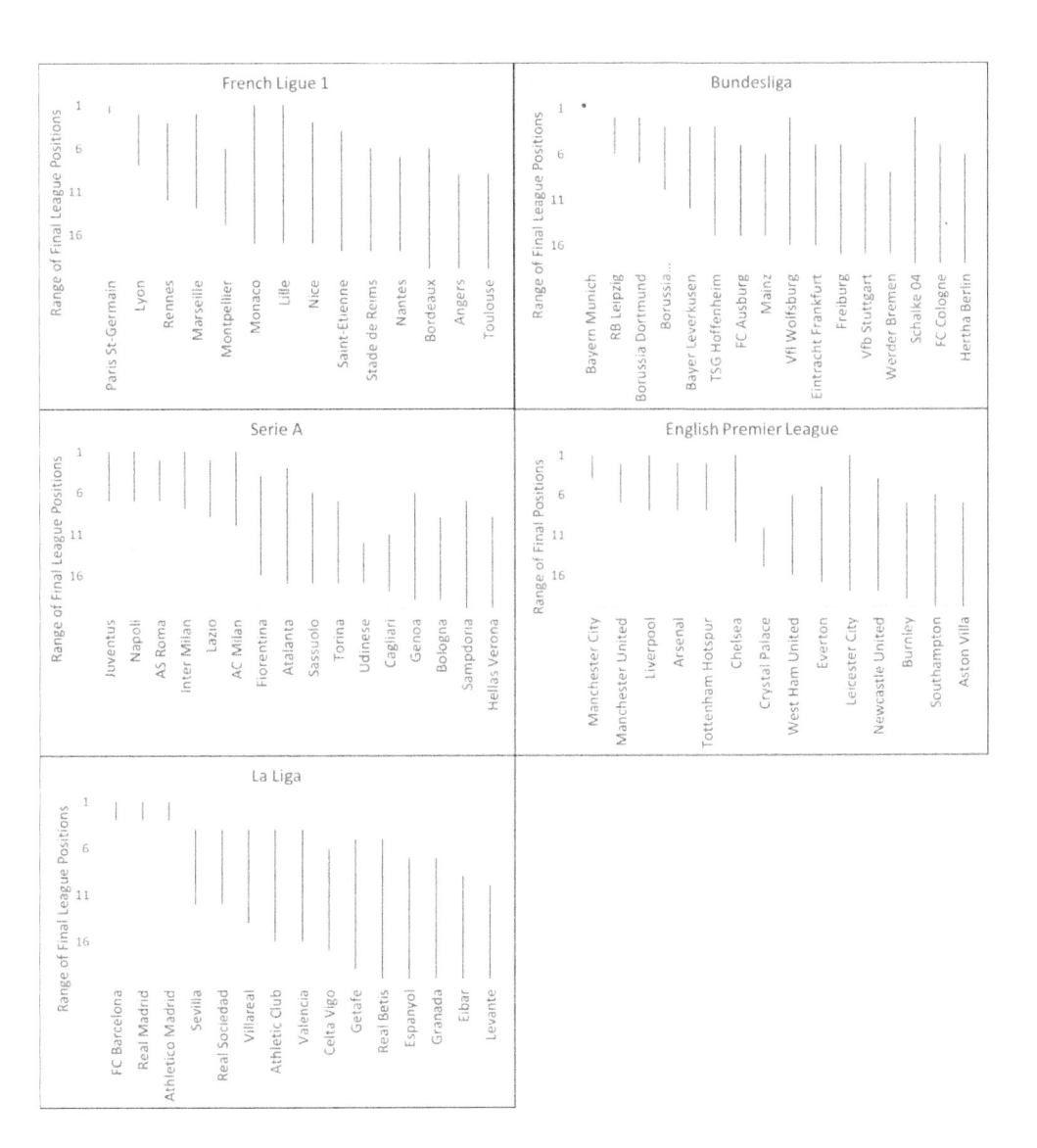

Figure 6.5. Range of final league positions of regularly competing teams from the leading domestic European football leagues over the past ten completed seasons.

6. Underdogs Unleashed: A Comparative Look into Upsets

American professional sport operates at the complete other end of the spectrum, with various degrees of salary caps, luxury taxes and drafts ensuring a large amount of parity and a good possibility of moving up and down the standings in any given year. In all these leagues, the lowest-performing teams get the best draft picks to select the better players entering the league the following season. Among the traditional four major leagues, all had seven or eight different champions between 2013–14 and 2022–23, and league movement above 40 percent of the maximum. The NFL, the most fluid league of the lot, boasted an incredible 51 percent of maximum movement (Table 6.5, Figure 6.6). The NFL and National Hockey League (NHL) have hard salary caps which help to promote equity. Major League Baseball has no salary cap (but does impose a luxury tax on excessive player spending), yet still has a lot of movement. The NBA has a soft salary cap, with numerous exemptions in place to circumvent it.

While dynasties have arisen in American professional sports, the restrictions put in place through caps, taxes, and drafts have clearly worked to foster competitions where even this year's cellar-dwellers can dream of glory next season.

Table 6.5. Number of different champions, most successful teams, PMM and highest- and lowest- moving teams in the four traditional American professional sports leagues over the past ten completed seasons.

League	Different Champions	Most Titles	PMM
NFL	7	3 - New England Patriots	51%
MLB	8	2 - Red Sox and Astros	46%
NHL	8	2 - Penguins and Lightning	45%
NBA	7	4 - Golden State Warriors	41%

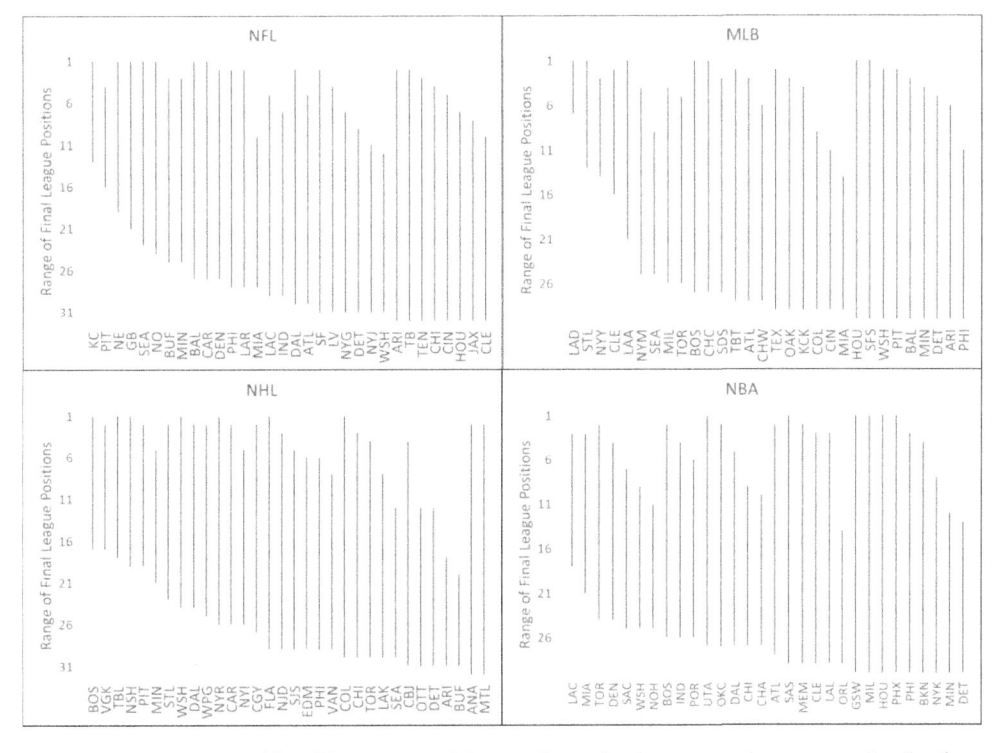

Figure 6.6. Range of final league positions of regularly competing teams in the four traditional American professional sports leagues over the past ten completed seasons.

6. Underdogs Unleashed: A Comparative Look into Upsets

Jumping around the globe, another useful comparison is the Indian Premier League (IPL, Table 6.6). This cricket league operates similarly to the U.S. professional leagues in that it's a franchise-based league with a salary cap. Perhaps unsurprisingly, much like the similarly structured U.S. professional leagues, the IPL allows a lot of movement (PMM of 53 percent). What Table 6.6 clearly shows is that rugby competitions tend to sit in the middle of the spectrum in terms of PMM. The franchise-based, salary-capped leagues tend to allow the most movement season to season, while the European soccer leagues tend to allow the least.

Table 6.6. *Number of different champions, most successful teams, PMM and highest- and lowest- moving teams from a selection of major global sports leagues over the past ten completed seasons.*

Sport	League	Different Champions	Most Titles	PMM
Cricket	Indian Premier League	5	4 - Mumbai Indians	53%
American Football	NFL	7	3 - New England Patriots	51%
Baseball	MLB	8	2 - Red Sox and Astros	46%
Ice Hockey	NHL	8	2 - Penguins and Lightning	45%
Rugby	Top 14	7	3 - Toulouse	44%
Rugby	English Premiership	5	5 - Saracens	42%
Rugby	Super Rugby	6	5 - Crusaders	41%
Basketball	NBA	7	4 - Golden State Warriors	41%
Football	Ligue 1	3	8 - Paris St Germain	38%
Rugby	United Rugby Championship	6	5 - Leinster	36%
Football	Bundesliga	1	10 - Bayern Munich	36%
Football	Serie A	4	7 - Juventus	33%
Rugby	Japan League One	4	5 - Wild Knights	31%
Football	English Premier League	4	6 - Manchester City	31%
Football	La Liga	3	5 - Barcelona	30%

Key:
Rugby
Football
Major Leagues / Cricket

Betting odds

As we covered earlier, arguably the best way to assess a sport's predictability is to compare bookmakers' odds to what actually transpired. For example, upsets are relatively rare in Rugby World Cup pool stages, and bookmakers' accuracy in predicting the correct winner is extremely high at 90 percent. This contrasts with the more competitive knockout rounds of Rugby World Cups where bookmaker accuracy falls to 75 percent.

This is helpful for getting a general sense of how things will (or should) turn out, but there are different levels of certainty in betting. As an example, the opening game of the 2023 Rugby World Cup was a blockbuster between hosts France and the All Blacks. With two of the main title contenders going head-to-head, the bookmakers weren't sure of the outcome, and set odds of $1.85 for France and $2.02 for the All Blacks; this can be converted into an implied probability of victory of 52 percent for France versus 48 percent for the All Blacks. So, according to the bookmakers, the match was essentially a coin flip in terms of who would prevail. Contrast that to the second game of the Cup—Italy versus Namibia—where favourites Italy were given odds of $1.01 versus $14.67 for Namibia. In this case, the bookmakers were 94 percent certain that Italy would be victorious.

Figure 6.7 outlines how certain the bookmakers are of the results of Rugby World Cup pool versus playoff matches based on the odds that they are setting. As would be expected, it shows that bookmakers are generally far more certain

6. Underdogs Unleashed: A Comparative Look into Upsets

of the results of pool matches than playoff games. For the majority of pool matches, the odds set indicate that they are more than 90 percent certain that the favourite will prevail. For knockout games, their certainty on the favourite winning is usually closer to 70 percent.

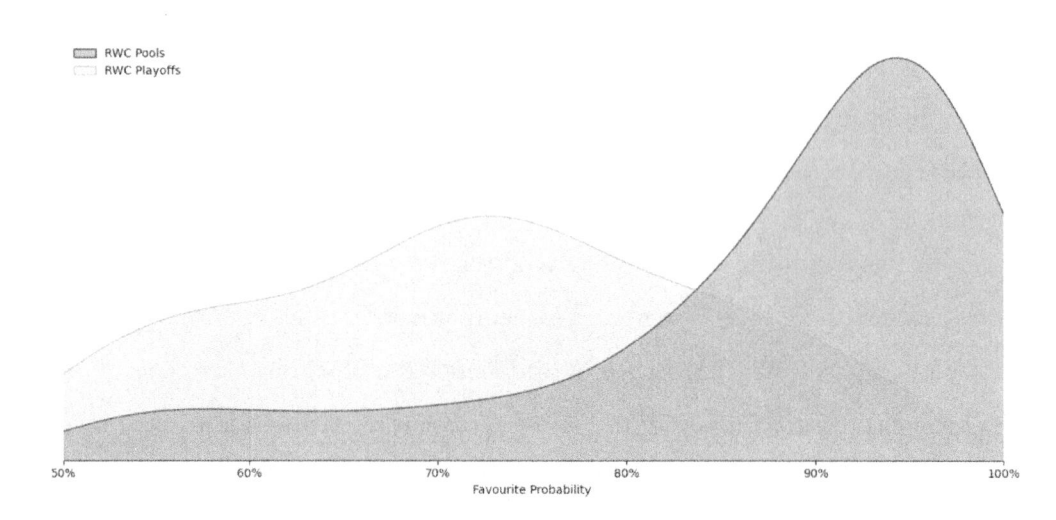

Figure 6.7. Distribution of bookmaker probabilities of the favourites winning across all matches in the past four Rugby World Cups.

We can also assess the bookmakers' accuracy using a metric called the Brier score, which offers a way to compare the accuracy of bookmakers' predictions (based on the odds they set) against actual results. A lower Brier score indicates more accurate odds-setting, as the Brier score essentially penalises the bookmakers the further their odds are from the actual result. Big upsets can really increase the score. For example, if the All Blacks, who were very slight underdogs, had beaten France in the 2023 World Cup opener, the Brier score would have only increased by 0.08. However, if Namibia had upset Italy, it would have increased by 1.76. For Rugby World Cup pool matches, the average Brier score is 0.16, versus 0.29 for the knockout stages.

Now let's apply these comparative measures to the Six Nations and Rugby Championship. In the Six Nations, the bookmakers' favourite has won 75 percent of matches, and the Brier score is 0.31. The Rugby Championship is slightly less predictable, with bookmakers being correct 72 percent of the time, with a Brier score of 0.33. This is a little surprising given that the final standings in the Rugby Championship have been much more stable over the years (as outlined earlier in this chapter).

Figure 6.8 shows that bookmakers tend to feel more confident in their predictions of Rugby Championship matches versus Six Nations matches, as evidenced by higher favourite probabilities. It's interesting, then, that they are slightly less accurate when picking the correct outcomes of this competition, despite their higher confidence levels.

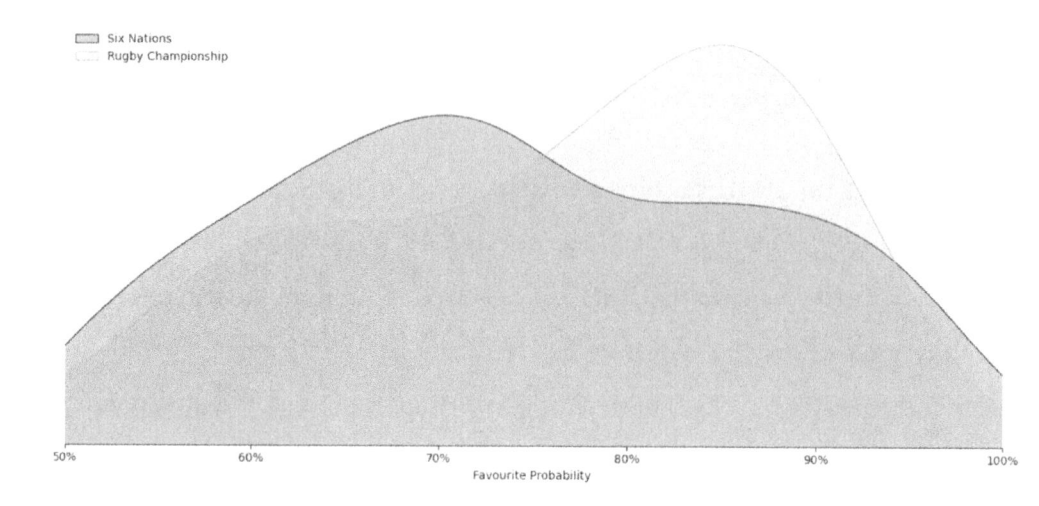

6. Underdogs Unleashed: A Comparative Look into Upsets

Figure 6.8. Distribution of bookmaker probabilities of the favourites winning across all matches in the past ten completed seasons of the Six Nations and Rugby Championship.

When it comes to comparing bookmaker accuracy across sports, it isn't possible to directly compare rugby with football (soccer). This is because football has a viable third possible result, the draw, which occurs frequently. While draws are possible in rugby too, they're so rare (approximately one in every 50 matches) that they don't overly impact the results. In football, they occur in around one in every four matches.

Comparing rugby competitions against other, non-football sporting leagues, we can see that rugby tends to be more predictable than the franchise-based U.S. major leagues and the Indian Premier League cricket (Table 6.7). You can also see from the table that as bookmaker accuracy decreases, both the Brier score and the PMM increases.

Table 6.7. Comparison of bookmaker accuracy, Brier score and PMM across different global sporting competitions. PMM not calculated for World Cup competitions where final standings across all teams are not available, and the makeup of competing teams in successive competitions changes.

Sport	Competition	Bookmaker Accuracy	Brier Score	PMM
Rugby	Rugby World Cup Pools	90%	0.16	
Cricket	One Day World Cup	81%	0.29	
Rugby	Japan League One	77%	0.31	31%
Rugby	Six Nations	75%	0.31	40%
Rugby	Rugby World Cup Playoffs	75%	0.29	
Rugby	Super Rugby	75%	0.34	41%
Rugby	Rugby Championship	72%	0.33	33%
Rugby	English Premiership	72%	0.39	42%
Rugby	Top 14	72%	0.36	44%
Rugby	United Rugby Championship	70%	0.36	36%
Cricket	T20 World Cup	70%	0.38	
Basketball	NBA	66%	0.43	41%
American Football	NFL	65%	0.42	51%
Baseball	MLB	59%	0.48	46%
Cricket	Indian Premier League	52%	0.50	53%

Key:
Rugby
Cricket
Major Leagues

For those interested, Table 6.8 shows the same information for the five major football leagues. But remember that the bookmaker accuracy and Brier scores are not directly comparable to the competitions in the previous table due to the prevalence of draws in football.

6. Underdogs Unleashed: A Comparative Look into Upsets

Table 6.8. Comparison of bookmaker accuracy, Brier score and PMM across the leading domestic European football leagues.

Sport	Competition	Bookmaker Accuracy	Brier Score	PMM
Football	Bundesliga	57%	0.60	36%
Football	La Liga	57%	0.59	30%
Football	Ligue 1	57%	0.57	38%
Football	Premier League	56%	0.59	31%
Football	Serie A	51%	0.62	33%

In competitions where the bookmakers are less certain, teams have a much greater ability to move up or down the table between seasons. This relationship between bookmaker accuracy and PMM can be seen in Figure 6.9. It confirms that the PMM index is a useful barometer for assessing how competitive sporting leagues are. And importantly, with PMM, football can be included as a relevant comparison, whereas due to the confounding impact of draws, it can't for bookmaker odds.

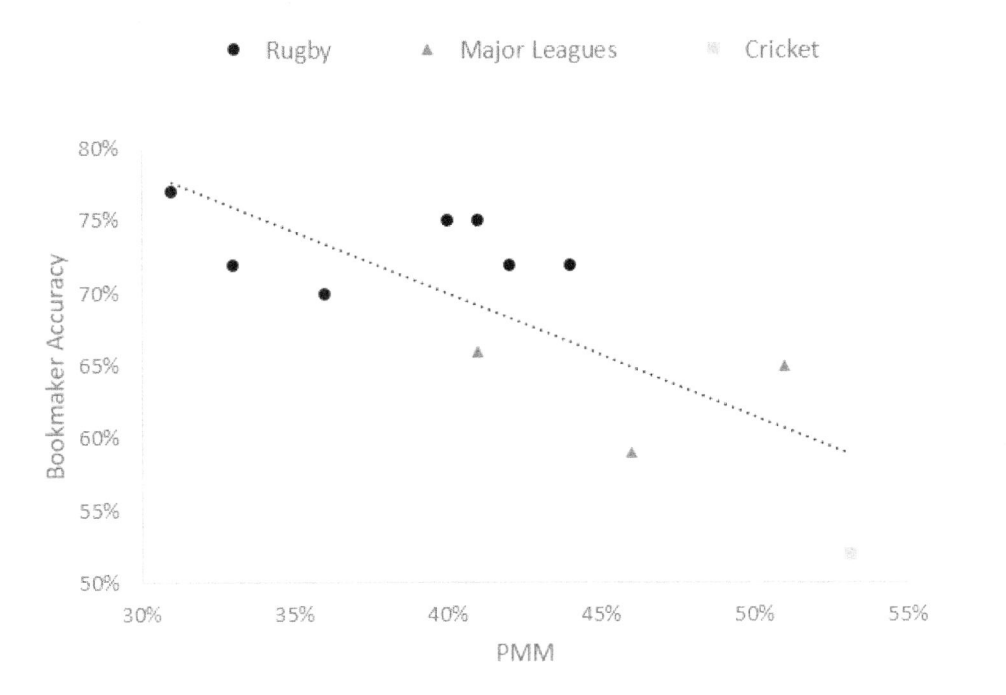

Figure 6.9. Relationship between bookmaker accuracy and PMM across selected major global sporting competitions.

The breakdown

When it comes to the likelihood of upsets occurring and the potential for a handful of teams to dominate their league/competition, rugby sits somewhere in the middle of the sporting landscape. Football leagues tend to have the lowest potential for movement and are dominated by the lucky few, whereas the franchise-based U.S. professional leagues and the Indian Premier League offer teams plenty of scope to climb up or down the standings from season to season.

6. Underdogs Unleashed: A Comparative Look into Upsets

This suggests that rugby is well balanced between parity and dominance. What effect expanding the Rugby World Cup to more teams could have on both is the topic for Chapter 9.

7. No Roar, Same Score? Rugby's Home Advantage During the Pandemic

The outbreak of the COVID-19 pandemic transformed the world in so many ways. During the truly unprecedented global crisis, sport wasn't spared from its severe disruptions, with empty stadiums quickly becoming a symbol of 'the new normal' as 2020 unfolded. However, as strange as this sight was, it presented a unique opportunity to explore an age-old question in sports science: the influence of home-ground advantage on match outcomes.

The enforced absence of crowds created a natural experiment that was previously impossible to run. With no (or very sparse) crowds during the pandemic, the effect of the actual crowd could now be isolated from other influencing factors of home-field advantage, such as travel fatigue and venue familiarity. Statisticians could finally quantify the impact that the actual crowd has on the match outcome, and which areas of performance the crowd influences.

In this chapter, I use data drawn from two major Northern Hemisphere domestic competitions— English Premiership Rugby and the French Top 14— to analyse crowd influence on professional rugby matches. During the 2020-21 season, both of these competitions played all of their games with no (or very

7. No Roar, Same Score? Rugby's Home Advantage During the Pandemic

limited) crowds. In contrast, in all of the other seasons between 2017–2018 and 2022–2023 where spectators were present, each competition typically attracted home crowds averaging 15,000 people per match. When spectators were present during this period, the home-ground win rate was 72 percent in the Top 14 and 63 percent in the Premiership.

In contrast, as you can see from Figure 7.1, the home-ground win rate in each competition dropped to its lowest level in recent history during the 2020–21 season. In the Top 14, home teams won just 59 percent of games without crowds, while for the Premiership, the rate dropped to 57 percent. This drop in home-win rate was statistically significant overall and for the Top 14, but not for Premiership Rugby by itself.

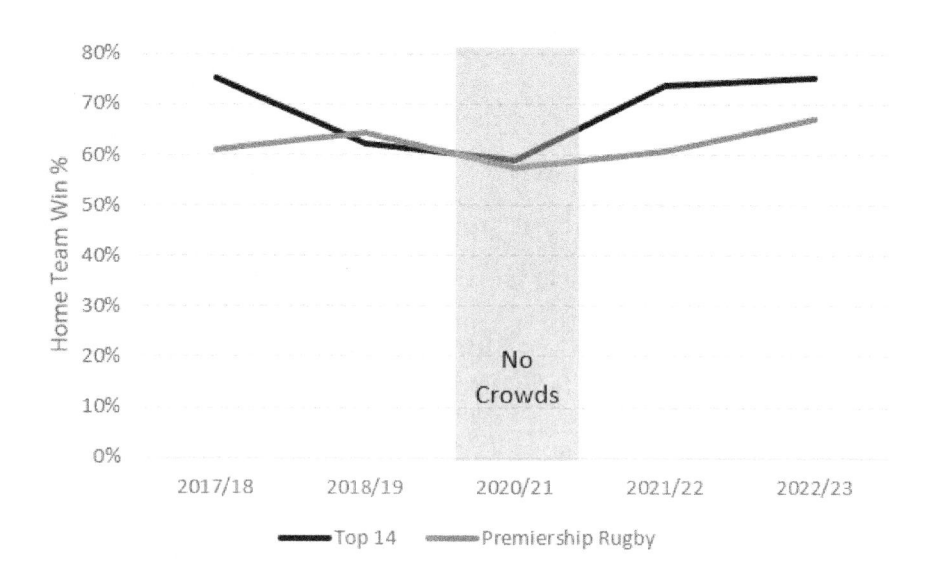

Figure 7.1. Home team winning percentage in the Top 14 and Premiership Rugby between the 2017–2018 and 2022–23 seasons.

Perhaps not surprisingly, the average score differential between home and away teams also narrowed in matches when crowds were absent, although the effect is not statistically significant (Figure 7.2). In the Top 14, the home team had an average points margin of +9.0 when crowds were present but +6.5 points without them. In the Premiership, this impact was far less pronounced: from +4.8 points with crowds to +4.1 without.

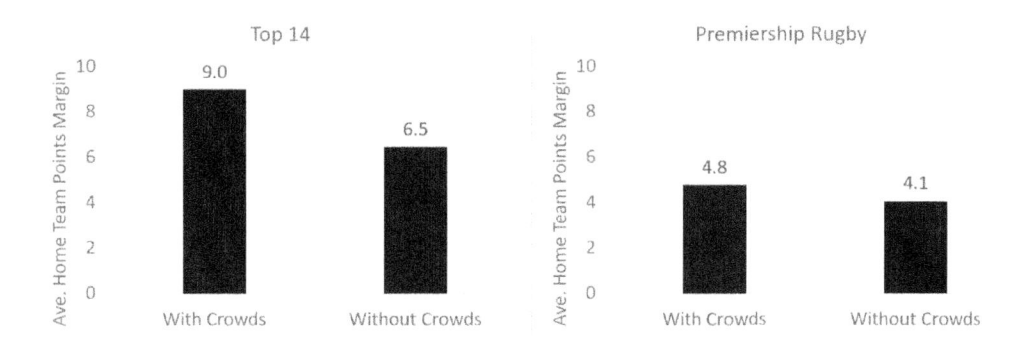

Figure 7.2. Average home team points margin with and without crowds in the Top 14 and Premiership Rugby from the 2017–2018 to 2022–23 seasons.

The data strongly implies that crowds play a role in helping the home team—in other words, the conventional wisdom is right. What's far more interesting to me though is *why* this advantage exists. Is it possible to quantify home-ground advantage beyond, well, positive vibes? You no doubt know what I'm going to say, but I'll say it anyway: let's go ahead and try!

When it comes to home-ground advantage, the most important element is typically said to be the home crowd's influence over referees. This matters especially in rugby, where refs come under more intense scrutiny than most

7. No Roar, Same Score? Rugby's Home Advantage During the Pandemic

other sports due to the complex nature of the rules and their reliance on individual interpretation. So it may not surprise many that the number one statistic that changes between matches with and without crowds is... *drum roll please*... penalties conceded.

As we can see from Figure 7.3, in the five seasons of our focus, home teams in Premiership Rugby and the Top 14 received 1.3 additional penalties when crowds were present but just 0.5 when crowds were absent. Therefore, the presence of crowds leads to an average increase of 0.8 penalties per match awarded to the home team.

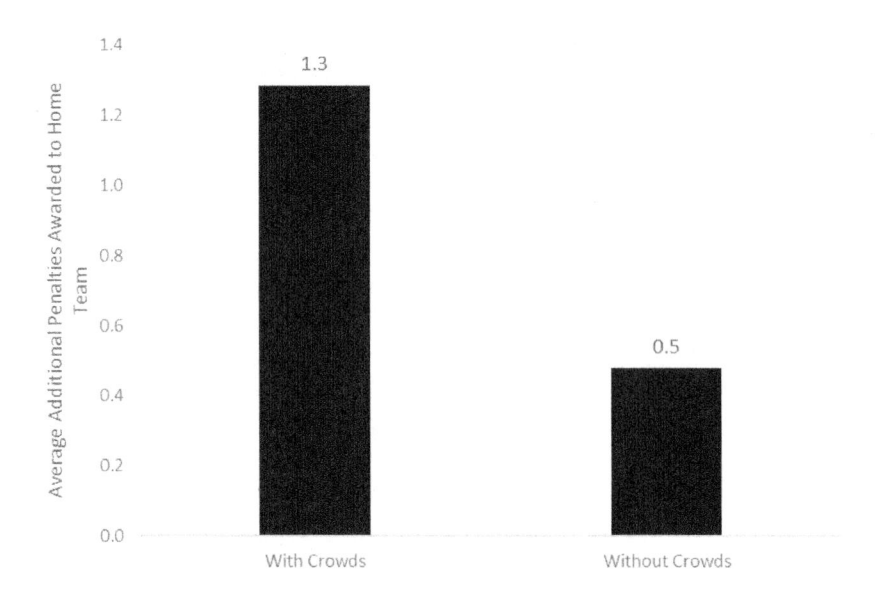

Figure 7.3. Average additional penalties awarded to the home team with and without crowds, in the Top 14 and Premiership Rugby from the 2017–2018 to 2022–23 seasons.

Now, we can't just attribute all of the observed difference in penalty count (an extra 0.8 penalties per match) to crowd pressure on the referees. For example, the home team may excel in other facets of the game with the crowd support, like possession and territory, that put them in a position to earn more penalties. Numerous other team performance metrics also change when there are no crowds, and many of them would also affect penalties. To disentangle these effects, I built a statistical regression model that isolates the direct influence of crowd presence on penalty count. This model also accounts for the impact of other key-performance metrics on penalty count (listed in Table 7.1), thereby isolating the specific contribution of the crowd.

Table 7.1. Team performance metrics used in a regression model to determine home crowd influence on penalty count.

Crowd presence	Possession	Territory	Number of passes
Number of runs	Number of kicks	Penalty goals kicked	Penalty tries
% of rucks won	% of mauls won	Turnovers conceded	Yellow cards
Clean breaks	Tackle success %	% of scrums won	% of lineouts won

The model determined that the specific impact of the crowd on the penalty advantage of the home team was 0.5 penalties per match. So while we saw from Figure 7.3 that when crowds were present, the home team received 0.8 additional penalties per match, according to the model we can attribute 0.5 of these additional penalties solely to the crowd influence on the referee. The

7. No Roar, Same Score? Rugby's Home Advantage During the Pandemic

remaining 0.3 penalties per match are earned due to the home teams higher performance in other areas which also impact penalty decisions (e.g., they have more possession and territory).

Figure 7.4 shows how a selection of performance metrics affect home advantage, both with and without crowds. You can see how the home team's winning percentage drops with crowds absent; this is consistent with a drop in the penalty advantage that they receive, as well as in yellow cards conceded by the visiting team.

The possession advantage of the home team also disappears when the home crowd does, but curiously, this only occurs in the second half. In the first half, the home team maintains a possession advantage of two percent on average even when the home crowd is absent.

It's the same with territory. The home team appears to get a lot of the benefit from home-crowd support during the final push for victory in the second half. When crowds are absent, the second-half territory advantage tends to favour the visiting team.

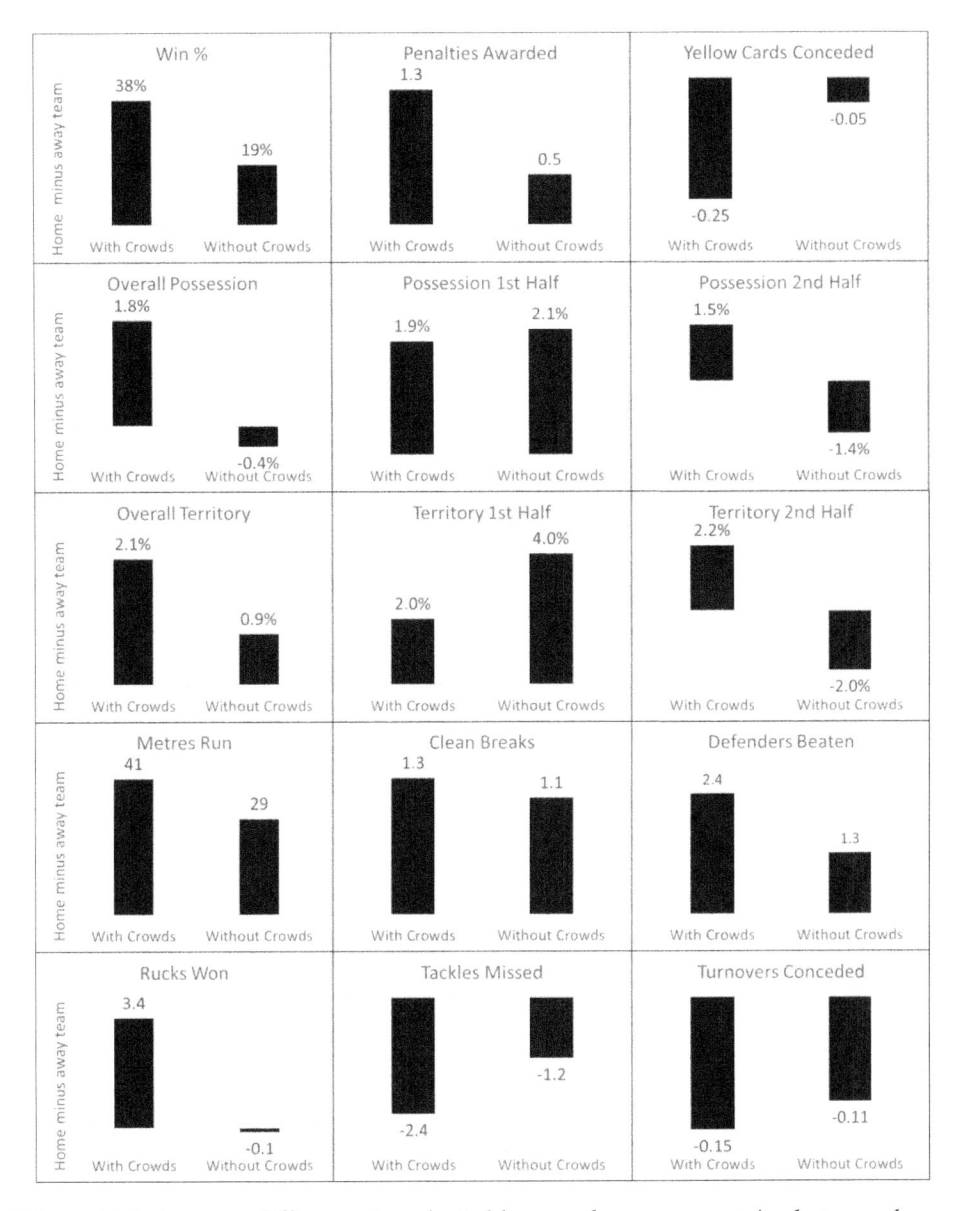

Figure 7.4. Average difference in selected key-performance metrics between home team and away team when crowds are present versus when they are absent. Data from Premiership Rugby and Top 14 from the 2017–2018 to 2022–23 seasons.

7. No Roar, Same Score? Rugby's Home Advantage During the Pandemic

A different type of statistical model (two-way ANOVA) can tell us the statistical significance of the home-team advantage in these performance metrics, and whether the presence of crowds has a significant impact (Table 7.2). Here's how it works.

The **Significance** column tells us if home advantage has a statistically significant impact on a metric, regardless of whether crowds are present or not (see Table Key for a description of the asterisk symbols). As you can see, almost all of the metrics are considered statistically significant (and in favour of the home team).

The **Interaction Significance** column informs us if the presence of crowds significantly enhances the home-team advantage. It reveals that only Win %, Penalties Awarded, Yellow Cards, Overall Possession, Possession 2nd Half and Territory 2nd Half have enough of an impact to be considered statistically significant.

Table 7.2. *Two-way ANOVA model measuring the effect of home advantage and the presence of crowds on selected key-performance metrics from Premiership Rugby and Top 14 between the 2017–2018 and 2022–23 seasons.*

Category	Metric	Home Advantage	Significance	Home Advantage With Crowds	Home Advantage Without Crowds	Interaction Significance
Result	Win %	33%	***	38%	19%	***
Discipline	Penalties Awarded	1.2	***	1.3	0.5	*
	Yellow Cards Conceded	-0.22	***	-0.25	-0.05	*
	Red Cards Conceded	-0.001	NS	-0.004	0.014	NS
	Total Free Kicks Conceded	-0.001	NS	-0.001	0.000	NS
Possession	Overall Possession	1.4%	***	1.8%	-0.4%	*
	Possession 1st Half	2.0%	***	1.9%	2.1%	NS
	Possession 2nd Half	0.9%	.	1.5%	-1.4%	*
Territory	Overall Territory	1.9%	***	2.1%	0.9%	NS
	Territory 1st Half	2.5%	***	2.0%	4.0%	NS
	Territory 2nd Half	1.3%	*	2.2%	-2.0%	*
Performance	Meters Run	39	***	41	29	NS
	Clean Breaks	1.3	***	1.3	1.1	NS
	Defenders Beaten	2.3	***	2.4	1.3	NS
	Rucks Won	2.8	***	3.4	-0.1	NS
	Tackles Missed	-2.2	***	-2.4	-1.2	NS
	Turnovers Conceded	-0.14	NS	-0.15	-0.11	NS

Table Key:

* = Pretty sure: there's a strong indication that what was observed is not just by chance (more than 95 percent confidence).

*** = Very sure: the evidence is very strong that what was observed is real and not just a random occurrence (more than 99.9 percent confidence).

NS (Not Significant) = not so sure; can't confidently say that what was observed isn't just due to chance.

7. No Roar, Same Score? Rugby's Home Advantage During the Pandemic

The breakdown

The COVID-19 pandemic, as devastating and disruptive as it was, created an unforeseen laboratory for exploring the phenomenon of home-ground advantage in rugby. The analysis in this chapter, which focused on the English Premiership and French Top 14 leagues during their crowd-less 2020–21 season, illuminated several fascinating elements of this phenomenon that could never before be tested (and likely never be able to again).

Most significantly, the findings revealed a notable decline in home-ground win rates when roaring crowds were replaced by empty seats. This shift was not just a number on a stats sheet; it was a silent testament to the power of thousands of cheering supporters. The Top 14's home-win rate dipped from 72 percent to 59 percent over the crowd-less 2020–21 season, while the Premiership saw a decrease from 63 percent to 57 percent. This underscores the psychological and atmospheric impact that crowds have on both players and match outcomes.

Influence on the referee was found to be a significant part of home-ground advantage, as evidenced by the big changes in penalty and yellow-card decisions made when crowds were absent. But it's clear that there are many other interrelated performance metrics that also contribute to the effect. Home- team domination decreases in a lot of areas beyond just the impact of the referee.

Above all else, what this chapter really demonstrates is how much fans matter to their teams. Many sporting competitions across the globe had been battling declining crowd attendance even prior to the pandemic. The pandemic helped to prove that every single fan who turns up to cheer on their side is making a contribution to the success of their beloved team.

8. Navigating the Knockout Gauntlet: The Importance of the Rugby World Cup Draw

The fate of the 2019 Rugby World Cup may well have been determined on the tournament's second day. That evening, a dejected Springboks team trudged off Yokohama Stadium, convincingly vanquished by the defending champions and tournament favourite, the New Zealand All Blacks. South Africa was no doubt well aware that no team prior to 2019 had ever lost a pool game and gone on to win the World Cup. A key reason for this, as we'll discover in this chapter, is that no team had survived a tough quarter-final in tournament history and gone on to prevail.

As a result of their loss against their Group B opponent, the Springboks all but expected to face the number one-ranked team in the world, Ireland, in the quarter-finals. That's what was meant to have happened if everything had gone to form in the neighbouring Group A. But a series of sensational results, including hosts Japan's (ranked tenth) beating of both Ireland and Scotland (seventh), turned the group and the fortunes of the World Cup on its head. Suddenly New Zealand, who thought they'd earned themselves a more favourable draw by winning Group B, faced the prospect of a clash against Ireland, setting up a match between the two top-ranked teams in the world. Meanwhile, South Africa got a far more palatable quarter-final match against the tenth-ranked Japanese. The Springboks' feelings of despair may have been premature.

The idea for this chapter came after that 2019 World Cup when the All Blacks matched up against Ireland in a titanic quarter-final clash. The All Blacks put in a landmark performance, prevailing 46–14 and installing themselves as heavy favourites to lift the William Webb Ellis trophy. However, the following week, despite the bookmakers giving them a 71 percent chance of victory, the All Blacks were soundly beaten by England in the semi-final, with an immense performance from England completely flattening the previously unstoppable All Blacks.

Suddenly England assumed the 'favourite' tag for the final against South Africa. The bookmakers rated England a 69 percent chance to back up their enormous semi-final performance in the final. Once again though, the heavy favourites couldn't seem to extend their mammoth performance to consecutive weeks, and it was South Africa who ran away with a famously comfortable 32–12 final victory—and the World Cup trophy.

It was a head-spinning, precedent-busting tournament. And it got me thinking about how difficult it is for rugby teams to put in consecutive big performances week after week. Rugby is an extremely physical game, so being able to back up three huge knockout-match performances in consecutive weeks is a massive ask, especially after surviving a torrid pool stage. And then there's the mental pressure of having to perform week after week in the pinnacle event of the sport while under intense public pressure and scrutiny.

8. Navigating the Knockout Gauntlet: The Importance of the Rugby World Cup Draw

So, if it is indeed difficult for rugby teams to put together back-to-back big performances at the knockout stage of the Rugby World Cup, does this mean who they play matters? This was my preliminary conclusion. On the other hand, among many players and pundits, conventional wisdom is that in the world of tournament sport, the draw is interesting but irrelevant. 'You have to beat everyone at some stage anyway', was Irish winger James Lowe's reaction to the horror 2023 Rugby World Cup draw that saw Ireland on a quarter-final collision course with heavyweights France or New Zealand.

But as Ireland found out, it *does* matter. The results of Rugby World Cups prove this, as we'll learn in this chapter.

You can think of the knockout stages of tournaments as a bit like poker. Both are a series of probabilities, and the more the odds are stacked in your favour, the far more likely you are to prevail. Top poker players don't consistently win because they are consistently luckier. They are constantly calculating their probability of success and usually only playing hands when the odds are favourable. When repeated over multiple hands, they come out on top more often than not.

To visualise how this works in rugby, think about the following example from a knockout tournament that has quarter-finals, semi-finals and a final (three knockout matches to win). Imagine a team that is dominant and has an 80 percent likelihood (i.e., four in five chance) to win each of their knockout games. On the surface, you would probably think this team should win the tournament practically every time, since they're so favoured in each match. However, even with an 80 percent likelihood of winning each match, their *overall probability* to win all three consecutive knockout matches and be crowned champions is just 51 percent (80 percent x 80 percent x 80 percent). In other words, despite being such heavy favourites in each individual knockout match, they are essentially just as likely as a flip of a coin to emerge as the ultimate victors and lift the Cup. Kinda wild, right?

As a real-life example, the All Blacks were the overwhelming favourites to advance in each of their knockout games in the 2015 World Cup. They faced a quarter-final against France (as 84 percent bookmaker favourites), a semi-final against South Africa (79 percent favourites) and the final against Australia (71 percent favourites). Despite their strongly favourable position in each of those individual knockout games, the overall probability of the All Blacks winning all three of those knockout matches was just *47 percent*.

That's why the draw is so important. A team that has a 50 percent chance in each of the three knockout rounds only has a 12.5 percent probability of winning all three, and the tournament. Change only their quarter-final matchup to a 90 percent probability, and their overall odds almost double, to 22.5 percent. Add to this the fact that rugby is a physically tough sport with injuries galore, and we see that in a condensed tournament format, it's proven to be extremely difficult for teams to get up for immense battles weekend after weekend after weekend.

Take these stats from the six tournaments that have been held since 2003

8. Navigating the Knockout Gauntlet: The Importance of the Rugby World Cup Draw

when World Rugby's rankings system was established:

- World Cup champions have never had to face and beat three teams ranked higher than seventh in the knockout stages.
- In four of the six tournaments, the eventual champions faced the lowest-ranked of the eight quarter-finalists (the exceptions were in 2015 and 2023).
- From 2003 to 2019, semi-finalists who had faced and beaten the highest-ranked quarter-final opponent went on to lose their semi-final. This trend was halted in 2023 by New Zealand, who beat number one-ranked Ireland and went on to win their semi-final but lose the final.

You can see from Table 8.1 that it's very rare for Rugby World Cup champions to face top-ranked opposition right through the knockout stages. Now don't get me wrong; at this level of play, all of the teams are very, very good. But it's fascinating to consider how rarely eventual champions survive a gauntlet of top-ranked opposition week after week. Even the Springboks' victory in 2023, labelled the 'toughest draw ever' because they faced all the other nations ranked in the top five during the tournament, did not feature consecutive matches against top-ranked opposition. New Zealand is the only side to have ever won consecutive knockout matches against top-four opposition, in both 2011 and 2015.

Table 8.1. Path to victory in the knockout stages of Rugby World Cups since 2003, when rankings began.

Tournament	Champion	Champions Pre-Tournament Ranking	QF Opponent's Ranking	SF Opponent's Ranking	Final Opponent's Ranking	Knockout Phase Opponents' Ave. Ranking
2003	England	1	10	5	4	6.3
2007	South Africa	4	13	6	7	8.7
2011	New Zealand	1	9	2	4	5.0
2015	New Zealand	1	7	3	2	4.0
2019	South Africa	4	10	5	3	6.0
2023	South Africa	2	3	8	4	5.0

Table 8.2 evaluates the overall probability of the last four World Cup Champions successfully navigating their knockout rounds, based on the bookmaker odds for their quarter-final, semi-final and final matchups. It shows that even teams that were overwhelming favourites in each of their individual knockout-round matches, like New Zealand in 2011 and 2015, were far from overwhelming favourites to survive all three. It also highlights how against-the-odds the Springboks' victories were in 2019 and 2023, coming in at slightly lower than the probability of getting through the entire *Oppenheimer* film on Netflix in a single sitting!

8. Navigating the Knockout Gauntlet: The Importance of the Rugby World Cup Draw

Table 8.2. World Cup champions' probability of winning each knockout round match, and overall probability of winning all three knockout round matches. Probabilities derived from bookmaker odds over the last four Rugby World Cups.

Tournament	Champion	Probability vs QF Opponent	Probability vs SF Opponent	Probability vs Final Opponent	Overall Knockout Rounds Probability
2011	New Zealand	94%	70%	87%	58%
2015	New Zealand	84%	79%	71%	47%
2019	South Africa	85%	73%	31%	19%
2023	South Africa	45%	82%	48%	18%

The case for excluding the 2023 tournament from the analysis

I wrote this chapter before the 2023 Rugby World Cup, and the data I had on hand told a nice story which I was excited to publish. The 2023 tournament meant additional data, which a statistician should always welcome. However, the 2023 draw threw a big, honking curveball. To start, its matchups seemed to be planned using geological timelines rather than those appropriate for the World Cup cycle. Made three years in advance and seeded in an attempt to balance the pools, the draw couldn't have foreseen the tectonic shift in team rankings that occurred in the subsequent three years. This resulted in the top five teams getting bunched together in the World Cup pools, turning one corner of the draw (with Pool A and Pool B) into the rugby equivalent of a heavyweight boxing ring. It would only be possible for two of these five to progress to the semi-finals, as they were destined to collide at the quarter-final stage.

It wasn't just that these teams were ranked as the top five, though. The gulf between them and the rest was much larger than it had ever been going into a World Cup (Table 8.3, Figure 8.1): there was a massive 9.1 difference in ranking points, on average, between them and the next five teams. The only previous time that the ranking points imbalance had exceeded 1.5 points between different sides of a Rugby World Cup draw was in 2007, and even then it was just three points.[8]

Table 8.3. World Rugby rankings and ranking points immediately prior to the 2023 Rugby World Cup.

Ranking	Team	Ranking Points	Pool	Side of Draw
1	Ireland	91.8	B	A
2	South Africa	91.1	B	A
3	France	89.2	A	A
4	New Zealand	89.1	A	A
5	Scotland	84.0	B	A
6	Argentina	80.9	D	B
7	Fiji	80.3	C	B
8	England	80.0	D	B
9	Australia	79.9	C	B
10	Wales	78.3	C	B

---

[8] A 'side' referred to here is the half of the World Cup draw that leads to two semi-finalists emerging. Generally, Pool A and Pool B crossover at the quarter-final stage, so Pool A and B combine to form a 'side' of the draw from which only two semi-finalists can possibly emerge.

8. Navigating the Knockout Gauntlet: The Importance of the Rugby World Cup Draw

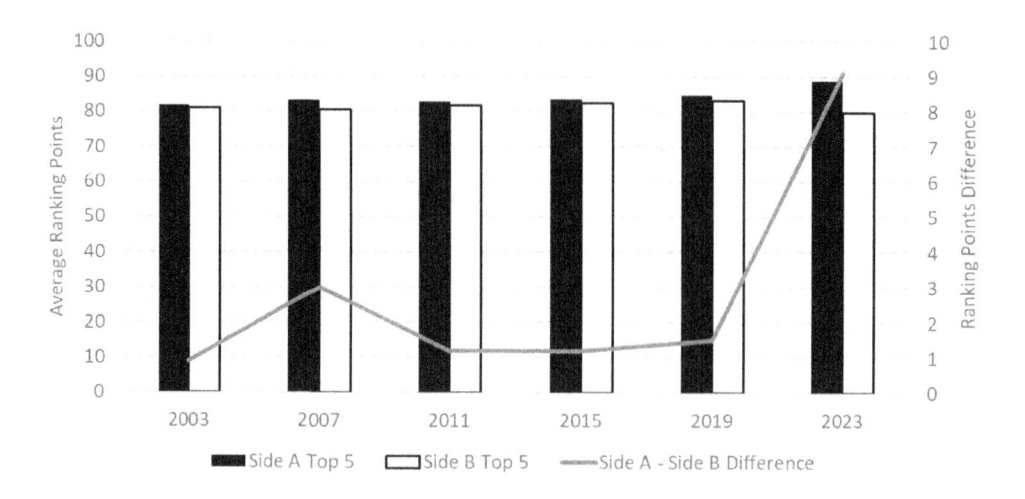

Figure 8.1. The average World Rugby ranking points of the top five teams on each 'side' of the draw (e.g., Side A contains Pools A and B, Side B contains Pools C and D) in six Rugby World Cups.

It was odds-on that whoever emerged from the titanic quarter-finals played between Pools A and B would go on to contest the final due to the relatively weak semi-final opposition they would face. And this proved to be the case, with South Africa and New Zealand fighting their way through to contest the final.

The impact of a tough quarter-final

While one of the premises of this chapter is that it's been very difficult to overcome a hard quarter-final opponent and win the Cup, the 2023 draw all but ensured that the finalists would be teams that had overcome tough quarter-final opposition. Factoring in the events of 2023 does change the complexion of historical trends, so my analysis both includes and omits the results of 2023 (which, due to the draw, did seem like an anomaly).

2003–2019 World Cups only

We can see from Figure 8.2a that if we split the semi-finalists into semi-final winners and semi-final losers, there is nothing to differentiate them in terms of their own average ranking points. We would expect the semi-final winners to consistently be the better-ranked team, but at 86.8 vs 85.0, the advantage is only slight and not statistically significant.

However, the respective quarter-final opponents that they had to overcome were quite different. The semi-final winners faced quarter-final opponents averaging 78.5 ranking points, whereas the semi-final losers had just come through a battle with quarter-final opponents averaging 83.6 ranking points (Figure 8.2b). This difference of 5.1 ranking points in opponents faced between the groups is statistically significant.

You can see from Figure 8.2c that the teams which went on to win their semi-final had enjoyed, on average, an 8.2 ranking-point advantage over their quarter-final opponents the prior week (compared to 1.5 for the semi-final losers). So, while there is little to separate the semi-final winners and losers themselves in terms of ranking points, the winners tended to face much lower-ranked quarter-final opponents the week before.

8. Navigating the Knockout Gauntlet: The Importance of the Rugby World Cup Draw

a. Ranking Points of Semi-Finalists

- SF Winners: 86.8
- SF Losers: 85.0

b. Ranking Points of Quarter-Final Opponents

- SF Winners: 78.5
- SF Losers: 83.6

c. Ranking Points Advantage over Quarter-Final Opponents

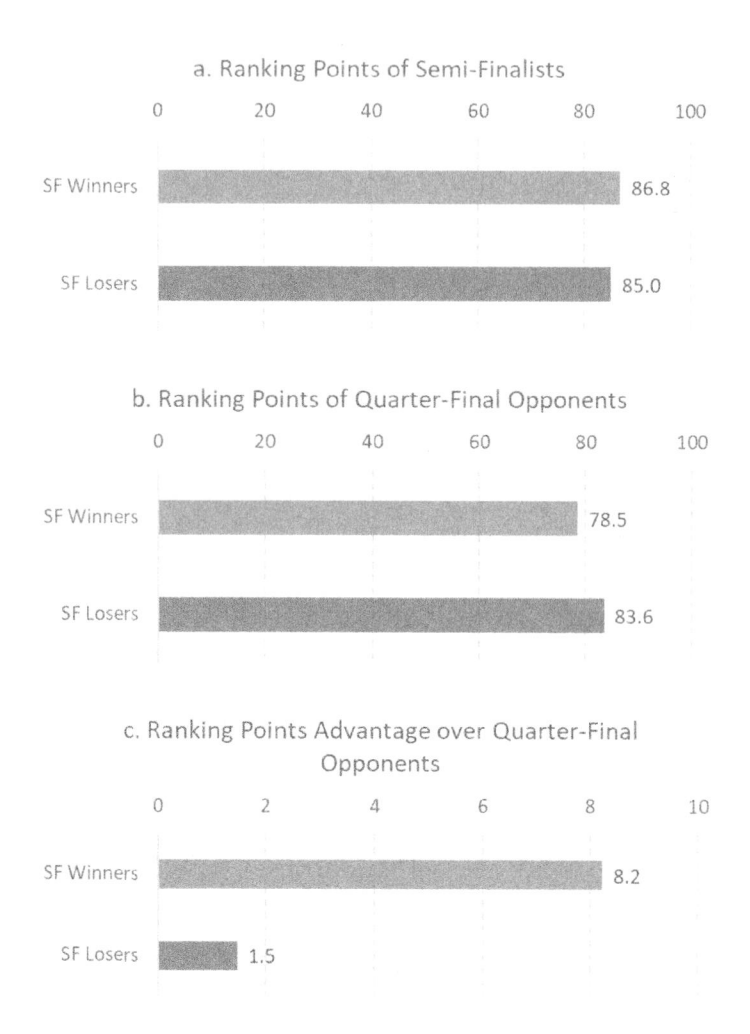

- SF Winners: 8.2
- SF Losers: 1.5

Figure 8.2. Average World Rugby ranking points comparing semi-final winners to semi-final losers across all Rugby World Cups between 2003 and 2019. Figure 8.2a compares the average ranking points of the semi-finalists themselves. Figure 8.2b compares the average ranking points of their quarter-final opponents. Figure 8.2c compares the average ranking points discrepancy between the semi-finalist and their quarter-final opponents.

It's a slightly different story with the finalists. The final winners have had on average a five-ranking-point advantage over the losers, which is statistically significant (Figure 8.3a). The final winners have tended to face weaker quarter-final opponents, averaging 76.2 ranking points versus 80.9 for the final losers (Figure 8.3b). This is not a statistically significant difference, however. And at semi-final time, there is no difference in opponent strength between final winners and losers (Figure 8.3c).

8. Navigating the Knockout Gauntlet: The Importance of the Rugby World Cup Draw

a. Ranking Points of Finalists

- Final Winners: 89.3
- Final Losers: 84.2

b. Ranking Points of Quarter-Final Opponents

- Final Winners: 76.2
- Final Losers: 80.9

c. Ranking Points of Semi-Final Opponents

- Final Winners: 85.0
- Final Losers: 85.0

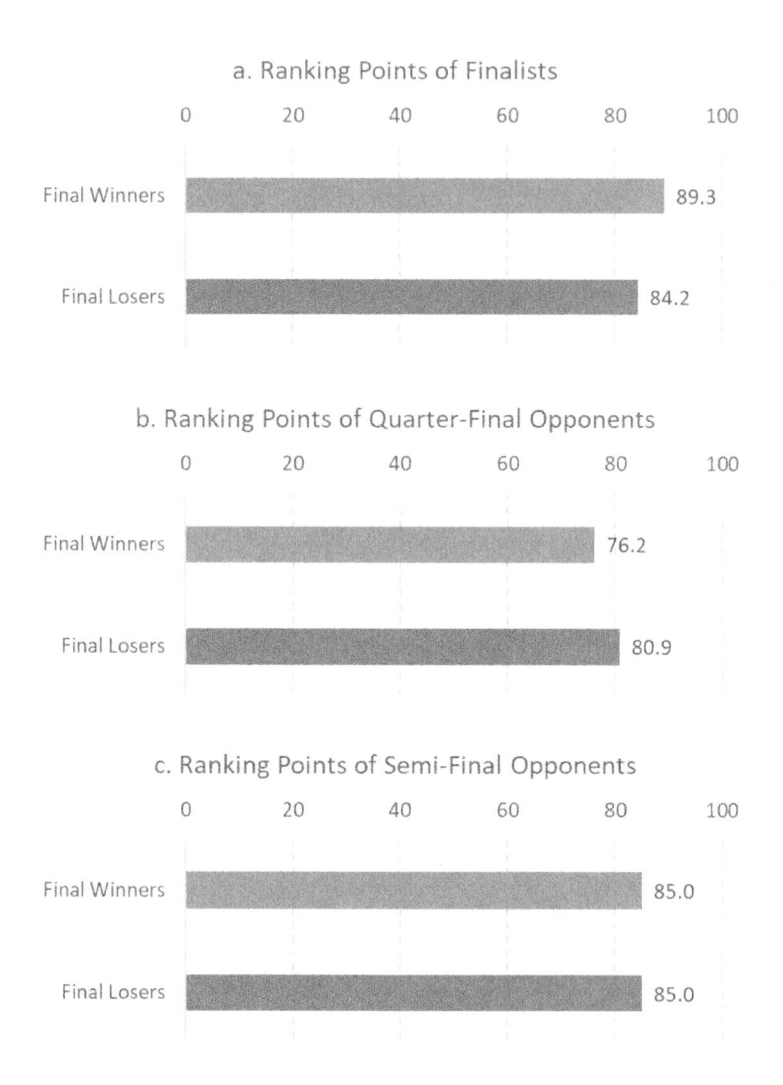

Figure 8.3. *Average World Rugby ranking points comparing final winners to final losers across all Rugby World Cups between 2003 and 2019. Figure 8.3a compares the average ranking points of the finalists themselves. Figure 8.3b compares the average ranking points of their quarter-final opponents. Figure 8.3c compares the average ranking points of their semi-final opponents.*

Okay, but now let's see 2023...

Just to reiterate again, the 2023 draw was historically exceptional. Due to its odd nature, the semi-final winners all survived highly ranked quarter-final opponents (and the losers had beaten low-ranked opponents in the quarter-finals). Figure 8.4 shows where the semi-finalists rank in World Cup history, and reinforces the fact that 2023 pitted two of the highest-ever ranked semi-finalists (by World Rugby ranking points) against two of the lowest-ever ranked.

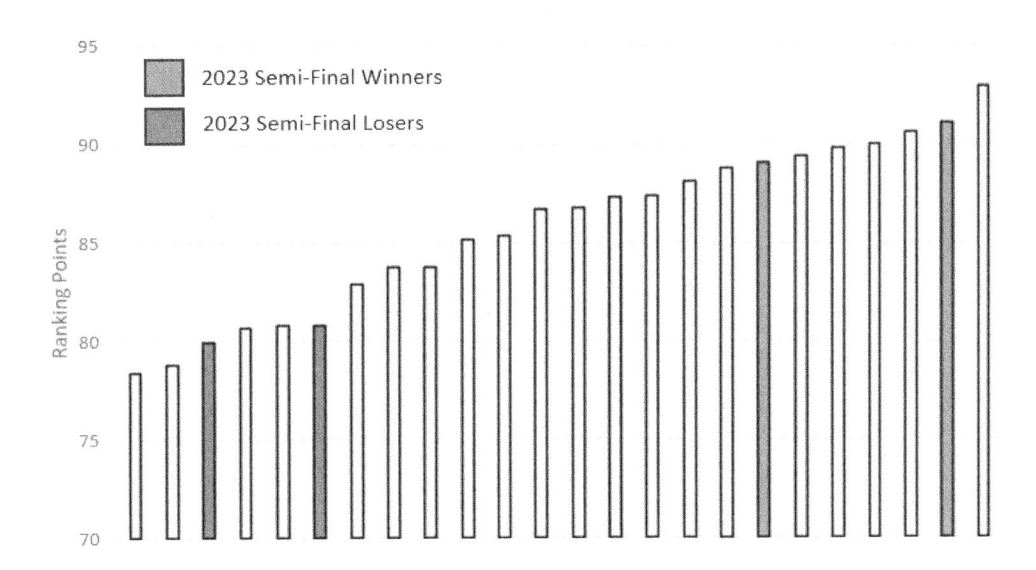

Figure 8.4. World Rugby ranking points of all semi-finalists in Rugby World Cups between 2003 and 2023.

8. Navigating the Knockout Gauntlet: The Importance of the Rugby World Cup Draw

Sure enough, including 2023 in our analysis levels the playing field considerably when it comes to the relative strength of quarter-final opponents. You can see from Figure 8.5a that a meaningful difference in ranking points begins to emerge between semi-final winners (87.3) and semi-final losers (84.2). While the difference isn't quite statistically significant, it's close ($p<0.08$, for the fellow propeller-heads). The ranking points of quarter-final opponents narrows to just 2.3, and while the semi-final winners still had a slightly easier quarter-final path, it's no longer significantly so (Figure 8.5b).

Rugbynomics

a. Ranking Points of Semi-Finalists

- SF Winner: 87.3
- SF Loser: 84.2

b. Ranking Points of Quarter-Final Opponents

- SF Winner: 80.5
- SF Loser: 82.8

c. Ranking Points Advantage over Quarter-Final Opponents

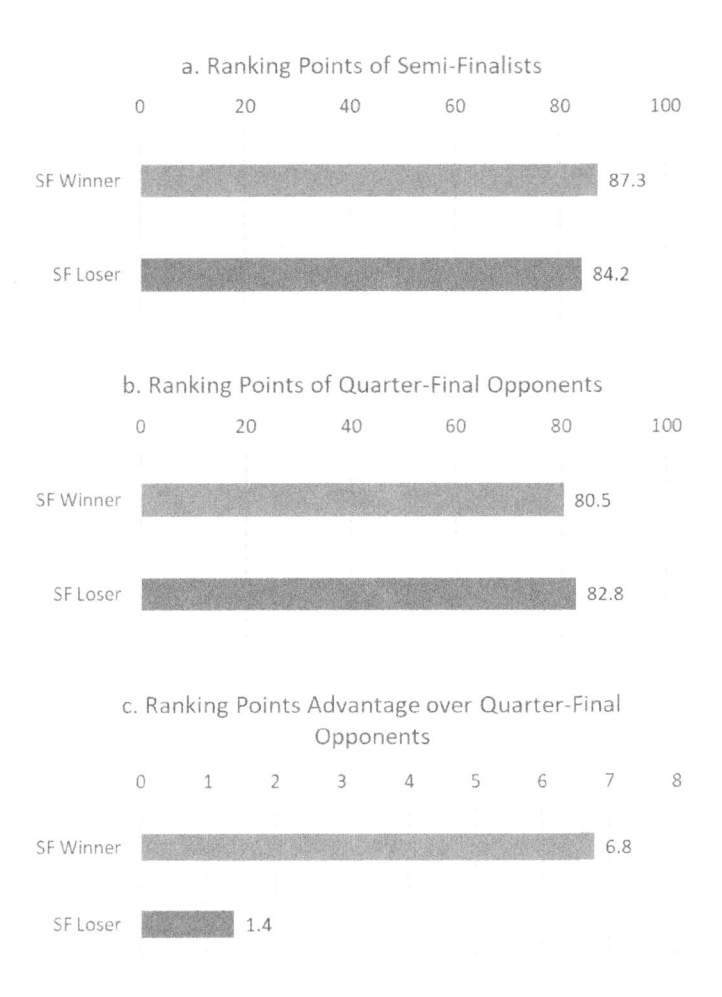

- SF Winner: 6.8
- SF Loser: 1.4

Figure 8.5. Average World Rugby ranking points comparing semi-final winners to semi-final losers across all Rugby World Cups between 2003 and 2023. Figure 8.5a compares the average ranking points of the semi-finalists themselves. Figure 8.5b compares the average ranking points of their quarter-final opponents. Figure 8.5c compares the average ranking points discrepancy between the semi-finalist and their quarter-final opponents.

8. Navigating the Knockout Gauntlet: The Importance of the Rugby World Cup Draw

When comparing the final winners and losers, the trends are essentially the same as before, even with 2023 included (Figure 8.6). The final winners have tended to have a statistically significant ranking advantage over the runners-up (Figure 8.6a). While they have faced relatively lower-ranked quarter-final opponents, this is still not statistically significant (Figure 8.6b). And again, there is no difference in the relative ranking of their semi-final opposition (Figure 8.6c).

Rugbynomics

a. Ranking Points of Finalists

Final Winner: 89.6
Final Loser: 85.0

b. Ranking Points of Quarter-Final Opponents

Final Winner: 78.4
Final Loser: 82.7

c. Ranking Points of Semi-Final Opponents

Final Winner: 84.1
Final Loser: 84.3

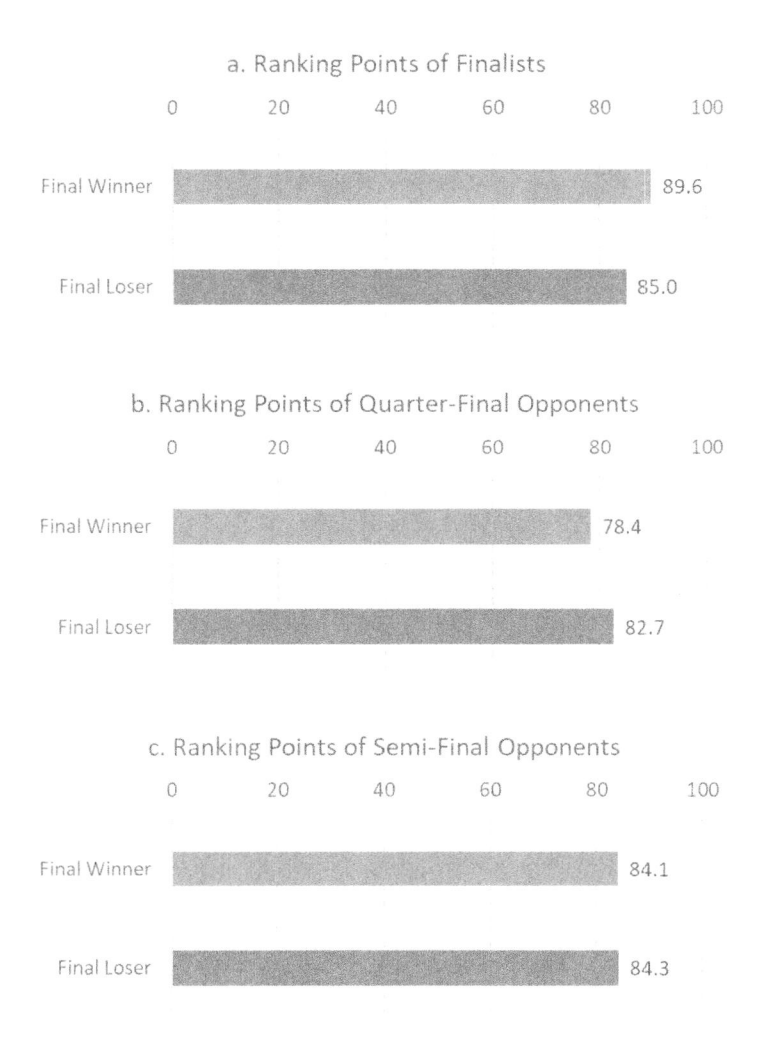

Figure 8.6. Average World Rugby ranking points comparing final winners and final losers across all Rugby World Cups between 2003 and 2023. Figure 8.6a compares the average ranking points of the finalists themselves. Figure 8.6b compares the average ranking points of their quarter-final opponents. Figure 8.6c compares the average ranking points of their semi-final opponents.

8. Navigating the Knockout Gauntlet: The Importance of the Rugby World Cup Draw

The randomness of sport

This is as good a place as any to discuss another important point about how we tend to think about and rationalise sports results. As I've outlined in this chapter, the path to a Rugby World Cup title is fraught with serious obstacles to navigate, and the odds are seldom in the eventual winner's favour from the start. But we humans tend to want to rationalise outcomes as being almost fatalistic. We like to perceive events as having been more predictable—almost inevitable—once they've actually happened.

We can visualise what this hindsight bias looks like with Figure 8.7. If Team X wins a rugby match over Team Y by seven points, afterwards humans like to rationalise that they are the better team and that if the game was played 100 times over that same day, the exact same result would occur.

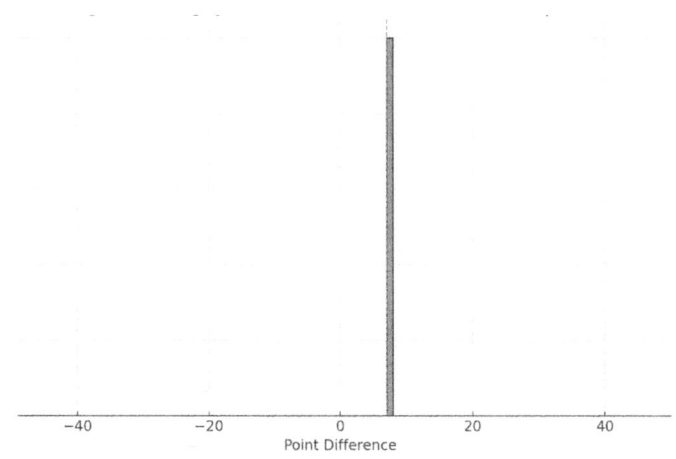

Figure 8.7. An example of a fatalistic interpretation of match results: a belief that all 100 matches played by the same teams on the same day would result in the same seven-point victory by the winner.

In reality, any sport, and especially rugby, is a combination of almost infinite micro-moments that each impact the end result. Added up, they create a diverse range of possible outcomes for any given match. These micro-moments are things like the bounce of the ball, the referee's interpretation of every single ruck and maul, a player deciding to step left instead of right, and even how each player is feeling that day. Contrary to what we might think, the *actual* graph of 100 matches played by the same teams at the same ground on the same day would look more like Figure 8.8. Even though Team X did win by seven points (indicated by the red line), that's just one of a plethora of possible outcomes that could have occurred. It just happened to be that all the random micro-moments added up to that particular outcome... this time. But there's a lot of randomness and uncertainty in the potential outcome. That's the beauty of sport!

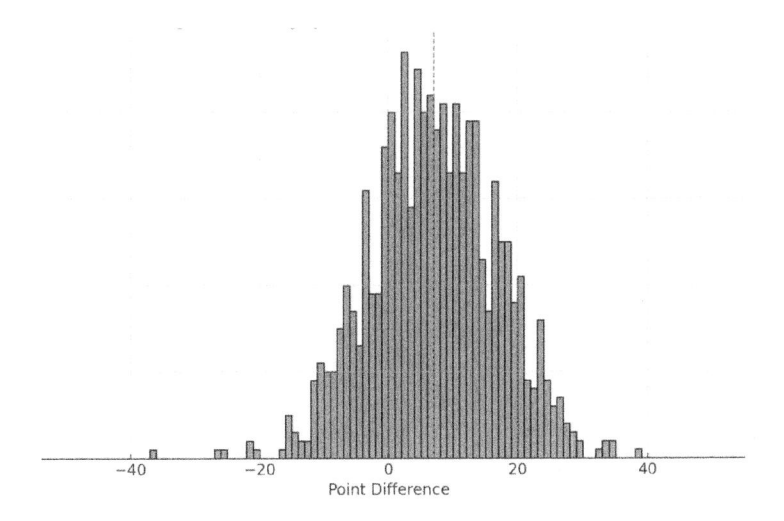

Figure 8.8. *Example of a more realistic interpretation of sports results: an acknowledgement that 100 matches played between the same teams on the same day will have a wide range of potential outcomes.*

8. Navigating the Knockout Gauntlet: The Importance of the Rugby World Cup Draw

The breakdown

While the 2023 Rugby World Cup tournament did throw somewhat of a spanner in the works of my statistical analysis, the evidence is still compelling that an 'easier' quarter-final is almost always crucial to advancing at the Rugby World Cup. Excluding the 2023 tournament, there has been a massive gulf in the difficulty of quarter-final opponents faced by the semi-final winners and losers. Backing up after a huge quarter-final clash against opposition of a similar standard has proven to be almost impossible during Rugby World Cups. The fact that prior to 2023 no tournament champion had ever had to overcome a team ranked higher than seven at the quarter-final stage speaks volumes. Only once has even a World Cup runner-up had to overcome top-five quarter-final opposition, when England upset number 2-ranked Australia in 2007 on their way to the final.

Hopefully this chapter has helped dispel that myth that 'you have to beat everyone at some stage to win a tournament anyway'. If you hear that tired old line being trotted out again, kindly point the misguided soul to this chapter.

9. Rugby's Global Stretch: Should the World Cup Have 24 Teams?

Much has been made of the competitiveness of World Cup pool matches—or rather, the lack thereof. For instance, the 2023 tournament infamously saw a number of one-sided 'cricket scores' being run up. This included an astonishing scoreline in a match between two Tier-1 nations when New Zealand thumped Italy 96–17.

The Rugby World Cup debuted in 1987 with 16 teams. This was expanded to 20 from the fourth edition (1999) onwards. For years, World Rugby had been considering the possibility of expanding to 24 teams in 2027, and immediately following the 2023 tournament the expansion was formally ratified at a World Rugby Council meeting. The official line was that this was done to grow the game and give more nations the chance to shine on the international stage. The extremely cynical suspected that it was purely for financial reasons, especially with potential commercial giant the United States missing out on qualifying for 2023 and due to host the tournament in 2031.

Whatever the true reason, this move has sparked quite a bit of controversy. Sure, it's in everyone's interest to see the game grow globally. And the exploits of plucky underdogs have been some of the most memorable highlights of World Cup tournaments. Think Japan beating South Africa in 2015, or Japan's run to the quarter-finals in 2019, or Portugal's famous victory over Fiji in 2023

9. Rugby's Global Stretch: Should the World Cup Have 24 Teams?

(coupled with those incredible airport scenes on their return home). The minnows always provide the magic when it comes to World Cup tournaments, and this is true in all sports. Cameroon and Morocco instantly spring to mind in men's football (soccer).

But the unsavoury side of expansion is the inevitable mismatches. Those matches often descend into a barely opposed training run for the top teams and can be uncomfortable viewing. The days of the 145–17 trouncing that the All Blacks put on Japan in 1995, where they averaged a try every four minutes, mercifully appear to be over. But in 2023, we still saw two teams come dangerously close to cracking the ton on the scoreboard. And there was a plethora of scores in the seventies and eighties.

All of this raises the important question: how competitive really is the Rugby World Cup, and how has this changed through the editions? Well, let's have a look.

Figure 9.1 shows the average score margins and the percentage of close games (defined as matches where opponents' scores were within seven points) for each of the Rugby World Cups from 1987 through to 2023. Note that for the first two editions, points have been converted into today's point allocation (i.e., five points for a try).

The first expansion in 1999 appears to have had a major impact on the points spread; that year, the average-score margin (including knockout matches) increased to 28 points, and only 17 percent of games were close. This trend continued into the 2003 tournament, which has been the worst to date in terms of parity. That year the average-score margin rose to 33 points, and only one in every seven games (15 percent) was close.

However, over the next three tournaments, levels of parity increased. By 2015, the average margin of victory had fallen to 22 points, and close games were a relatively healthy one in every four (23 percent). This trend reversed somewhat in the following two editions (2019 and 2023); the 28-point margin in 2023 was the highest since 2003. On the other hand, 2023 produced a lot of very tight games among the blowouts including some memorable upsets thrown in for good measure. 27 percent of games in 2023 were 'close'—the highest percentage since 2011 and fourth highest in the tournament's history.

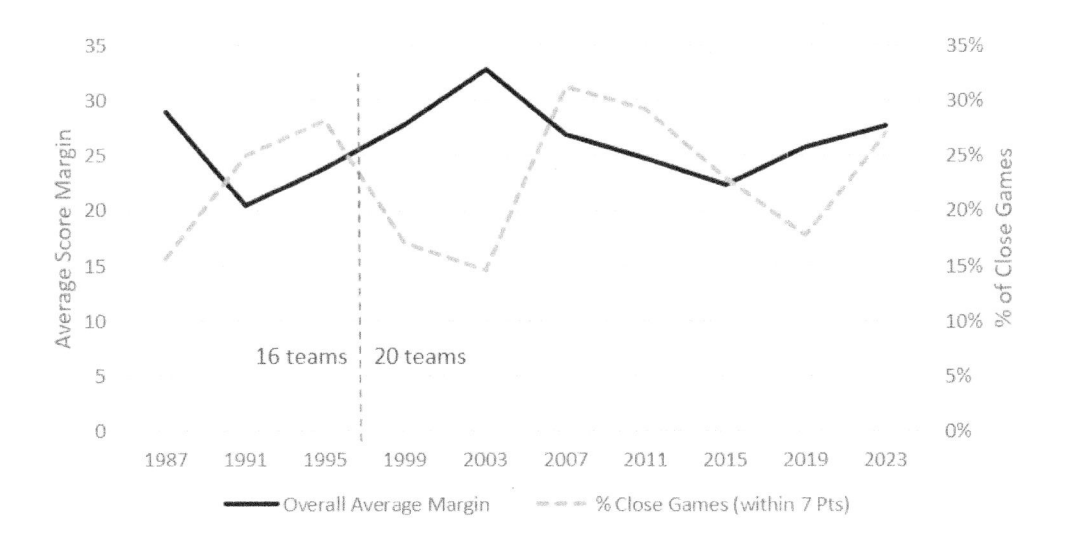

Figure 9.1. Average-score margin and percentage of close games at each Rugby World Cup between 1987 and 2023 (1987 and 1991 tries converted to five points).

9. Rugby's Global Stretch: Should the World Cup Have 24 Teams?

What do the bookies say?

As always, another way to look at the impact of these changes is through bookmakers' odds. As mentioned in Chapter 6, bookmakers are pretty good at predicting winners (their livelihoods depend on it!), and the way they set their odds gives us insight into how favoured each team is to win a match. If the bookies are more confident, then the favourites' probability of winning (derived from their odds) would be close to 100 percent. Less confident and it's closer to a 50:50 matchup.

Figure 9.2, which draws from the available data between 2011 and 2023, indicates that bookmakers were less certain about the outcomes of the 2023 tournament pool stages than in any previous tournament. The chart shows the distribution of the odds the bookmakers set on the favourites for every pool match (with the bookmakers' odds converted into the probability of winning). All four tournaments have a large peak above 90 percent, indicating that the majority of matches were mismatched fixtures where there was an overwhelming favourite. The 2023 tournament has the lowest peak here, indicating a lower proportion of matches that had such overwhelming favouritism. Contrast that to the 2011 tournament which comfortably has the highest peak above 90 percent.

Each tournament in Figure 9.2 also has a second, much lower peak between 50 and 70 percent. These indicate there was a smaller portion of evenly matched games where the bookmakers found it harder to predict the winner.

The 2023 tournament had a reasonable portion of games where the bookmakers' favourite was given less than a 60 percent chance to prevail. Conversely, the secondary peak for the 2011 tournament occurs at the 70 percent mark, indicating that even the more evenly matched games that year were still considered to be fairly predictable.

Of course, the tournament draw will also influence match predictability, as it can group together more evenly matched teams. Remember from Chapter 8 that the 2023 tournament had a very lopsided draw between the different pools, but within each pool this caused a lot more competitiveness.

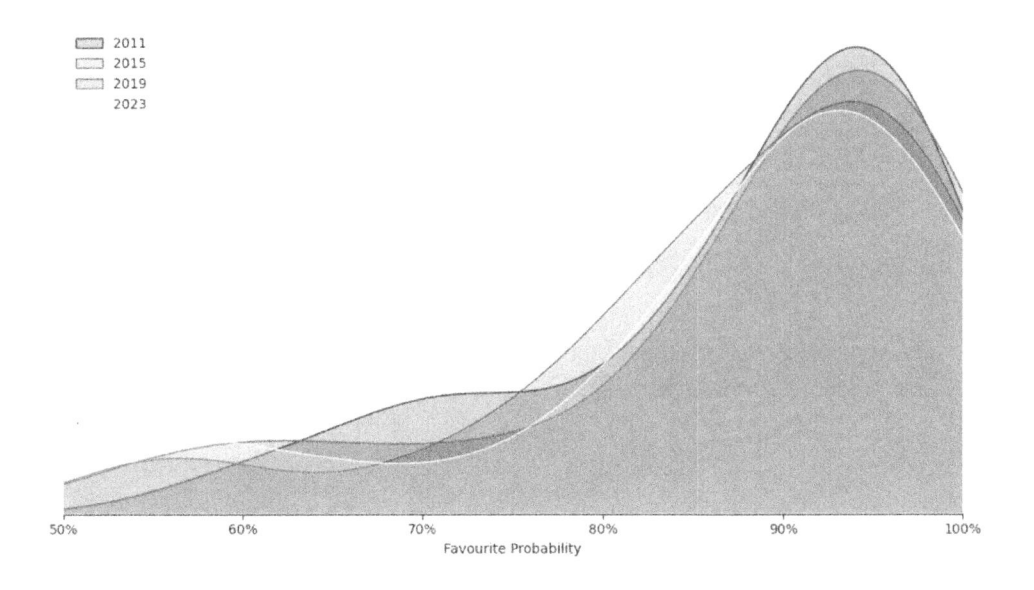

Figure 9.2. Probability, derived from bookmaker odds, of the favourite winning across all pool stage matches of the 2011, 2015, 2019 and 2023 Rugby World Cups.

9. Rugby's Global Stretch: Should the World Cup Have 24 Teams?

Actual upsets (based on the bookmakers' favourite) in pool play are very rare. Across the last four World Cup pool stages, there have been just 18 upsets in total, averaging 11.5 percent of matches (Table 9.1). This means that approximately one in every nine pool matches has delivered an upset. 2015 had the most upsets, followed by the recent 2023 edition.

The bookmakers' Brier score is included in Table 9.1 too. Remember from Chapter 6 that this is a measure of how accurate their odds are across all matches, with a lower score indicating greater accuracy. While the scores are close among the four tournaments, they back up the fact that the 2015 tournament was the least certain, and 2011 seemed to be the most certain (despite having one more upset than 2019).

Table 9.1. Pool stage upsets and bookmakers' Brier scores from the 2011, 2015, 2019 and 2023 Rugby World Cups. Note that in 2019 three pool games were cancelled because of Typhoon Hagibis.

Year	Pool Matches	Upsets	Upset %	Brier Score
2011	40	4	10%	0.16
2015	40	6	15%	0.19
2019	37	3	8%	0.17
2023	40	5	13%	0.17
TOTAL	157	18	11%	0.17

Formatting error?

The other factor to consider with Rugby World Cup expansion is the new format for 2027 and beyond. The four pools of five teams will be gone, replaced with six pools of four teams and a new round of 16 added to the knockout stages. This format change will tend to further separate the top teams in pool play (Table 9.2).

In 2023, eight of the 40 pool games (one in every five) were between Tier-1 teams. With the ten Tier-1 teams spread across six pools in 2027, in all likelihood two of the pools will contain only one Tier-1 team, with the other four containing two. That means there will only be four Tier-1 clashes in pool play out of a total of 36 pool games. In other words, we're likely to go from one in five pool games being a clash of Tier-1 teams to one in nine.

And then there's the new round-of-16 format to factor in. The eight matchups at this stage will likely only have two or three Tier-1 clashes, depending on where teams qualify from the pool phase. Taking the average (2.5), that means a Tier-1 clash should only occur once every seven matches in the new, combined 44-match pool stage and round-of-16 format.

In my view, this change in format is required. Even with four pools of five, the old format was becoming bloated, especially with a pool-play bye introduced in 2023. The 2023 tournament kicked off during a late-summer European heatwave, with water breaks hastily introduced to help teams cope with the 35+ degree temperatures; the final game was played on a cold and wet Parisian night

9. Rugby's Global Stretch: Should the World Cup Have 24 Teams?

at the very end of October, a whole seven weeks later. Adding another week on top of this was not really a viable option. If World Rugby had simply decided to just add another team to each of the existing four pools, we would have seen eight Tier-1 clashes spread across 60 pool games. That's one in every 7.5 games.

Table 9.2. Summary of different Rugby World Cup formats, and how many matches and Tier-1 clashes each format would likely produce prior to the quarter-final stage.

No. of Teams	Format	No. Matches Prior to Quarter-Final Stage	Average No. of Tier-1 Clashes	% of Tier-1 Clashes
20	Four pools of five teams	40	8	20%
24	Six pools of four teams	36	4	11%
24	Six pools of four teams, with a round of 16	44	6.5	15%
24	Four pools of six teams	60	8	13%
24	Four pools of six teams, with a round of 16	68	10.5	15%

So while a new format is definitely needed to accommodate the four additional teams joining the tournament and allow it to finish in a timely manner, an unintended consequence may be that we're treated to a dearth of heavyweight clashes until the very pointy end.

The breakdown

If history is anything to go by, the 2027 expansion and adjusted pool structure will undoubtedly increase the frequency of blowouts and create an environment of less competitive fixtures, at least in the short term. It took three tournaments following the last expansion in 1999 for the prior level of parity to be restored.

The adjusted pool structure will also have a negative impact when it comes to the highly prized clashes between Tier-1 heavyweights.

It's a tough balancing act, though. Among the procession of one-sided pool stage fixtures, we've been treated to some absolute humdingers of matches and moments that can define World Cups. Without the expansion to 20 teams in 1999, would we have seen Tonga's famous win over Italy that year, or Uruguay notch their first World Cup win over Spain in the same tournament? Would Japan have grown into the force they have, capable of upsetting top-tier nations regularly on the biggest stage? Would Georgia have developed into a leading Tier-2 nation, capable of testing even the best on their day? And would we have been treated to those airport scenes from Lisbon? Definitely not.

World Rugby has proclaimed that it is committed to raising the standards of the Tier-2 nations to increase the competitiveness of the tournament. It's something we've heard before, so let's see if it comes to fruition as the memories of the 2023 heroics of Portugal, Chile and Uruguay gradually begin to fade.

As it turns out, one relatively cheap way to strengthen parity is through data. A 2023 article from the BBC highlighted how FIFA democratised the use of football analytics data in advance of the 2022 World Cup, making rich and real-time data accessible to all participants. Gaining access to this data was credited as one of the reasons why the 2022 edition was perhaps the most evenly contested FIFA World Cup in history, with unfancied Croatia and Morocco progressing all the way to the semi-finals. As we continue to understand and

9. Rugby's Global Stretch: Should the World Cup Have 24 Teams?

unlock the value of data in sports performance, it's a strategy that World Rugby would be wise to follow.

10. Regressing to the Mean— Of Rugby Players and Fighter Pilots

What do elite rugby players have in common with air force fighter pilots? Quite a lot in terms of being at the very top of their chosen profession, and working in extremely stressful environments requiring split-second decisions that have huge consequences (the consequences are obviously amplified for the fighter pilots where actual lives are on the line!). Another thing that they have in common is that they're subject to a phenomenon known as 'regression to the mean'. This is a fancy term for a concept that was popularised by Daniel Kahneman (2011) in his seminal book *Thinking Fast and Slow*.

Regression to the mean is the phenomenon that any performance which is subject to random fluctuations in quality will eventually revert to the average level of performance over the long term. There will be performances that greatly exceed or fall short of expectations along the way, but rather than being indicative of a new trend in expected performance, these are aberrations that will even out over time.

A famous example from Kahneman's book was when he was working with an air force squadron. The squadron commander claimed that if a pilot performed manoeuvres poorly, then when he gave them a right good 'bollocking', they almost always performed better on the next flight. However, in the squadron commander's experience, if the pilot performed their

10. Regressing to the Mean—Of Rugby Players and Fighter Pilots

manoeuvres exceptionally well, he was better to be minimal with his praise. Experience had shown him that when he praised his pilot's exceptional performance too much, their next flight was inevitably worse than the last one.

Kahneman recognised this as not a function of the squadron commander's fury or praise, but instead the pilots regressing back to their natural mean. Independent of any feedback from their commander, an especially good flight was more than likely to be followed by one that was not as good. And a particularly bad flight would almost inevitably be followed by a better one.

If we substitute squadron commander with rugby head coach, and fighter pilots with rugby players, would the same results apply? You can imagine the grizzled, old-school rugby coach tearing his players a new one at halftime if their performance is not up to scratch, and being quietly satisfied as he watches his charges perform appreciably better in the second half. And the same coach being reserved in his praise of an excellent first-half performance for fear that complacency might set in during the second half.

Kahneman reinforces that our human minds are strongly biased towards causal explanations. We touched on this in Chapter 8 when outlining that a game of rugby is a series of micro-moments, with each having multiple potential results. When added together, these micro-moments create a range of possible match outcomes, and this is the randomness of sports which compels us to watch. But us humans, we are programmed to seek out a reason why the things that we observed happened. Why did the team that looked gone for all money at halftime come storming back in the second half to win the game? 'Regressing back to their long-term expected performance' isn't usually a satisfactory explanation!

To investigate regression to the mean in rugby, I compared the first-half performance of teams against their second-half performance. The performance is evaluated by the points difference at both half and fulltime versus the expected point spread according to the bookmaker odds.

Why use the performance against the expected points spread rather than simply just the score? Because the perception of under or over-performance would greatly vary depending on the opposition. For example, with all due respect to the Flying Fijians and their outstanding performance at the 2023 Rugby World Cup, if they were to face the All Blacks in a test in New Zealand, Fiji would probably be reasonably satisfied to go into the sheds at halftime 'only' ten points down. On the other hand, the All Blacks and their home crowd would likely be rather unhappy with how the game was unfolding. Conversely, if the Springboks found themselves ten points down at halftime in a test against the All Blacks, it's the Springboks who would be looking to turn their second-half performance around, while the All Blacks would likely be quite satisfied with their 40 minutes of work. The expectations of each game matters greatly here, and as we've seen in previous chapters, the bookmakers' odds provide an excellent gauge on what those expectations should be.

I conducted this analysis on almost 700 matches across the Top 14, Rugby Premiership, Super Rugby, Six Nations, Rugby Championship and Rugby World Cup knockout stage. The results outlined here are for the home team

10. Regressing to the Mean—Of Rugby Players and Fighter Pilots

only. This is because, for every team that is overperforming at halftime by ten points, there's an opposition that is therefore underperforming by ten points. The away team results are simply an inverse of the home team results.

What happens when the home team finds themselves well behind where they're expected to be on the scoreboard at halftime? In most situations, they likely get a good dressing-down from the coaching staff and captain in the changing rooms, and their fans probably let them know in no uncertain terms that they're expecting better. And sure enough, they generally turn their performance around in the second half. When home teams were more than a converted try (>7 points) behind where the points spread predicted they should be at halftime, they turned it around in the second half to beat the expected performance by an average of one point.

This analysis uses the same betting odds for each half, so there's been no adjustment in scoring expectation based on the first-half performance. These teams have simply tended to perform far better, going from underperforming against expectations in the first half by an average of 13 points, to overperforming by one point in the second half. 84 percent of the teams performed relatively better in the second half against the spread than they did in the first (Figure 10.1). This is a huge turnaround in performance. Is it the brilliance of the halftime pep talk? Is the home crowd galvanising their team? Is it complacency of the opposition kicking in? Or is it simply regression to the mean (i.e., that their performance is reverting back to its long-term expectation)?

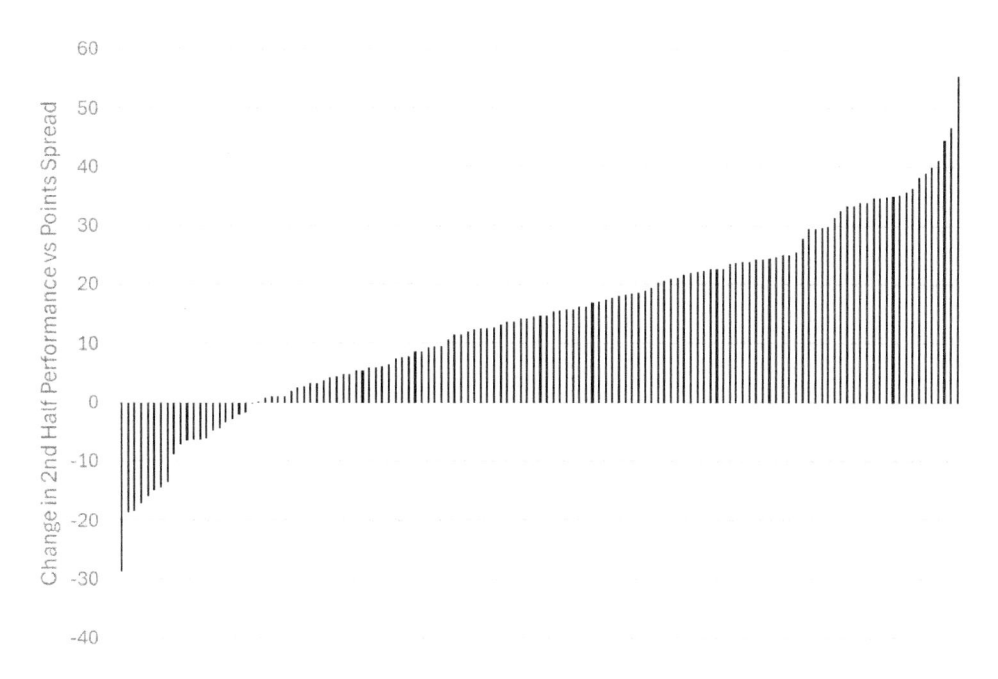

Figure 10.1. Change in second-half performance versus first-half performance for home teams that underperformed against the predicted points spread in the first half by greater than seven points. Data from matches in the Top 14, Premiership Rugby, Super Rugby, Six Nations, Rugby Championship and Rugby World Cup knockout rounds.

Let's look at the opposite scenario. When the home team is outperforming expectations at halftime by greater than seven points, we see the exact opposite pattern. In those matches, the home team beat the points spread expectation by an average of 12 points in the first half, but underperformed by 1.6 points in the second half. They performed relatively worse in the second half (compared

10. Regressing to the Mean—Of Rugby Players and Fighter Pilots

to the first) in 82% of matches (Figure 10.2). Suddenly, the coach's halftime pep talk, or the home crowds, don't seem to be having such a positive impact if the home team was doing well!

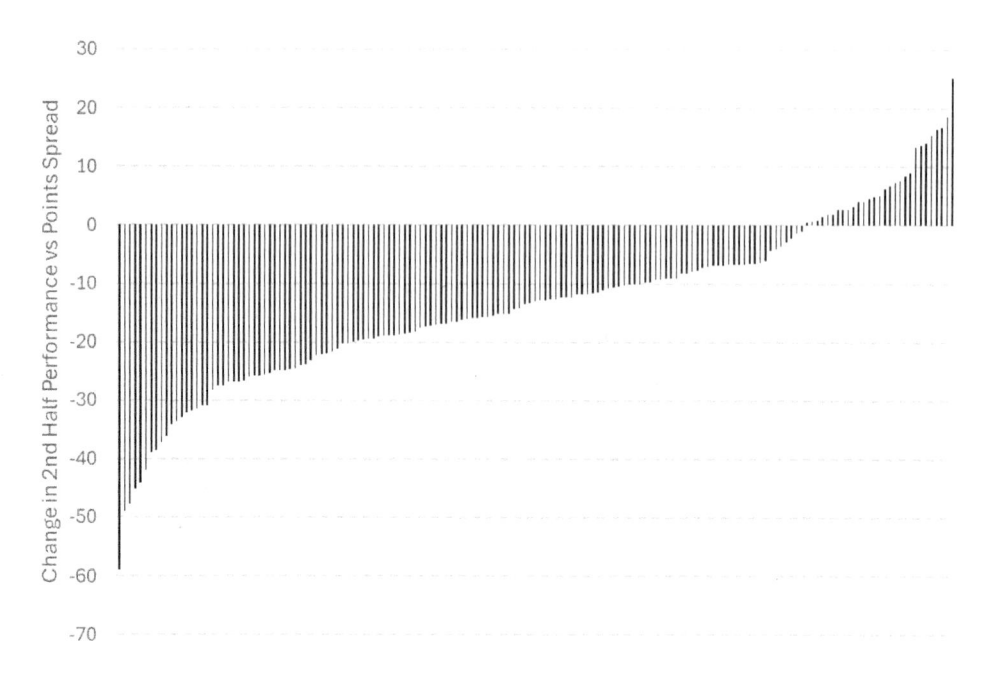

Figure 10.2. Change in second-half performance versus first-half performance for home teams that overperformed against the predicted points spread in the first half by greater than seven points. Data from matches in the Top 14, Premiership Rugby, Super Rugby, Six Nations, Rugby Championship and Rugby World Cup knockout rounds.

What about matches that are going almost to expectation at halftime? There is much variation across individual matches (as would be expected), but on average, for games that are within three points of the expected scoreline at halftime, the second half continues to go as expected. The average deviation from expectation in these games is just 0.1 points in the first half, and 0.4 in the second. As seen in Figure 10.3, the matches are evenly split between relatively better or worse second-half performance.

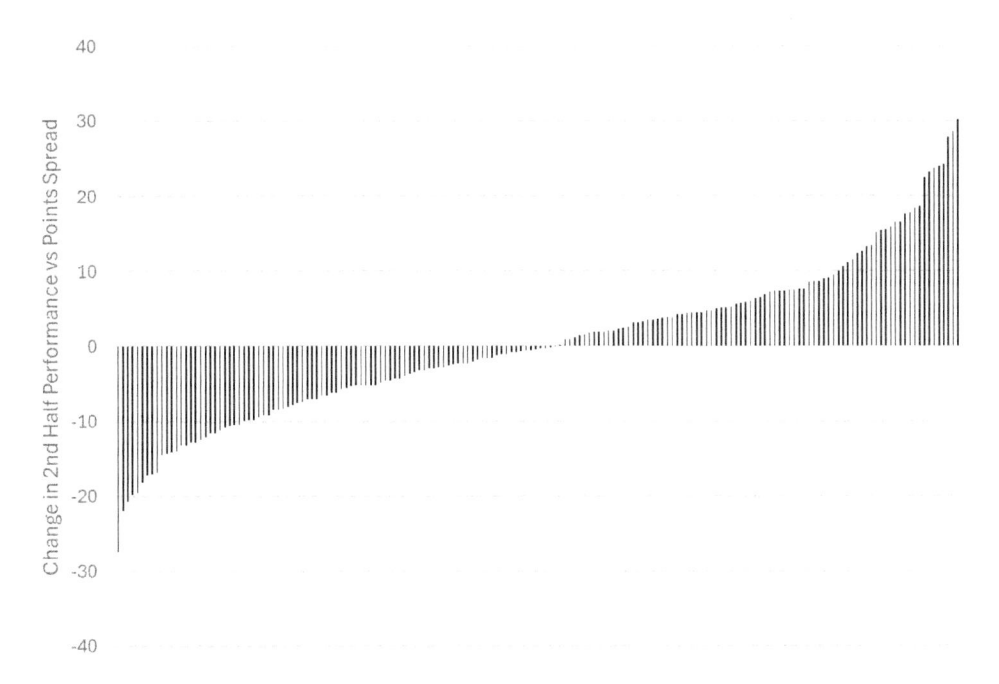

Figure 10.3. Change in second-half performance versus first-half performance for home teams that were within three points of the predicted points spread at halftime. Data from matches in the Top 14, Premiership Rugby, Super Rugby, Six Nations, Rugby Championship and Rugby World Cup knockout rounds.

The three charts demonstrate classic regression to the mean in rugby performances. Better than expected first-half performance generally leads to a

10. Regressing to the Mean—Of Rugby Players and Fighter Pilots

worse second-half performance. Worse than expected first-half performance generally leads to a better second-half performance. And when first-half performance meets expectation, the second-half performance on average does too. There is even a statistically significant difference between the overall second-half performance and the first-half performance across all 700 matches.

Still not convinced? Kahneman had a clever way to further demonstrate regression to the mean using golf as an example. Because regression to the mean is not causal (i.e., the initial performance is not impacting the subsequent performance), he examined rounds of professional golf. When players performed better than expected in the first round, their second round was generally worse than their first. He attributed this to the luck that had contributed to their excellent first round eluding them in the second, and they performed closer to their expected level. Since Kahneman's theory is that the golfer's performance in each of these rounds is independent of each other, he then reversed the analysis and predicted the first-round performance based on what happened in the second round. It makes no sense that the first round would be impacted by what occurs the next day in the second round. Yet he found the exact same pattern. When golfers performed better than expected in their second rounds, their first rounds had usually been worse.

We can apply the exact same logic to rugby! Let's look at the performance of teams in the first half, relative to how they performed in the second. I'm sure by now you can guess where I'm going with this. But sure enough, if we reverse the halves and compare performance, *we get the exact same results!* Teams that performed more than seven points worse than expected in the second half performed on average one point better in the first. 90 percent of those teams performed better in the first half than they had in the second (Figure 10.4).

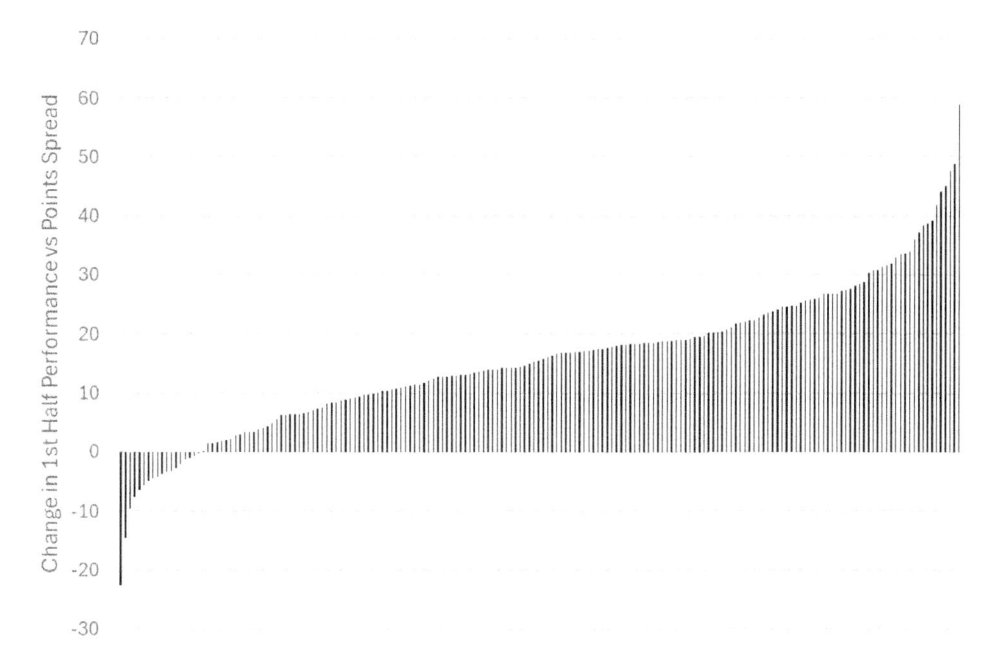

Figure 10.4. Change in first-half performance versus second-half performance for home teams that underperformed against the predicted points spread in the second half by greater than seven points. Data from matches in the Top 14, Premiership Rugby, Super Rugby, Six Nations, Rugby Championship and Rugby World Cup knockout rounds.

And teams that performed more than seven points better than expected in the second half had overwhelmingly underperformed in the first half, by an average of two points worse than expected. In 96% of those matches, the teams

10. Regressing to the Mean—Of Rugby Players and Fighter Pilots

performed better in the second half than they had in the first (Figure 10.5).

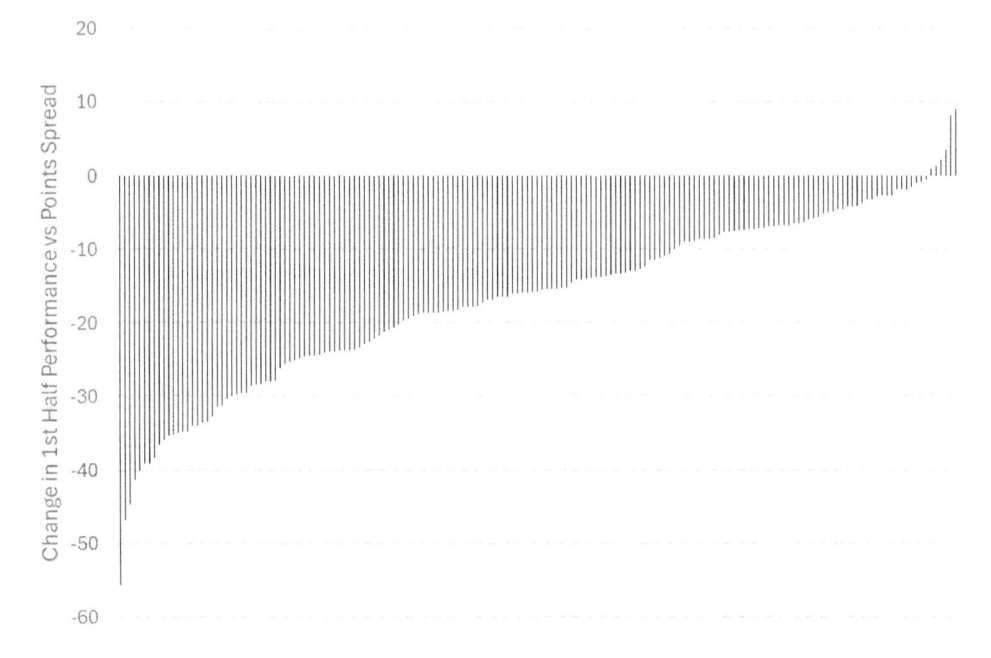

Figure 10.5. Change in first-half performance versus second-half performance against the points spread for home teams that overperformed against the spread in the second half by greater than seven points. Data from matches in the Top 14, Premiership Rugby, Super Rugby, Six Nations, Rugby Championship and Rugby World Cup knockout rounds.

The fact that we can reverse the order and still predict a trend that happened beforehand is good evidence that this relationship is not causal. Sorry coaching staff, but unless you can bend the space-time continuum and deliver your team talk for the first half based on what you know will transpire in the second, then the change in performance can't be caused by you.

The breakdown

In fact, some rugby teams have cottoned on to performance being independent of the team talk in the change room. Back in the mid-2000s, then All Blacks captain Tana Umaga took his coach, Graham Henry, out for what I can only imagine was a rather awkward coffee. Umaga allegedly informed Henry that his team talks were 'meaningless', and to his credit, Henry listened to the feedback and abandoned doing team talks before and during games. His successor as All Blacks coach, Steve Hansen, continued this philosophy, saying that if a team talk is required on game day, it's already too late. The preparation happens during the week, and the All Blacks' players were largely left to manage their own performance on game day. There was no Al Pacino-style *Any Given Sunday* speech for a while in the All Blacks then, and they've certainly done okay over those years!

Hansen did feel the need to deliver what was described by hooker Dane Coles as an old-school, nine out of ten on the dressing room Richter scale verbal spray at halftime of the All Blacks World Cup match against Namibia in 2019. Coles noted that it was rare and unusual for Hansen to do this, but the team needed it. The heavily favoured All Blacks were leading 24–9 at halftime, which clearly wasn't to Hansen's satisfaction. They piled on 47 unanswered points in the second half to win 71–9, finishing right on the expected points margin. Was it the epic halftime spray, or regression to the mean that led to this turnaround in performance. You be the judge!

11. Black Tide Rising: Flipping the Script in the All Blacks vs Springboks Saga

The Springboks versus the All Blacks: it's arguably the greatest rivalry in rugby. It took on almost mythical status back in the days when the two nations only met during periodic tours, and the tension only increased during the Apartheid era when contests were few and far between. The Springboks were famous for being the All Blacks' Achilles' heel, and rightfully so; for most of the All Blacks' history, they were the only team that could boast a winning record against the fearsome men in black.

My, how times have changed. Since the Professional era began in 1996, this rivalry has been absolutely turned on its head with the All Blacks dominating their big Southern Hemisphere rivals. This might sound like a strange statement to be making in early 2024, off the back of the All Blacks' record 2023 towelling by the Springboks at Twickenham followed by their defeat in the 2023 Rugby World Cup final. But I'm looking at the bigger picture, which is that since professionalisation, New Zealand has dominated their old foes (Figure 11.1).

The first 70 years of the rivalry were shaded by the Springboks, who largely maintained an overall winning record against the All Blacks. In the 42 tests played between 1921 and rugby turning professional in 1996, the Springboks won 21 to the All Blacks' 18 (with three draws). However, in the years since, the Springboks have only won 19 of 64 tests. The All Blacks have prevailed 44 times, with three draws. Figure 11.1 puts this reversal of fortune into sharp focus, as you can see that the rivalry win advantage has shot up in the All Blacks' favour.

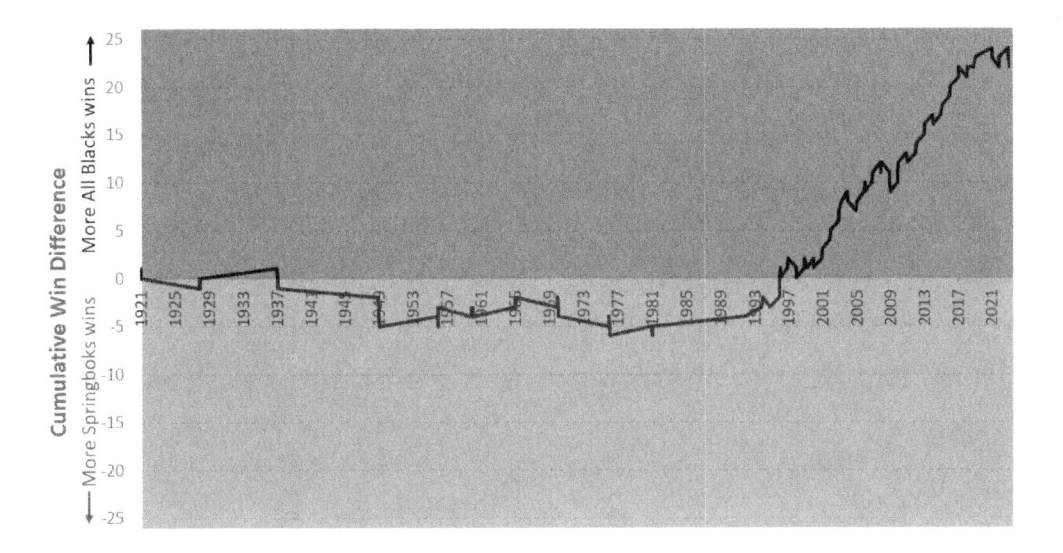

Figure 11.1. Cumulative test rugby win difference over time between the New Zealand All Blacks and the South Africa Springboks.

The purpose of this chapter isn't to gloat about this new order to Springboks fans. They are, after all, feeling justifiably smug with themselves after netting their record-breaking fourth World Cup in 2023. I'm much more interested in examining what the data can tell us about this rivalry—namely, why it has transformed so rapidly and decisively. There are a lot of theories ripe for us to explore, confirm, debunk or discount. Here are a few of the less crazy ones, posed in the form of questions:

11. Black Tide Rising: Flipping the Script in the All Blacks vs Springboks Saga

- Have the Springboks become significantly worse since 1996?
- Have the All Blacks become significantly better since 1996?
- Have neutral referees had an impact?
- Have the All Blacks figured out how to play and win in South Africa, and particularly at altitude (South Africa's big home-ground advantage)?
- Has the fact that the teams meet on a regular basis at both international and club levels had an effect?

Let's dissect these one by one.

Have the Springboks become significantly worse since 1996?

Far more has gone on in South Africa since the mid-1990s than just rugby turning professional, to say the least. Most obviously (and significantly), the country underwent monumental political and social change with the end of the Apartheid era in 1994. It goes without saying that rugby is a mere triviality within the broader context of the pursuit of freedom and equality for the majority of the South African population. But any conversation on Springbok rugby performance during the Professional era must consider this seismic shift in the country during the same period.

On the one hand, after Apartheid the Springboks were able to tap into a much larger player pool. Integration was fast-tracked by the periodic implementation of quota systems designed to bring players of all races into the sport. During Apartheid, rugby in South Africa was largely the domain of the white population. The Springboks' World Cup-winning 1995 squad featured a single player of colour, winger Chester Williams. Their 2023 equivalents, also World Cup winners, contained ten players of colour, including the captain and many of the team's biggest stars.

But on the other hand, continued political upheaval at home, combined with the weakness of the South African rand, has made the lure of professional money overseas disproportionately attractive to many South African players. Their exodus to high-paying European and Japanese leagues has been somewhat mitigated by the fact that overseas-based players are still eligible for the national team (the Springboks' 2023 World Cup roster contained 19 players who earned their living outside of South Africa). New Zealand, conversely, does not currently allow overseas-based players to represent the country.

Could the decentralised nature of modern-day South African rugby, with so much talent based overseas, have had a detrimental impact on the performance of the national team? On the surface, Figure 11.2 would suggest that it has. The Springboks' winning percentage against traditional Tier-1 teams has fallen from 60 percent before 1996 to 53 percent in the (current) Professional era.[9]

---

[9] I deliberately excluded Italy and Argentina as Tier-1 teams in this analysis since the Springboks only played them five times before 1996 and have played them 47 times since. Including them would artificially raise the Springboks' winning percentage in the Professional era relative to pre-1996, as since 1996 they have enjoyed an 89 percent win rate against these teams.

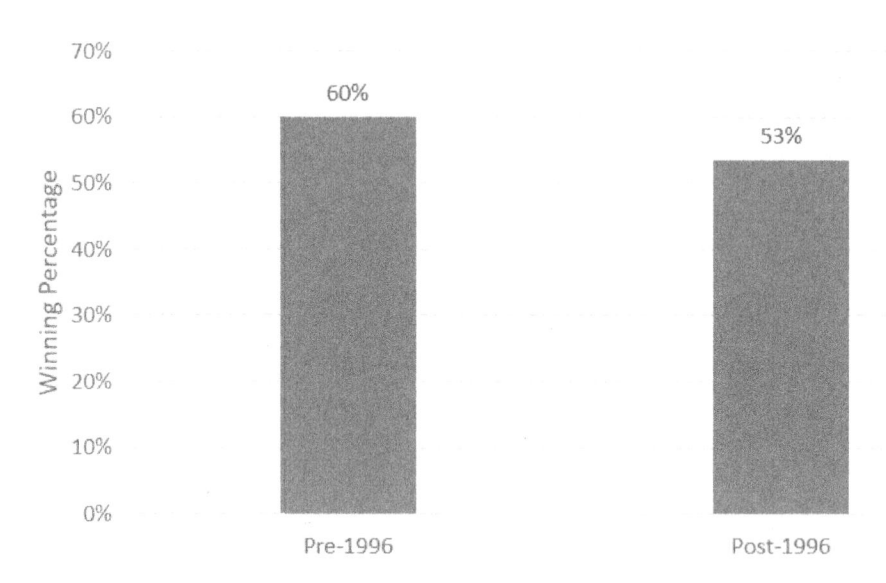

11. Black Tide Rising: Flipping the Script in the All Blacks vs Springboks Saga

Figure 11.2. The Springboks' test rugby winning percentage pre- and post-professionalisation, against the traditional Tier-1 teams of New Zealand, Australia, England, France, Wales, Ireland, Scotland and the British & Irish Lions.

Then again, we know that the All Blacks have enjoyed huge success against the Springboks since 1996. Is it possible that the Springboks' success against the other Tier-1 opponents continued after 1996? Indeed, if we exclude the All Blacks, the Springboks' win rate against the other Tier-1 nations barely changes, going from 63 percent to 61 percent (Figure 11.3).

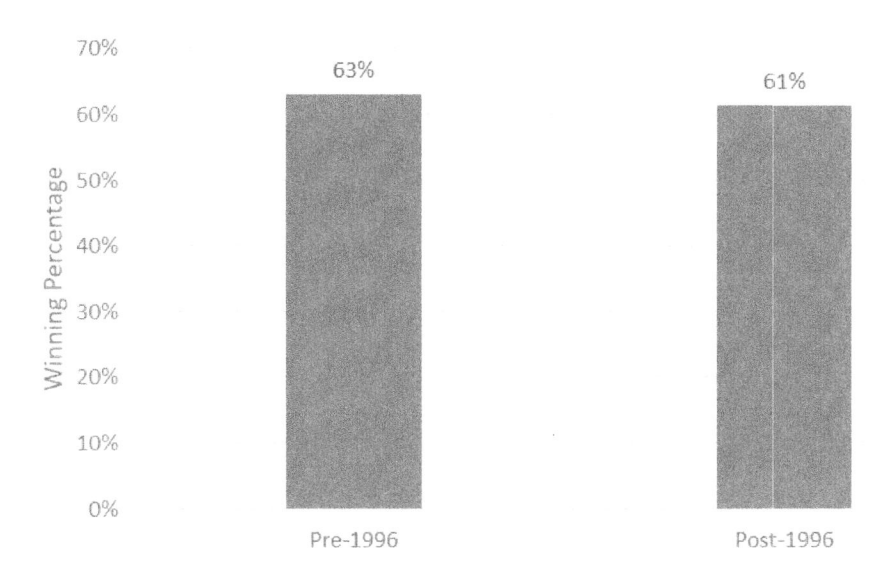

[Bar chart showing Winning Percentage: Pre-1996 at 63%, Post-1996 at 61%]

Figure 11.3. The Springboks' test rugby winning percentage, pre- and post-professionalisation, against all traditional Tier-1 teams except New Zealand.

So, it appears that, apart from their tussles with the All Blacks, the Springboks have enjoyed a similar level of success against the other 'big guns' of world rugby since 1996. The theory that the Springboks have become a lot worse since professionalisation doesn't seem to hold much water.

Have the All Blacks become significantly better since 1996?

If we look at the All Blacks' record against the same traditional Tier-1 set, we can see that their winning percentage has increased from 70 percent prior to 1996 to 77 percent in the Professional era (Figure 11.4).

11. Black Tide Rising: Flipping the Script in the All Blacks vs Springboks Saga

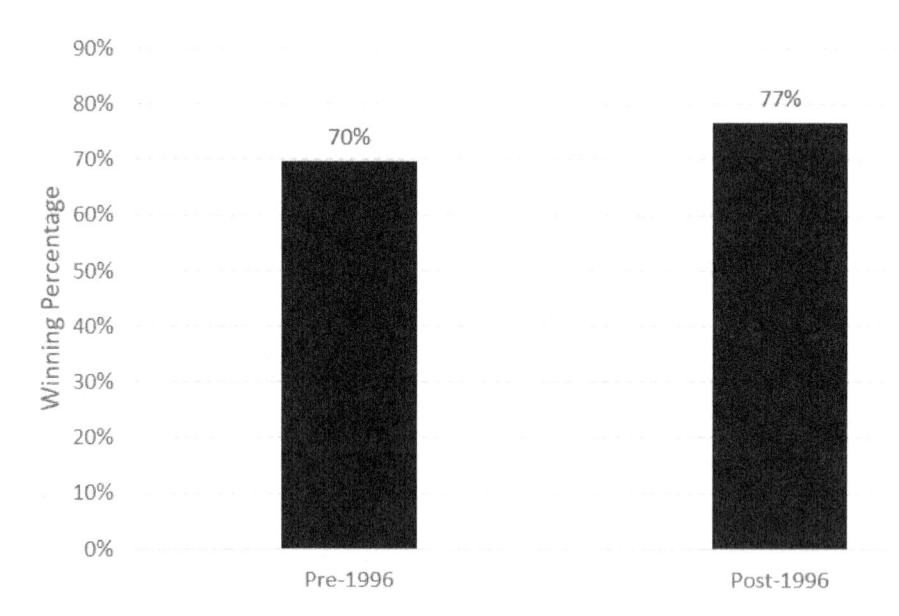

Figure 11.4. The All Blacks' test rugby winning percentage, pre- and post-professionalism in 1996, against the traditional Tier-1 teams of South Africa, Australia, England, France, Wales, Ireland, Scotland and the British & Irish Lions.

However, if we remove South Africa from this equation, the percentage increase is milder (Figure 11.5), changing from 75 percent to 79 percent (not enough to be statistically significant). So, while the All Blacks' record has become slightly better against the other traditional Tier-1 teams, it's not even close to explaining the level of their improvement against South Africa specifically.

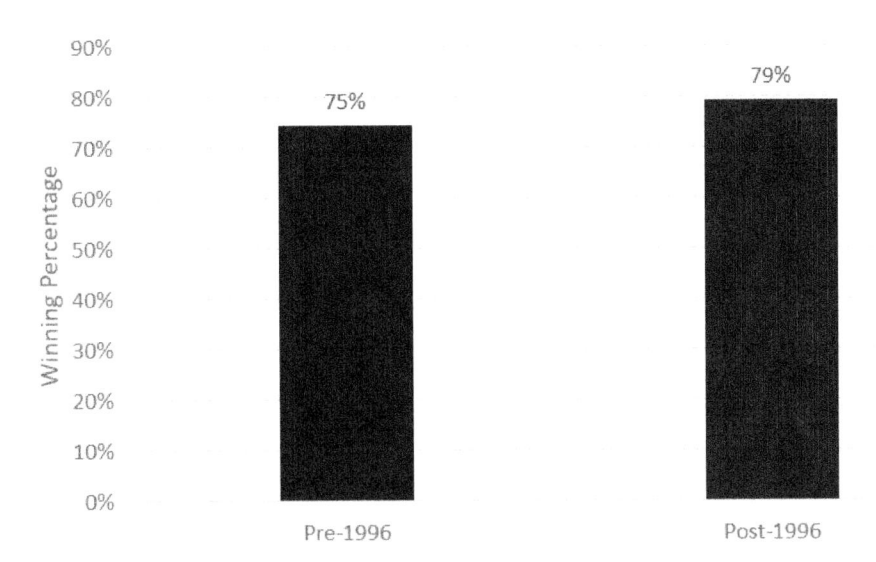

[Bar chart: Pre-1996: 75%; Post-1996: 79%]

Figure 11.5. The All Blacks' test rugby winning percentage, pre- and post-professionalisation in 1996, against traditional Tier-1 teams except South Africa.

And what improvement they've made! When we examine the All Blacks' record against each individual Tier-1 country (Figure 11.6), we see that after 1996, their win rate has improved the most against none other than their old rival.

11. Black Tide Rising: Flipping the Script in the All Blacks vs Springboks Saga

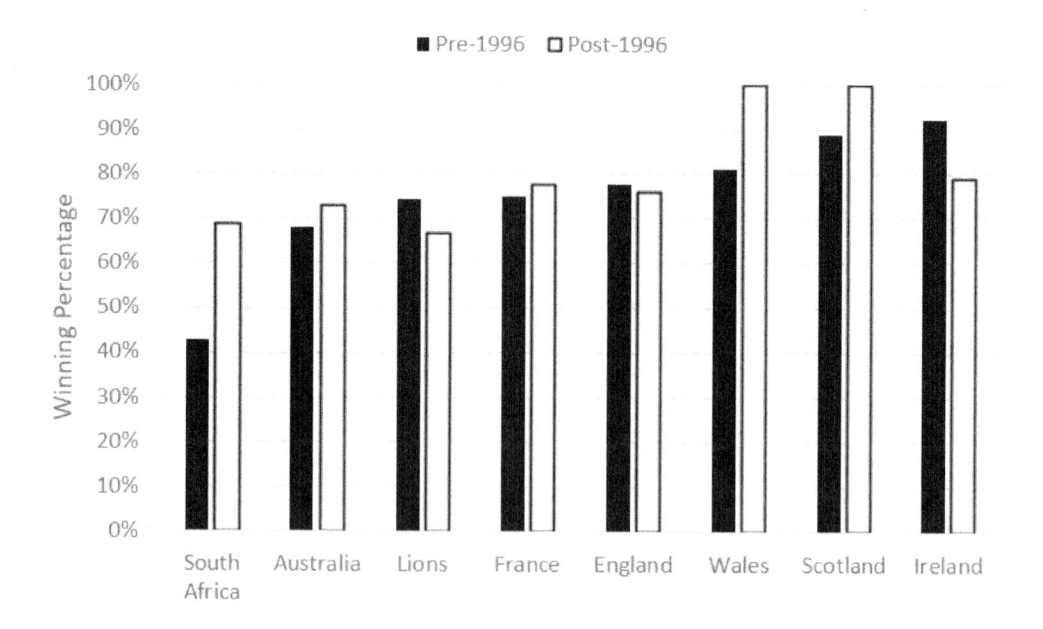

Figure 11.6. Comparison of the All Blacks' test rugby winning percentage against traditional Tier-1 teams before and after 1996.

The All Blacks' increased success rate against South Africa is a huge outlier compared to the rest of the traditional Tier-1 teams. We need to keep looking.

Have neutral referees had an impact?

When it comes to officiating, the gripes from both sides are legendary. The Springboks were famously incensed by the lenient home refereeing during their 1956 tour, especially after New Zealand called in retired All Black and heavyweight boxing champion Kevin Skinner as an enforcer for the third and fourth tests. Skinner admitted to punching each of the opposing props, helping to check the Springbok aggression as the All Blacks won both tests and their first-ever series against the South Africans.

On the other side, a series-deciding penalty awarded to the home side in Johannesburg in 1976 still rankles the All Blacks involved. (The referee allegedly conceded to the All Blacks' players afterwards that he was obliged to award it the way he did because, while they could go home to New Zealand, he had to live in South Africa!)

Removing even a whiff of hometown bias is undoubtedly a good thing. What do the numbers tell us about its impact on the longstanding New Zealand/South Africa rivalry? One way to analyse this is to break down the matches into three distinctive refereeing periods:

1. 1921–1976: Amateur era with home referees.
2. 1981–1995: Amateur era with neutral referees.
3. 1996–present: Professional era with neutral referees.

Table 11.1 outlines the results of these periods for tests played in each country. There isn't a big enough sample size in the middle period, 1981–1995, to provide definitive conclusions. But overall, it doesn't appear that neutral referees are the reason for the turnaround in the All Blacks' success. While the All Blacks' record in South Africa has undoubtedly improved since neutral referees were appointed, it has also massively improved in New Zealand. The All Blacks won only 57 percent of tests on home soil when game officials were fellow kiwis. But since 1996, they've won a whopping 81 percent of tests against the Springboks in New Zealand, despite the referees being neutral. Figure 11.7 charts the cumulative win difference for tests played in each country. The line shifts upwards in favour of the All Blacks for tests in both countries after 1996.

11. Black Tide Rising: Flipping the Script in the All Blacks vs Springboks Saga

Table 11.1. *Comparison of test results in South Africa and New Zealand under home and neutral referees.*

Years	Referees	Era	In South Africa Home Wins	Away Wins	Draws	Home Win %	In New Zealand Home Wins	Away Wins	Draws	Home Win %
1921 - 1976	Home	Amateur	14	5	1	70%	8	5	1	57%
1981 - 1995	Neutral	Amateur	1	1	0	50%	4	1	1	67%
1996 - 2023	Neutral	Professional	11	19	0	37%	21	4	1	81%

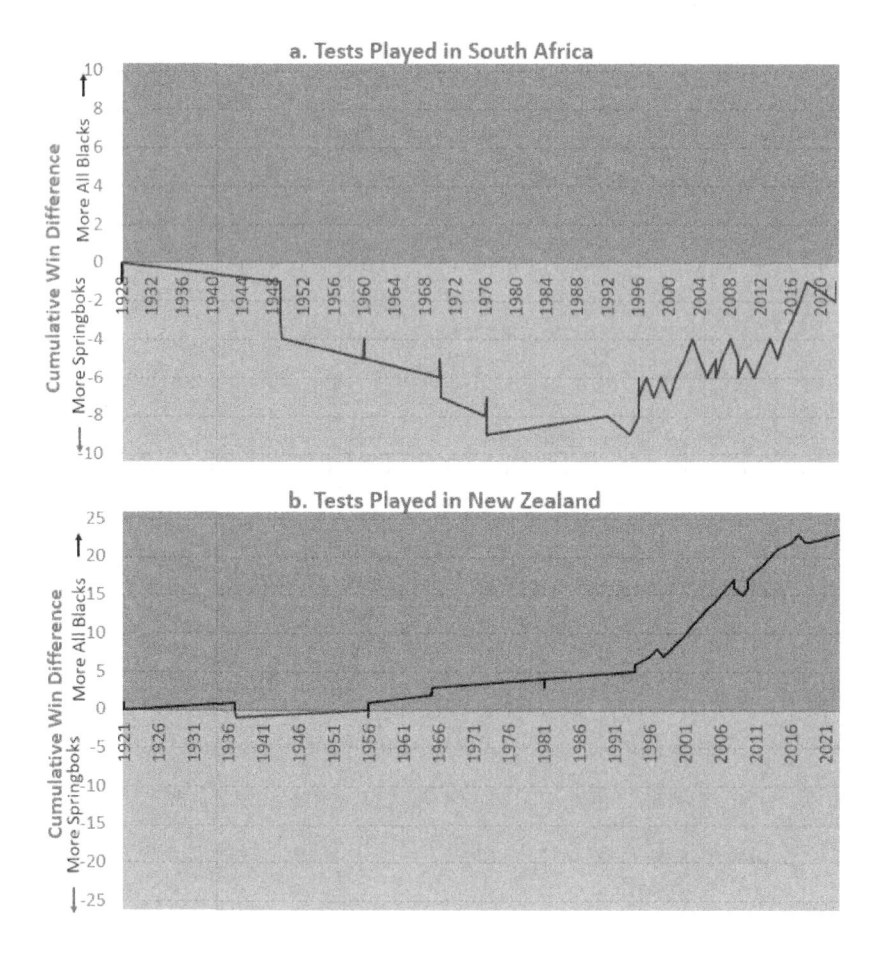

Figure 11.7. *Cumulative test rugby win difference between the New Zealand All Blacks and South Africa Springboks in the two countries. Figure 11.7a represents tests played in South Africa. Figure 11.7b represents tests played in New Zealand.*

Taken together, the evidence doesn't seem to support the theory that refereeing is the cause of the All Blacks' recent domination. Moving along…

Have the All Blacks figured out how to play and win in South Africa, and particularly at altitude (South Africa's big home-ground advantage)?

It's not easy to get to South Africa from New Zealand. Even today, it involves 20 hours of travel with at least one stopover while crossing 11 time zones. In the early days of the rugby rivalry, tours to South Africa involved up to 30 matches and took multiple months to complete. Many members of the touring party had never left New Zealand before, let alone set foot on the other side of the world in a place as unfamiliar as Africa. And the lung-busting, rarified air of the Highveld would have felt even more foreign to the players. Table 11.1 highlights the All Blacks' struggles in South Africa prior to 1996, a period during which they won just 6 of 22 tests.

A series win in South Africa—the last great mountain remaining for the All Blacks to climb—was achieved immediately upon rugby's professionalisation in 1996. The All Blacks have gone on to dominate the ledger even on South African soil in the modern Professional era, winning an incredible 63 percent of test matches played in South Africa.

When embarking on this chapter, I was fairly certain that a key ingredient to the turnaround in the All Blacks' fortunes would be a newfound ability to win in South Africa, and especially on the Highveld. Why? It seemed logical that a more professional approach and better sports science would help the team

11. Black Tide Rising: Flipping the Script in the All Blacks vs Springboks Saga

perform in an environment they'd struggled in. For example, in earlier years the All Blacks used to try and acclimatise to the altitude immediately, heading up to the Highveld as soon as possible to spend the week training and familiarising themselves with the thinner air. Soon after professionalisation, this strategy was flipped on its head, with teams opting to remain at sea level as long as possible and only venturing up to the venue the day before the game (i.e., there was no attempt to acclimatise). The theory was that a week wasn't enough time to acclimatise anyway, but the week spent training at altitude exhausted the players too much before the match had even started.

We already saw in Table 11.1 and Figure 11.7 that, while the All Blacks have performed substantially better on South African soil since 1996, they've also improved on home soil during the same period. Table 11.2 summarises the All Blacks' record against the Springboks across the Amateur and Professional eras, in each country overall and at the different altitudes in South Africa.

Table 11.2. Comparison of test results in South Africa on the Highveld and in New Zealand in the Amateur and Professional rugby eras.

Venue	Amateur Era Matches	Amateur Era NZ Win %	Professional Era Matches	Professional Era NZ Win %	NZ Win % Difference
All Tests in South Africa	22	27%	30	63%	36%
Highveld Tests in South Africa	10	30%	18	61%	31%
Low Altitude Tests in South Africa	12	25%	12	67%	42%
All Tests in New Zealand	20	60%	26	81%	21%
Overall (incl. neutral venues)	42	43%	64	69%	26%

Indeed, the increase in the All Blacks' winning percentage has been slightly more pronounced in South Africa than in New Zealand, although this difference is not statistically significant. Most interestingly, and certainly against my expectation, the All Blacks have actually made larger gains in low-altitude tests in South Africa than in the vaunted tests played on the Highveld.

Has the fact that the teams meet on a regular basis at both international and club levels had an impact?

When it came to the Springboks/All Blacks rivalry, the Professional era didn't just mean that the players were now openly compensated for their toil. It fundamentally changed the frequency of meetings between the two teams, and, by extension, the rivalry's overall dynamic. This didn't just occur at the international level either; the Super 12 club competition, launched in 1996, began the process of players regularly touring and clashing with each other at the domestic level as well. (The club clashes technically first began in 1993 with the Super 10 competition, but this was restricted to specific teams and played in pools, so matches between New Zealand and South African teams were much more limited.)

The barcode chart (Figure 11.8) provides a nice visual representation of how the frequency of Springboks/All Blacks test matches has changed. Each line represents a test (with lines grouped together into thicker lines during test series). You can see that until the barrier-breaking Johannesburg test of 1992, meetings were few and far between. Since 1994, the COVID-impacted 2020 season is the only one that hasn't featured at least one Springboks-All Blacks test.

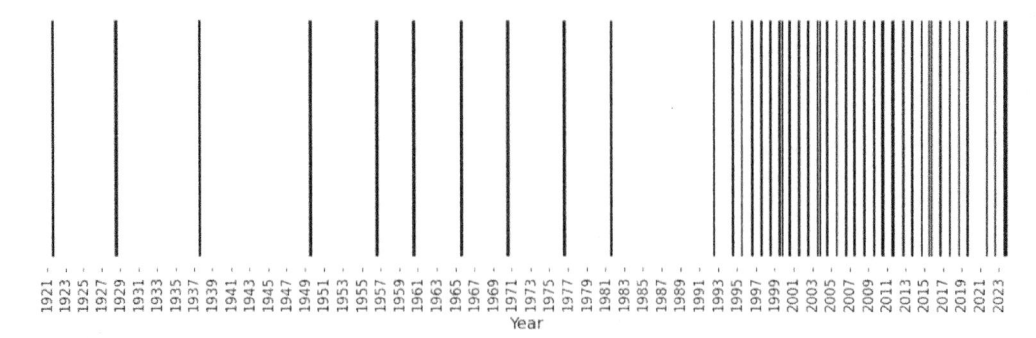

11. Black Tide Rising: Flipping the Script in the All Blacks vs Springboks Saga

Figure 11.8. Rugby test matches played between the All Blacks and the Springboks from 1921 to 2023.

Could the increased frequency of this rivalry somehow have worked in the All Blacks' favour? The previously mythical Springbok beasts were perhaps cut down to size as regular interactions proved that they were, well, mortal after all?

To try and find out, let's look to another country who also received a healthy dose of Springboks competition since the dawn of professionalisation: fellow Tri-Nations' combatants, the Australian Wallabies. How have they fared against the Springboks over the same period? They've certainly had a similar fixture profile over the years, though Springboks/Wallabies clashes were even rarer prior to the 1990s (Figure 11.9).

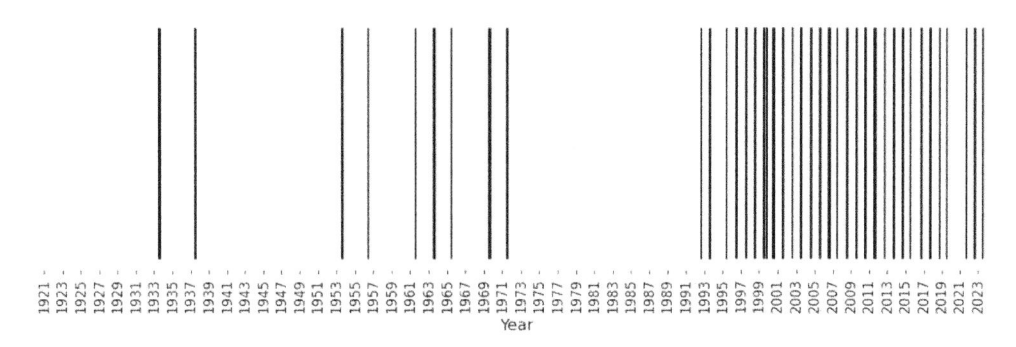

Figure 11.9. Rugby test matches played between the Wallabies and the Springboks from 1934 to 2023.

There's a fair bit of 'noise' in the Wallabies/Springboks rivalry data, especially in the early years where fixtures were such a rarity (Figure 11.10).

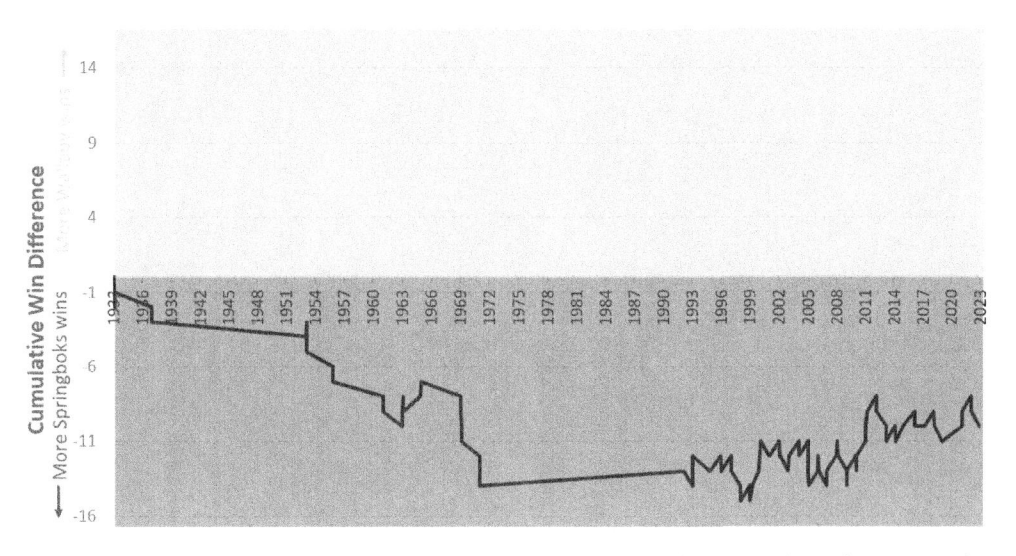

Figure 11.10. Cumulative test rugby win difference over time between the Australian Wallabies and South African Springboks.

11. Black Tide Rising: Flipping the Script in the All Blacks vs Springboks Saga

While the Wallabies have never edged the overall head-to-head record, they have fared far better in the Professional era than they did previously. The Wallabies' winning percentage against the Springboks has increased by 20 percent since 1996, from 30 percent to 50 percent (Figure 11.11). Their win-loss record in the Professional era against the Springboks is 30–27 (with three draws), compared to a 10–23 win-loss record before 1996.

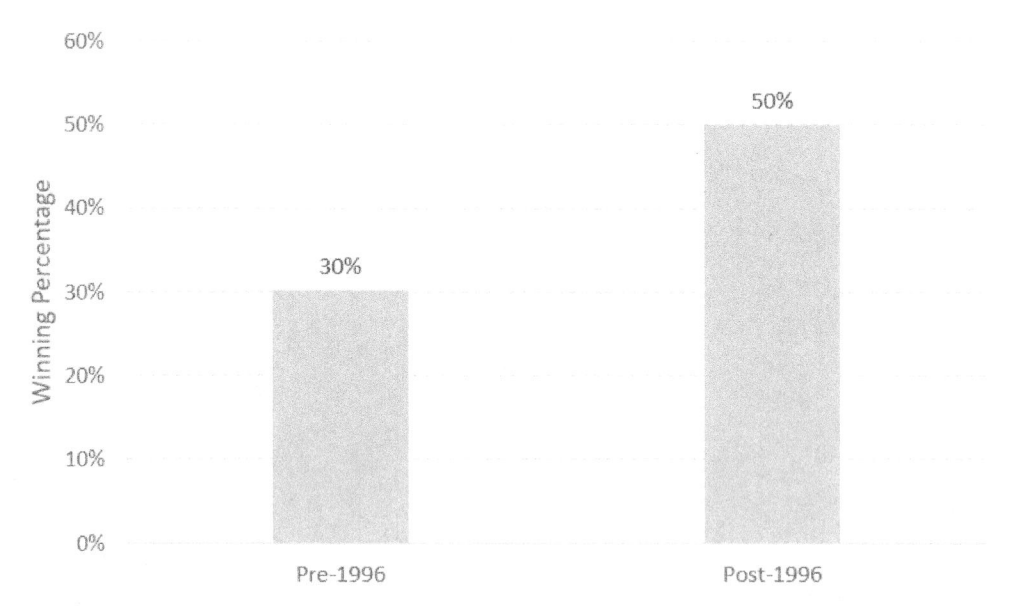

Figure 11.11. Comparison of the Wallabies' test-winning percentage against the Springboks, pre- versus post-1996.

Argentina's history may provide additional useful context. The Southern Hemisphere nation joined the 'party' in 2012 when it became a member of the expanded Rugby Championship (which replaced the Tri-Nations). This meant that Argentina also got to play the Springboks multiple times each year. The

Argentinian Jaguares club team also got exposure to South African club teams in an expanded annual Super Rugby competition that ran between 2016 and 2020.

Argentina doesn't have the history against the Springboks that New Zealand or Australia does, having only played an official test for the first time in 1993. The sides played 13 times from 1993 until 2011, with the Springboks winning all 13. Since the Pumas (the Argentine national team) were admitted to the Rugby Championship, they've met a further 23 times with Argentina recording three wins and a draw to the Springboks' 19 wins. There haven't been enough matches to determine if their modest success is a statistically relevant change, but the three wins and a draw certainly suggest that increased playing frequency has helped Argentina, much like it may have helped New Zealand and Australia.

So the Southern Hemisphere heavyweights, who now have regular matches against South Africa, have seen their records against the Springboks improve considerably. What about other Tier-1 nations who haven't faced the Springboks so regularly? Figure 11.12 shows that the only other top nation that the Springboks' performance has fallen off against to the same extent is Ireland.

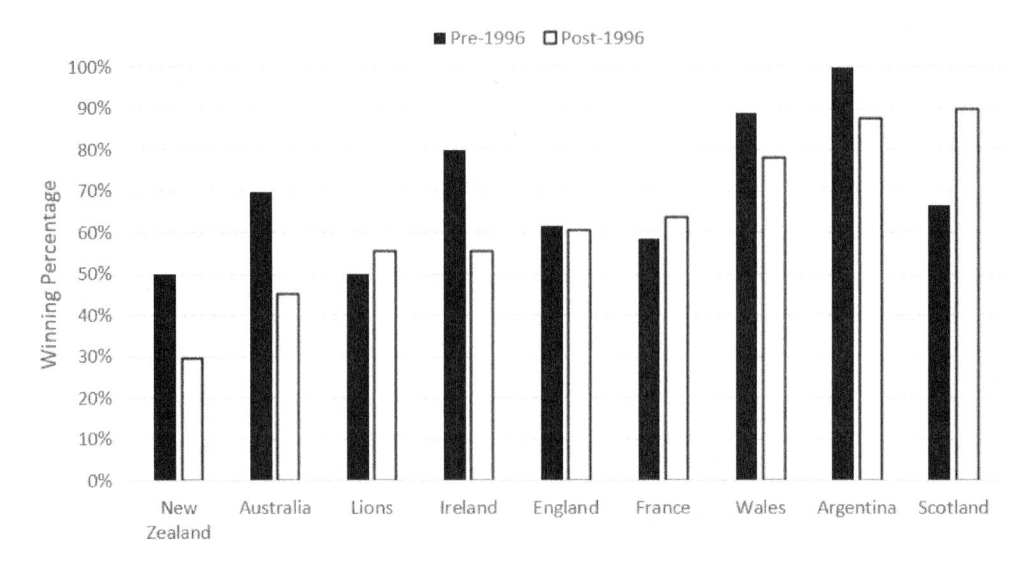

11. Black Tide Rising: Flipping the Script in the All Blacks vs Springboks Saga

Figure 11.12. Comparison of the Springboks' test rugby winning percentage against traditional Tier-1 teams (including Argentina) before and after 1996.

The Springboks' winning percentage against the Irish has fallen from 80 percent in the Amateur era to just over half (56 percent) in the Professional era. The two teams met ten times in the Amateur era, during which Ireland notched a single win coupled with a draw. The Professional era, however, is a tale of two halves. The Springboks dominated the initial period through 2004, peeling off six straight wins. Since then, it is the Irish who have dominated, winning eight of the 12 contests.

This can't be due to any increased familiarity, as the teams have continued to meet only sporadically, and didn't play at all in the five-year period from 2017 to 2022. It's really a reflection of the fact that Irish rugby is a story in and unto itself. In recent years they've emerged as a global heavyweight of the game, winning 5 of the last 11 Six Nations and frequently appearing near the top of the World Rankings. They've transformed their record against most of world rugby's heavyweights in the years since 2005, with the exception of France and Argentina (Figure 11.13). Most relevant to our current discussion, their increased winning percentage has been highest against none other than—you guessed it—South Africa.

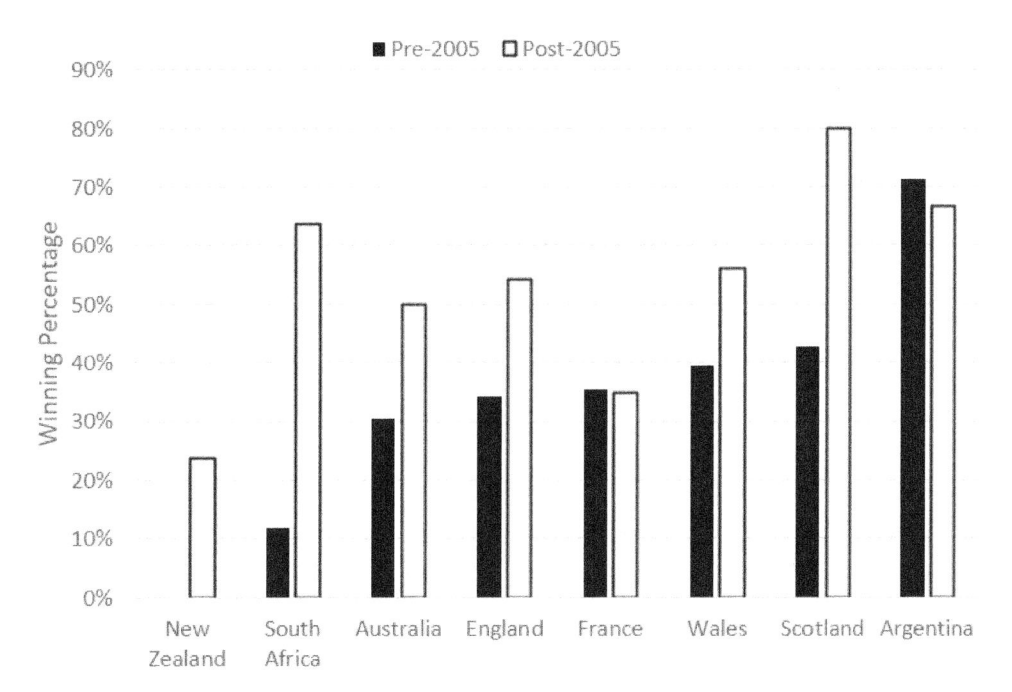

Figure 11.13. Comparison of Ireland's test rugby winning percentage against traditional Tier-1 teams (including Argentina) before and after 2005.

Getting back to the question at hand about the All Blacks versus the Springboks, there's one more data point we can look at while we're investigating the familiarity theory. I mentioned earlier that New Zealand players also get

11. Black Tide Rising: Flipping the Script in the All Blacks vs Springboks Saga

exposure to South African teams and conditions at club level via the Super Rugby competition. Well, in 2020 South African teams left Super Rugby to play in the United Rugby Championship based out of Europe. That same year, as you may have noticed in Figure 11.1, the All Blacks' win difference began flattening out. While the sample size of matches between the two juggernauts since then isn't huge, the data strongly suggests that New Zealand players' reduced exposure to their South African counterparts at the club level has impacted the All Blacks' success rate. Table 11.3 summarises this drop off. Since South African teams left Super Rugby, the All Blacks' winning percentage suddenly plummeted back to what it was in the amateur days. Quite interesting, right?

Let's not get carried away just yet; it's only a sample of seven test matches. But the lack of exposure to South African rugby and the different playing styles they bring is certainly causing angst among many New Zealand fans. We'll have to see how the rivalry continues to play out to know for sure if the angst is justified.

Table 11.3. The All Blacks' test win percentage against the Springboks, including the post-2020 period when South African club teams left Super Rugby.

Period	Tests	All Blacks Wins	All Blacks Win %
Pre-1996	42	18	43%
1996 - 2020	57	41	72%
Post 2020	7	3	43%

The breakdown

Of all the theories in this chapter speculating why the All Blacks have been able to flip the script in their rivalry with the Springboks, the familiarity theory appears to have the most compelling evidence. What I haven't answered is *why* this seems to be the case. Why does it seem to advantage New Zealand and not South Africa to be playing each other regularly?

I'm honestly not sure what the answer is. It may be that South Africa presents such a unique playing style challenge, so different to what New Zealand teams are used to facing, that regular meetings are needed to break it down and find ways to overcome it. This is certainly a ripe topic for the next edition of this book when more data is at hand—and, in the meantime, hours of spirited debate among rugby fans!

12. Cap-italising on Position: Which Rugby Positions (and Locations) Offer the Best Path to International Fame?

It's a cold, wet night in Auckland in 2015. Revellers who've had more than a few too many drinks are doing their best to sober up their demeanour as they approach the door. They're wise to show the bouncer appropriate respect; not only is he the sole arbiter on whether their big night out will continue, he also tips the scales at a whopping 170kg. They don't know it—nor does he—but his personal story will soon become a part of modern rugby folklore. For within three years, he'll swap the temporary respect of nightclub revellers just trying to get through the door for the adulation of millions of All Blacks fans as he dons the hallowed black jersey.

The meteoric rise of Karl Tu'inukuafe has been well documented in rugby circles. After his weight ballooned to that nightclubber-intimidating 170kg in the five years after leaving high school, he decided to take up rugby once again on doctors' advice, purely as a way to lose weight. It worked, and he 'slimmed down' to a much healthier 135kg. But his success didn't stop there. He began to quickly move through the rugby ranks, getting his first taste of professional rugby when he was selected to play for North Harbour in the New Zealand domestic competition. This put him on the radar of some Super Rugby franchises, and a spate of injuries on the Chiefs saw him called into the franchise in 2018. But Big Karl wasn't finished there.

With props going down left, right and centre, Tu'inukuafe received the call up to make his debut for the All Blacks that same year. His rise from not even playing rugby to All Blacks starter within the space of a few years got him nominated for World Rugby's Breakthrough Player of the Year award in 2018. His successful international career included 27 test appearances for the New Zealand All Blacks, and he currently plies his trade as a professional in the lucrative French Top 14 league.

While his story is a rare and extreme example of a player rising from relative obscurity, it got me thinking about which positions in a rugby team are more likely to lead to earning international honours. For the last decade in New Zealand, it has seemed that practically every Super Rugby prop has had a realistic chance to get the call up to the national team. On the surface, this seems completely logical: the position requires four players in every matchday squad and has a high potential for injuries.

I therefore expected prop to be the position most likely to earn international selection (in New Zealand at least). Somewhat surprisingly, I found it was scrum-half—a position at the opposite end of the attritional scale—that has had the highest odds of achieving international honours in the New Zealand game. Over half (53 percent) of eligible scrum-halves among the five New Zealand Super Rugby franchises in 2023 have represented the All Blacks (Table 12.1), while props come in second at 46 percent, closely followed

12. Cap-italising on Position: Which Rugby Positions (and Locations) Offer the Best Path to International Fame?

by midfielders (45 percent). For context, 38 percent of NZ-eligible Super Rugby players in 2023 had represented the All Blacks. It's a fairly high overall percentage, reflecting a combination of player eligibility and experimentation in the national side.

Table 12.1. *Number of eligible Super Rugby players from the five New Zealand franchises in 2023 that have represented the All Blacks, by position.*

Position	NZ Eligible	All Blacks	%
Prop	28	13	46%
Hooker	15	4	27%
Lock	24	7	29%
Loose Forward	34	11	32%
Scrum-Half	15	8	53%
Fly-Half	14	5	36%
Midfield	20	9	45%
Outside Back	28	10	36%
TOTAL	**178**	**67**	**38%**

When I first envisaged this chapter, I was expecting the same patterns to show up in other countries around the world. But this isn't the case, and in hindsight, that makes a lot of sense. For one thing, each team has a different personnel profile. As an example, New Zealand has been well-served by three outstanding world-class locks in recent years in Sam Whitelock, Brodie Retallick and Scott Barrett. There have been limited opportunities for others to force their way into the team, and with a maximum of only three locks in a matchday squad, lock has been one of the least likely positions in New Zealand for Super

Rugby players to achieve higher honours (29 percent).

The other key difference is the prevalence of eligible players. The 14 teams that comprise the top French league, while littered with foreign players, still contain twice the number of internationally eligible players that New Zealand, Australia and Ireland have at their disposal from their own domestic competitions (Table 12.2). With almost twice the number of scrum-halves to select from as New Zealand, it's little wonder that in France, scrum-half is an extremely tough position to crack for the national team. Never mind that France's team captain and one of the best players in the world, Antoine Dupont, is also the incumbent scrum-half.

(Sidenote: the nations selected for this analysis are the top-tier nations who select almost all their international players from their domestic teams. Hence nations like South Africa, Wales and Scotland are not included.)

12. Cap-italising on Position: Which Rugby Positions (and Locations) Offer the Best Path to International Fame?

Table 12.2. *Comparison of number of players eligible for their national team in the top domestic leagues of New Zealand, Australia, France, England and Ireland in 2023.*

Position	New Zealand	Australia	France	England	Ireland
Prop	28	26	58	50	27
Hooker	15	15	33	28	15
Lock	24	19	42	34	19
Loose Forward	34	26	67	39	27
Scrum-Half	15	13	29	18	14
Fly-Half	14	15	22	15	11
Midfield	20	22	39	33	20
Outside Back	28	22	56	49	25
TOTAL	**178**	**158**	**346**	**266**	**158**

As is so often the case with data exploration, while your initial theory may not prevail, interesting nuggets of information often arise during the search.

Taking another look at the percentage of eligible players that reach international honours (Table 12.3), we can see that the results are all over the map, with every position both a high-likelihood position in some countries and a low-likelihood position in others. There is a slight overall edge for forwards over backs, with 35 percent of eligible forwards across all nations earning international honours, versus 31 percent of backs. Almost half of the eligible players from Ireland's four professional teams have earned international honours (45 percent), while only 30 percent of English Premiership equivalents have.

Table 12.3. *Percentage of players in the top domestic leagues of New Zealand, Australia, France, England and Ireland in 2023 who were eligible for their national team and had earned international honours.*

Position	New Zealand	Australia	France	England	Ireland	OVERALL
Prop	46%	38%	38%	26%	44%	37%
Hooker	27%	47%	27%	36%	40%	34%
Lock	29%	42%	48%	32%	37%	38%
Loose Forward	32%	31%	31%	33%	44%	34%
Scrum-Half	53%	31%	28%	39%	43%	37%
Fly-Half	36%	27%	32%	27%	55%	34%
Midfield	45%	23%	28%	30%	40%	32%
Outside Back	36%	27%	30%	27%	56%	33%
TOTAL	**38%**	**33%**	**33%**	**30%**	**45%**	**35%**

Things start to get more interesting when we look at the raw numbers of eligible players in the domestic leagues during the 2023 season who have played international rugby (Table 12.4). To clarify, these are players who had earned at least one international test cap up until the end of 2023.

Table 12.4. *Number of players in the top domestic leagues of New Zealand, Australia, France, England and Ireland in 2023, by position, who have represented their national teams.*

Position	New Zealand	Australia	France	England	Ireland	OVERALL
Prop	13	10	22	13	12	70
Hooker	4	7	9	10	6	36
Lock	7	8	20	11	7	53
Loose Forward	11	8	21	13	12	65
Scrum-Half	8	4	8	7	6	33
Fly-Half	5	4	7	4	6	26
Midfield	9	5	11	10	8	43
Outside Back	10	6	17	13	14	60
TOTAL	**67**	**52**	**115**	**81**	**71**	**386**

12. Cap-italising on Position: Which Rugby Positions (and Locations) Offer the Best Path to International Fame?

The big outlier in Table 12.4 is France, who have selected substantially more players than any of the other nations. This is especially true at prop, lock and loose forward, where France has selected almost double the average of the other nations (Figure 12.1). And—supporting my original hypothesis, may I remind you!—prop is the most selected overall position, followed by loose forward.

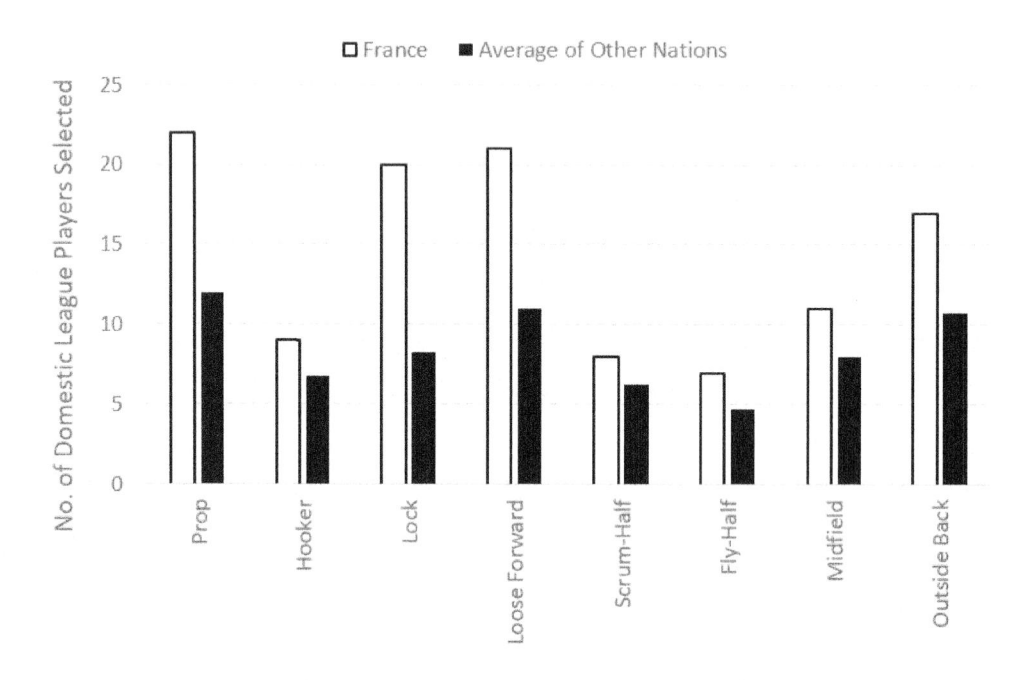

Figure 12.1. Comparison of the number of domestic players in 2023, by position, selected for their national teams between France and the average of New Zealand, Australia, England and Ireland.

France has the most eligible domestic players at their disposal, and they also select the most international players. Is this the paradox of choice, whereby when we're given too much choice, we tend to find it more difficult to make a decision? France has occasionally treated their summer tours, especially against lower-ranked opposition, as opportunities to blood new players. But then so have all the other top nations. Regardless, in the last two World Cup cycles, France has debuted 34 percent more players than any other traditional Tier-1 nation (Figure 12.2).

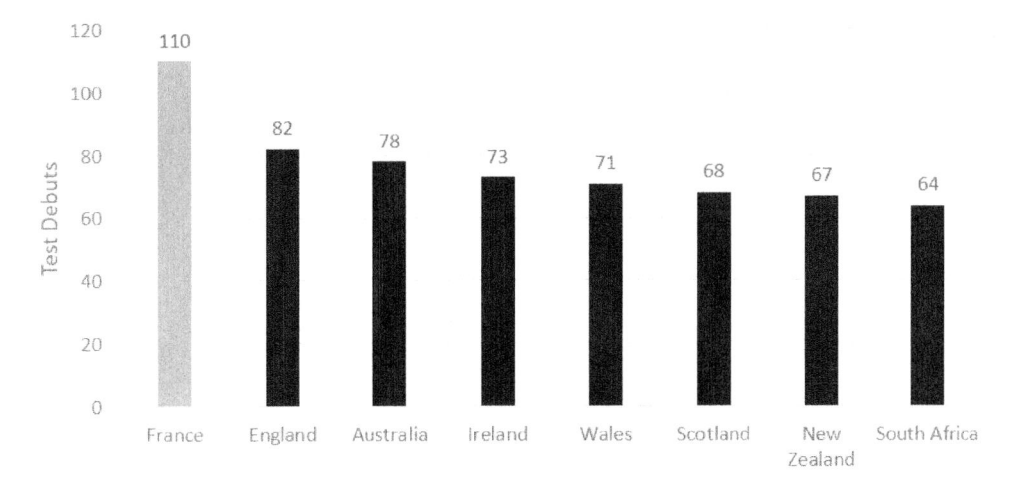

Figure 12.2. Comparison of the number of rugby test debutants by country between 2016 and 2023.

Perhaps this abundance in French caps being handed out was specific to the time period. They were gearing up to host the 2023 World Cup and may have wanted to leave no stone unturned in their quest to win it. Or maybe their coaching group at that time liked to tinker and experiment?

12. Cap-italising on Position: Which Rugby Positions (and Locations) Offer the Best Path to International Fame?

It turns out this approach is not a recent phenomenon. Look at the number of players who have achieved 100 test caps by nation, and you'll see that France is well down the list (Figure 12.3). France has fewer test centurions than Georgia, Romania and Russia, and are tied with Portugal. Additionally, for such a major test nation, France is seriously underrepresented in the Tier-1 records. Only Serge Blanco (19th in tries) is in the top 25 for either test caps, points scored or test tries!

It seems that longevity is not engrained in French rugby DNA. Whether this is due to the famous French flair and unpredictability extending to the selection table, I'm not sure.

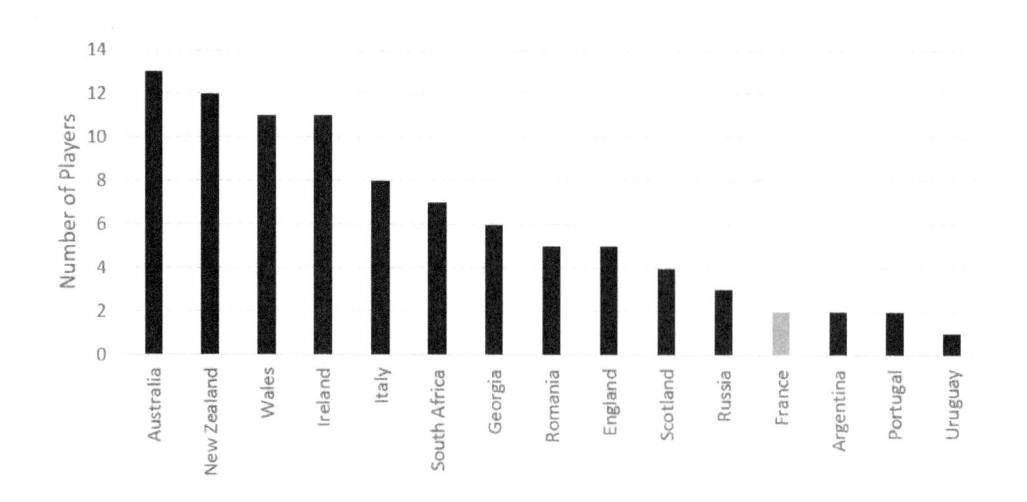

Figure 12.3. Number of rugby test centurions by nation at the end of 2023.

The breakdown

I began this chapter with a pretty basic question: which position would be most likely to land you a test cap? It turns out that the results are highly specific to each nation and their needs, and there's no 'one size fits all'. However, positions such as prop and loose forward do tend to receive the most selections.

But perhaps the overriding takeaway from this chapter is that if you're a promising rugby player who covets higher honours, move to France as soon as possible!

Fulltime

It's time to blow the fulltime whistle on this book. But before we part, I'll leave you with some speculation about the future of rugby.

Rugby now stands at a pivotal junction, faced with challenges and opportunities that will undoubtedly shape its future trajectory. Perhaps the most daunting—some might say existential—challenge looms from player lawsuits alleging that World Rugby hasn't done enough to protect them from the risk of brain injury. (These lawsuits are coming from both former professional players and current grassroots' club players.) The negative publicity around brain injuries and contact sport is seriously impacting playing numbers, especially among the next generation. While the figures touted by various governing bodies are often able to gloss this over by combining male playing numbers with the rapidly growing female side, as we've seen time and time again throughout this book, if you want the truth, you need to dive deeper into the data. And the truth is that the men's side of the game is not growing in playing numbers in most established rugby markets.

On the positive side, rugby is established now as an Olympic sport through Rugby Sevens. The men's World Cup is boldly expanding to 24 teams, and the United States is all but primed to become a major new market as it prepares to host the global showpiece tournament in 2031. World Rugby will be hoping that the 2031 tournament can have a similar impact that hosting the 1994 FIFA World Cup had on football (soccer) in the U.S.

While there is a lot of future uncertainty, one thing which appears guaranteed is that the importance of data and analytics will continue to grow. Rugby has been somewhat of a laggard in adopting analytics compared with the professional U.S. sports leagues, football and cricket. But this is changing, and the big professional teams all employ dedicated analytics staff nowadays.

Data and analytics may be especially useful when it comes to head injuries. Instrumented mouthguards are one promising technological development currently being tested by teams. They not only protect a player's pearly whites but also provide real-time data to the coaching team on the severity of head impacts. This could be game-changing in the quest to mitigate repeated head injuries, both in matches and in midweek training. Additionally, trials are underway at the community rugby level to lower tackle height to below the sternum. If these experiments show that they can reduce head injuries, they may very well help bring more players back into the game.

They will also undoubtedly change the game in unexpected ways. As we saw in Chapter 4, every law change can have unintended consequences on the game. What could the potential unintended consequences of head-injury-avoiding changes be? The data will ultimately tell us.

It's clear that the sport is navigating a period of massive transformation. But I'm confident it can and will adapt to meet the moment, as it's always done since William Webb Ellis first picked up the football and ran with it at Rugby School in 1823. The future may be fraught with challenges, but with the prudent application of data and analytics, rugby can not only navigate these obstacles but emerge stronger, safer and more vibrant than ever before.

References

Chapter 1

Barnsley, Roger & Thompson, Angus & Barnsley, PE (1985). Hockey success and birthdate: The relative age effect. *Canadian Association for Health, Physical Education and Recreation.* 51: 23-28.

Cauley, Alexander and Zax, Jeffrey S. (2018). Alphabetism: The Effects of Surname Initial and the Cost of Being Otherwise Undistinguished. Available at SSRN: https://ssrn.com/abstract=3272556 or http://dx.doi.org/10.2139/ssrn.3272556.

Grondin, S, Deshaies, P and Nault, LP (1984). Trimestre de naissance et participation au hockey et au volleyball. *Le revue Quebecoise de l'activite physique.* 2: 97-103.

Kelly AL, Till K, Jackson D, Barrell D, Burke K and Turnnidge J (2021) Talent Identification and Relative Age Effects in English Male Rugby Union Pathways: From Entry to Expertise. *Front. Sports Act. Living* 3:640607. doi: 10.3389/fspor.2021.640607

Simons, G., and Adams, L. (2017). The significance of birth dates of NZ 'All Blacks' — A comparison of the professional and amateur eras. *Scope.* 1: 164–170

Chapter 2

Rablen MD, Oswald AJ. (2008) Mortality and immortality: the Nobel Prize as an experiment into the effect of status upon longevity. *J Health Econ*. Dec;27(6):1462-71. doi: 10.1016/j.jhealeco.2008.06.001. Epub 2008 Jun 12. PMID: 18649962.

Redelmeier DA, Singh SM. (2001) Survival in Academy Award-winning actors and actresses. *Ann Intern Med*. May 15;134(10):955-62. doi: 10.7326/0003-4819-134-10-200105150-00009. PMID: 11352696.

Chapter 5

J.T. (2015) 'Why rugby teams should go for penalties not tries.' *The Economist*. October 16 2015. https://www.economist.com/game-theory/2015/10/16/why-rugby-teams-should-go-for-penalties-not-tries.

Chapter 9

Haywood, Rob. (2023) 'Democratising data — how FIFA primed World Cup underdogs to shock.' *BBC Sport*. December 21 2023. https://www.bbc.com/sport/football/67749259.

Chapter 10

Kahneman, D. (2011). *Thinking, Fast and Slow*. Farrar, Straus and Giroux.

Acknowledgements

This book would not have been possible without the support, encouragement and inspiration from a host of wonderful people. I am deeply grateful to everyone who has been part of this journey—your contributions have been invaluable.

I extend my profound gratitude to my editor, Adam Rosen, whose keen insight and invaluable suggestions have greatly improved this manuscript.

Additionally, John Coomer provided the critical final touches with his copy-editing and proofreading to get the manuscript into a publishable form. I'd like to thank Christian Storm for his excellent cover design.

I'd also like to specifically thank Mark McKenzie, Iain McGregor, Dr. Steve Fox and Dr. Glen Thompson for their advice, feedback, support and enthusiasm in this endeavour.

I'm also extremely grateful for the help I've received from the following individuals: Mark Baynes, Andrew Gebbie, Daniel Jones, George Berry, Tony Smith, Alysha Delany, Oliver Pitkin, Andrew Bradley, Dan Byrne, Angie Williams, Al Evans, Scott Stringer, Callum Ellwood, Kent Barnes, Matt Sturge, Liz Bissland and Chris Danrell.

Printed in Great Britain
by Amazon